D1138998

ROCKETS &
SPACECRAFT
HOW THEY WORK

.

Destination Moon: preparing to launch the Apollo manned spacecraft at
Cape Kennedy

ROCKETS AND SPACECRAFT

HOW THEY WORK

John W. R. Taylor

WITH 75 ILLUSTRATIONS
BY
JOHN W. WOOD AND WILLIAM HOBSON

J. M. DENT & SONS LTD
LONDON

BY THE SAME AUTHOR

C.F.S.
A Picture History of Flight
The Eagle Book of Aircraft
Great Moments in Flying
Wings for Tomorrow
Spitfire
Helicopters Work Like This
Jet Planes Work Like This
Jane's All the World's Aircraft
(annually, since 1960)
Combat Aircraft of the World
Aircraft Aircraft
The Lore of Flight
etc.

© *John W. R. Taylor* 1959, 1961, 1964, 1968, 1970

Printed in Great Britain
in 11 point Monotype Garamond, 2 points leaded, by
The Bowering Press of Plymouth for
J. M. DENT & SONS LTD
Aldine House · Bedford Street · London

First published with the title Rockets & Satellites Work Like This 1959
Revised editions 1961, 1964, 1968
Revised and Enlarged edition 1970

ISBN: 0 460 06417 7

Contents

Acknowledgments

Thank You

to Kenneth Gatland for permission to reproduce the illustrations on pages 39 and 41 (top); and to Donovan Brown of *Soviet News*, the U.S. Information Service in London and the British, U.S. and French aircraft industries for providing much valuable material.

Out into Space

THE sun rose four hours ago at Cape Kennedy in Florida; but this meant little to the men in the artificially-lit and air-conditioned control centre. Many of them had worked through the night, partnering the teams of skilled engineers whose workshop was the huge steel gantry at Launch Complex 39A.

Under the glare of powerful spotlights, focused across the concrete launch-site, the engineers had swarmed over platforms extending from the gantry, checking and rechecking every part of the great Saturn V rocket that would soon begin its journey into space.

Now they have finished. The rocket stands erect and alone on its firing platform, like a long white finger pointing to the sky. The whole scene appears suddenly to be lifeless. Not a sound, not a movement, disturbs the peace of the last few minutes of the rocket's life on Earth.

From the concrete safety of an underground blockhouse we can peer at it through periscopes or watch the flat unchanging picture of the firing area on a television screen high on one wall. The atmosphere is tense. Even the clock that marks away the seconds does it noiselessly, and the silence seems one with the little world outside.

Crew inside Apollo Command Module

7

It is always like this before one of the 'big birds' is launched. The men here have known the frustration and disappointment of seeing months of work destroyed in a flash when something has gone wrong at take-off, followed by the anti-climax of sorting over scraps of still-smoking wreckage to try to find the cause.

This time nothing must go wrong, for this rocket carries the most precious cargo ever aimed at the emptiness of space. In a tiny cabin near the nose sit three men, whose lives depend on the combined skills of the army of designers and engineers who built this strange craft and made it ready for flight.

No chances have been taken, for many years of research have led to this moment. The rocket and its motors have been proved by dozens of firings. The guidance system has already taken cameras and research instruments on journeys of discovery to the Moon. Two of the men have lived and worked in space for periods of several days while training for this mission.

Yet there is not an engineer at Cape Kennedy today who will feel happy or confident until the rocket has survived the first critical minutes of its long flight.

Only the captain feels calm. Long years of training, of difficult flights in jet fighters and supersonic research 'planes, of orbital journeys in Gemini two-man spacecraft, of endurance tests in spinning cabins and laboratory 'torture-chambers' on Earth have prepared him for this.

For so mighty a machine, the controls and instruments are simple, much of the work—even the navigation and guidance—being done for him by a cluster of 'black boxes' somewhere in the rocket below.

Below or behind? As he straps himself into the sturdy, well-padded couch he wonders momentarily, because he must lie on his back for take-off. Does it matter anyway? In space there is no up or down.

In space—a few moments now and that's where he'll be—all being well. Over his radio comes the flat-sounding voice of the firing officer:

'Thirty seconds.'

Just for a second he feels a flash of doubt, remembering films of rockets that dissolved into a cloud of flame and torn metal when the firing button was pressed. But once again his training overcomes his fear. At least he is not facing the great test alone, and he gives a 'thumbs up' signal to the two men strapped to the couches on each side of him.

'Ten seconds'—the final count-down—'nine . . . eight . . . seven . . . six . . . five . . .'

His eyes sweep over the levers and dials for the last time, then past them, through the narrow window, seeing nothing but the blue sky.

'. . . four . . . three . . . two . . . one . . . FIRE!'

Almost before he hears the shouted word, his body hunches into the couch. White smoke begins to billow angrily from the tail of the rocket, sending vibrations through its metal carcass that even the deep padding cannot conceal.

Slowly . . . so slowly that it seems the rocket must topple, it begins to thrust itself from the pad. The roar of its engines can be heard inside the blockhouse; the very ground trembles with their power.

The greatest adventure in all history has begun. This time it is 'Destination Moon'.

How a Rocket Works

WHY must we use anything so apparently dangerous and unpredictable as a rocket for space-flight? Why cannot we fit jet-engines or even propellers to our space-ships of the future?

The answer is contained in the word 'space'; because every type of engine yet fitted to an aircraft or rocket gets its power from fuel that is burned inside it. To burn anything we must have oxygen, and all the usual types of aircraft power plants—piston-engines, turbojets, turboprops, ramjets, pulsejets, and the rest—get their oxygen from nature's ready-made supply, the air.

As there is no air in space, these engines would be no more use than elastic bands to drive a spacecraft. In fact, the air is so 'thin' even at a mere 80,000 feet (15 miles) above the Earth that jet-engines are of little use above that altitude, while propellers find the air too 'thin' to work efficiently at half that height.

A rocket, on the other hand, does not need air from the atmosphere to support combustion, because it carries its own oxygen in the propellents that it burns.

Before going any further, it is important to make sure that you know what is meant by the power of an engine, and that you understand how a jet-engine or rocket pushes an aircraft forward. If you have read a book entitled *Jet Planes Work Like This* you will know already and can skip the next nine paragraphs.

As a start, a jet-engine or rocket is NOT pushed forward by the pressure of its exhaust gases against the air behind it. If this were so, a rocket could never work in space, where there is no air to push against.

Sir Isaac Newton knew better than this 250 years ago, when he stated in his Third Law of Motion that 'To every action there is an equal and opposite reaction'.

Even if you do not know precisely what he meant, you will probably have experienced the consequences of reaction—in the form of a ducking —if you have ever tried to jump too energetically from a boat to the bank of a river.

The object of pushing yourself forward with your foot was to propel your body towards land. This was the kind of 'action' to which Newton referred. The 'equal and opposite reaction' was the force exerted against the boat by your foot, which made it move away from the bank, and produced your ducking.

Now let us think in terms of rocket engines.

The force, corresponding with the effort which you put into your leap from the boat, is provided by burning the propellents. This flings a mass of exhaust gases towards the rear of the engine, which is the only way of escape for them, in the way that your body was flung towards the bank. And, just as reaction shoved the boat away in the opposite direction, so it pushes the rocket forward, together with any aeroplane or spacecraft to which it might be attached.

If we could tie a small rocket to a spring balance, we should be able to measure its 'push' in terms of pounds weight. So, for convenience, the 'push' of any jet or rocket engine which does its work by reaction-propulsion is given in 'pounds of thrust'.

Finally, it is important to remember that 'push' and power are two different things. Power is force (or 'push') multiplied by speed, and we can find the equivalent horsepower of a rocket engine by using a simple formula:

$$\text{Horsepower} = \frac{\text{Pounds thrust} \times \text{speed}}{375}$$

If, therefore, we have a rocket able to develop 6,000 lb. of thrust and fit it to an aeroplane able to fly at 500 m.p.h., it would give the equivalent of $\frac{6,000 \times 500}{375}$, or 8,000 h.p. at that speed.

As we have seen, the power of a jet-engine falls off quickly at great heights, because it cannot get sufficient oxygen from the air to work efficiently. The power of a rocket, on the other hand, increases as the air gets 'thinner', because there is less air resistance to slow it down and higher speed means greater power.

In fact a rocket works better in space, where there is no air at all, than anywhere else.

Unfortunately, there is a snag, because it is impossible to get something for nothing in the engineering world; and the snag with rockets is their tremendously high fuel consumption. Even a relatively small aircraft rocket engine, developing 8,000 lb. of thrust, can easily burn up to a ton of propellents every minute.

Shaded areas indicate fuel or propellent tanks of a motor-car, a long-range airliner and a rocket

Once again, we must get the picture into perspective by thinking in terms of power rather than thrust.

A rocket motor is a relatively simple and compact power plant, so that our 8,000 lb. thrust rocket might weigh only 300 lb. By comparison, a jet-engine of equivalent thrust would probably weigh about 2,000 lb. This saving in engine weight helps to offset the weight of fuel, and it soon becomes clear that when very high power is needed for brief periods the rocket motor is highly efficient, despite its apparently alarming fuel consumption.

So far as space-flight is concerned, we have already seen that there is

FUEL   TURBOJET

A turbojet engine often takes up more space than the fuel

FUEL   ROCKET ENGINE

A small rocket engine needs a great deal of fuel

no alternative at present to some form of rocket motor. Fuel consumption, except during take-off and landing, is not excessive, because once the spacecraft has been accelerated to a high speed beyond the atmosphere, less and less power is needed. With no air to slow it down, the spacecraft has only to offset the steadily decreasing pull of gravity that will continue to try to drag it back to Earth when it is far out in the depths of interplanetary space.

Rockets Are Not New

THE guided missiles and spacecraft of today and the future seem to have little in common with the simple firework rockets that we bang off so gleefully every Fifth of November in Britain or Fourth of July in the United States. Yet they all result from something that happened hundreds of years ago, probably in China.

We shall never know the true story of how the rocket was invented, but we do know that the Chinese were using gunpowder by the start of the thirteenth century, and it is easy to guess what might have occurred. The first rocket probably came into being by accident when a home-made bomb, produced by packing gunpowder into a strong paper tube, failed to explode and, burning slowly at one end, began streaking along the ground.

If there happened to be a war on at the time, the bomb-maker would almost certainly have dashed down the road to tell the local army commander about his newly discovered mobile incendiary bomb, which could propel itself at high speed into an enemy town without any need for the man who fired it to get within range of the defences.

Chinese soldier firing a rocket

A logical next step would have been for somebody to suggest tying the fire-bomb to an arrow, so that the tail-feathers would keep it on a straight course as it flew towards the target. It would soon have been discovered that the bomb flew straight even after the blast had burned away the feathers—and the result would have looked little different from a modern firework rocket on a long stick.

Whether or not we have guessed right, there is no doubt that rockets of this kind existed in the year 1232, when Mongol invaders were driven back from the city of Peiping by a well-directed rocket barrage.

From China, the technique of building war rockets spread first to India and then through the Saracen Empire to Europe. But with the development of cannon and small arms in the centuries that followed, the rocket seems to have fallen from favour to a certain extent, being less accurate than the new guns. So British soldiers in India must have received an unpleasant surprise in 1780, when their old enemy, Hyder Ali of Mysore, brought into action at Guntur iron-cased rockets weighing up to 12 lb. each and with a range of half a mile. Fired in hundreds, they won him a temporary victory, and rekindled an interest in rocket artillery in England.

The person chiefly responsible for the advances that followed was Colonel (later Sir) William Congreve, an artillery expert who was given permission to design and produce war rockets in the Royal Laboratory at Woolwich. He must have been a persuasive character as well as a clever inventor, for when the Navy set out for Boulogne in 1806, during the Napoleonic Wars, it took with it a fleet of twenty-four 'projector' ships built especially to fire Congreve rockets.

Before long, heavy salvoes of these missiles began falling on the town and among units of the French fleet. The results were devastating, because the rockets had pointed noses and when these stuck into the sides of wooden-hulled ships and buildings a fiery liquid was squeezed out through rings of holes, coating the target with flames in a matter of seconds.

Boulogne fell; and in the following year Copenhagen felt the weight of 25,000 Congreve rockets, some with incendiary warheads, some explosive, and some combining both types. Weighing 32 lb. each and with a range of up to two miles, they were very different from the earlier simple firework rockets, and the army was so impressed that it formed a special Rocket Brigade, which saw action at Waterloo in 1815.

The Americans, too, must have been impressed when missiles of this kind were used against them at Baltimore in 1814, for there is a reference to "the rockets' red glare" in their national anthem. Useful as Congreve's rockets were, however, they were poor by modern standards. They were propelled by burning a black powder of low efficiency and were unstable in flight, which spoiled their accuracy.

Improved accuracy came when the long wooden stick was replaced by stabilizing fins—an idea first suggested by a Frenchman named Frezier. Then, in 1815, the spin-stabilized rocket was invented in America, giving still greater accuracy. In this, some of the exhaust gases were taken out through a ring of small nozzles inclined at an angle round the main

Congreve incendiary rocket used as siege weapon

Guiding stick   Black powder   Delay fuse   Slow-burning incendiary filling

Shrapnel

Gunpowder charge

Congreve shrapnel rocket used against troop concentrations

Rocket life-line

exhaust, making the whole rocket spin, in the same way that rifling in the barrel of a gun makes a shell spin and so keeps it flying straight.

By the 1840's, rockets were being fired through tubes similar to a modern bazooka. Twenty years later, William Hale's spin-stabilized rockets became standard equipment in both the British and American armies: but even greater progress was being made with conventional artillery, and for the second time there was a gradual loss of interest in the rocket as a weapon of war. For other jobs, its usefulness was only beginning.

The Chinese realized the value of rockets for signalling almost as soon as they started to use them in battle, and attempts were made in many countries through the centuries to operate a primitive air freight service by tying small loads to rockets. This made them even less accurate, and as it is usually important to ensure that packages reach the right person, little progress was made until, in 1807, a Cornishman named Henry Trengrouse tied a light cord to the end of a rocket and so invented a new method of carrying life-lines to ships in distress. By hauling on the cord draped over their vessel by the rocket, sailors were able to drag over a heavier rope tied to the end and then clamber along this to safety.

The big snag was the low power and short burning life of the rockets of that time, and once again it was an idea of the Frenchman, Frezier, which provided the answer. He suggested putting rockets one behind the other, so that as the first burned itself out it would light the next one in front—an arrangement that we now call the multi-stage or step-rocket —to increase the range.

Frezier's ideas were used by Colonel Boxer to produce his famous two-stage life-line rocket of 1855, in which two ordinary powder charges were separated by a small charge of quick-burning powder in a single tube. It worked so well, and was so much more compact and transportable than the Manby mortar then in use round our coasts, that Boxer rockets were in service at every life-saving station in Britain by 1870. Weighing only 6 lb. each, they could carry a $\frac{1}{2}$-in. circumference hemp line a distance of over 1,000 feet, and this type of rocket is still in use all over the world.

No precise figures are available, but life-saving rockets have certainly helped to save a total of well over 15,000 lives around the coasts of Britain. So rockets have never been entirely destructive.

The next important developments took place in Russia, where Nikolai Kibaltchitch designed a rather primitive rocket-powered aircraft in 1881. He was already well known as an inventor, having designed and built the bombs used to blow up Tsar Alexander II, and he designed his aeroplane

Solid-propellent unguided rockets were fired from fighters against ground targets in the second world war

in prison while awaiting execution. His work came to an abrupt end, and it is Konstantin Tsiolkovsky rather than Kibaltchitch who is honoured in the Soviet Union as the great pioneer of space flight.

As early as 1903, Tsiolkovsky showed that a rocket could work in a vacuum, and made a model of a space-ship. A few years later, in France, Robert Esnault-Pelterie divided his time between building some of the first streamlined monoplanes and investigating the mathematical possibilities of space travel. In America, a scientist named Robert Goddard began to search for new rocket fuels.

The result marked a turning point in rocket design, because by the early

Goddard's first
liquid-propellent rocket

twenties Goddard had decided that the only way to produce sufficient power for flight beyond the atmosphere was to use liquid propellents such as liquid oxygen, instead of the powder fuels that had been in use for at least seven centuries.

In setting out to design a motor that would run on liquid propellents, he faced tremendous problems. In place of the simple 'firework' rocket, he had to have a strongly built firing chamber, tanks for the liquid oxygen and petrol propellents, pumps to supply them to the firing chamber, an ignition system to start them burning, and a series of valves and controls. Nor was his task made easier by the fact that the liquid oxygen had to be kept under pressure, for the simple reason that it would have boiled away if its temperature had been allowed to rise above minus 183 deg. C.

B   17

With only a grant of $5,000 from the Smithsonian Institution to help cover the cost, he produced by 1923 a small motor that worked satisfactorily on a test-bench. Three years later, on 16 March 1926, all was ready for the first flight test of a liquid-propellent rocket. It looked very different from the giant streamlined missiles of today. To keep it as light in weight and simple as possible, Goddard built it as a skeleton structure, some 10 feet long, consisting of the large liquid oxygen tank and smaller petrol tank linked by slim pipelines to the firing chamber.

Launched from a simple framework, on a farm at Auburn, Massachusetts, this frail-looking rocket covered a distance of 184 feet at a speed of 64 m.p.h. It was airborne for only $2\frac{1}{2}$ seconds, which may not seem very exciting nowadays; but it was a start, and Goddard was soon busy producing bigger, better, more streamlined rockets on the same lines.

Like the early pioneers of aeroplane flight, he received little encouragement from the press and public. The newspapers branded him a crank in 1919 when he included references to space travel in a serious technical paper entitled *A Method of Reaching Extreme Altitudes*. After his 1926 experiments he was declared to be a danger to public safety and was forbidden to make any further rocket launchings in Massachusetts.

One of the few Americans who realized the importance of what Goddard was doing was Charles Lindbergh, the famous Atlantic flyer, who persuaded the rich Daniel Guggenheim to provide $25,000 for further experiments. As a result, by 1935, Goddard progressed to an 85 lb. rocket, 15 feet long, which soared to 7,500 feet and attained a speed of 700 m.p.h. But by that time even more important events were taking place in Europe.

Back in 1922, Goddard had received a letter from a Rumanian professor named Hermann Oberth asking for a copy of the paper which he had written three years earlier. Oberth then produced a much more detailed book of his own entitled *The Rocket into Interplanetary Space*, which quickly became the bible of space flight or, to give it its proper name, the science of astronautics.

The main market for this book was in Germany, where flying was so restricted by the terms of the peace treaty that had ended the 1914–18 war that young designers and scientists welcomed the chance to tackle the new, exciting problems of rocketry. A group of them formed in June 1927 a society known as the *Verein für Raumschiffahrt* (*VfR*), devoted to a study of every aspect of astronautics, and within a year it had more than five hundred members, including Oberth.

They concentrated at first on the use of firework-type rockets to propel motor-cars and gliders, and for mail delivery in mountainous country: and it was not until 1930 that they began to experiment with liquid-propellent designs, based largely on Oberth's theories. Progress was, perhaps, too good, because soon after one of these rockets had been demonstrated to German army officers in 1933 the Gestapo closed down the *VfR*, and the Army Weapons Department set up a secret military rocket research establishment at Kummersdorf, south of Berlin.

Kummersdorf was put under the command of Major-General Walter Dornberger, with one of the most brilliant members of the *VfR*, the 20-year-old Wernher von Braun, as chief designer. For the first time in rocket history plenty of money was available for research, and tremendous achievements were made possible.

In 1934, a liquid-propellent rocket code-named A-2 reached a height of 6,500 feet. More important than the distance flown was that it was kept on a straight path by a gyroscope which operated tail control surfaces, because this pointed the way to greatly improved accuracy.

Three years later, the whole establishment was moved to the village of Peenemunde on the Baltic coast, far from prying eyes: and in 1939 a rocket known as A-5 covered 11 miles when fired from the new base. Far larger than anything previously tested, it was 25 feet long, with a weight of 1,650 lb. and it was steered in flight by small vanes which operated in the hot exhaust gases. These vanes made possible far better control at take-off, when the rocket was not moving fast enough for tail-fins to be effec-

Fuelling an A-4 (V-2) rocket

19

tive, and at high altitudes, where the air is too 'thin' for ordinary controls to work efficiently.

Impressed by the possibilities opened up by A-2, the German Army had meanwhile set Dornberger the fantastic task of developing quickly a rocket with a range of over 150 miles and able to deliver a one-ton high-explosive warhead with a high degree of accuracy. Overcoming countless problems and setbacks, the men of Peenemunde worked with even greater urgency after September 1939, when Germany was once more at war.

After partial successes, all was ready for the first full-scale test of the new rocket, which was code-named A-4, on 3 October 1942. It was an unforgettable sight as the great 46-foot missile, weighing over 12 tons, lifted itself from the firing pad and climbed away, slowly at first and then faster and faster until it was streaking upward at over 3,000 m.p.h.

For the first time, that day, a rocket travelled well over 100 miles. It was by no means perfect, and it took two more years and nearly 65,000 design changes before A-4 could be used as a weapon of war. But when the first A-4 (or V-2, as we then knew it) fell on Chiswick, London, on 8 September 1944, it marked the beginning of a new kind of warfare, waged by scientists with push-buttons and computers, rather than by men fighting in aeroplanes and tanks.

Of far greater value to mankind was that it also represented the first big stride in the direction of the exploration of space.

Propellents and Performance

ROBERT GODDARD spent no more than £71,300 during his entire thirty years of rocket research and experiment. By comparison, millions of pounds were needed to perfect Germany's wartime V-2, and every one fired against England cost a further £10,000–£16,000. The main reason was that the V-2 contained some 30,000 separate parts. Yet, with only a primitive guidance system it was much simpler than the long-range rockets of today, and it has been stated that America's Minuteman intercontinental ballistic missiles (ICBMs) cost around half a million pounds each, without their nuclear warheads.

It is easy to see how and why rockets have become so complex and costly when we study the job they are expected to do.

The war rockets used originally by the Chinese, and later by armies all over the world, were not intended to travel long distances or to carry a heavy warhead. Propellents like gunpowder were quite good enough and the main problem was to ensure even and steady burning.

Often the powder tended to burn faster on one side than on the other, slewing the rocket towards the side where the greatest weight of powder remained. Attachment of the stick prevented this, by imposing so much 'drag' when the rocket started to slew that it was soon pulled back onto a straight course.

More even burning and higher power resulted from hollowing out the powder to a cone shape, so that a greater area of powder caught fire at

Firework rocket, showing hollowed-out charge and venturi nozzle

once. This simple idea is still used in firework rockets, but was not good enough for the solid-propellent rockets fired from aircraft against ground targets in World War II, for which high speed and a longer range were essential. So, to ensure the greatest possible burning area in the American 12-inch Tiny Tim rocket, for example, the four separate sticks of solid propellent were moulded with a cruciform, instead of a circular, section.

By enabling a much greater area of propellent to be burned at once, such an arrangement produces a large volume of exhaust gas far more rapidly than simply burning away a single stick of propellent of the same weight from the rear towards the front. It does not in itself guarantee higher performance, for if the gases were not ejected at high speed from the nozzle at the tail of the rocket they would simply blow up the casing. A great deal depends on efficient nozzle design to get the gases away quickly.

If you look at a small firework rocket, you will see that the cardboard casing is pinched in at the rear, so that the gases escape through a hole much smaller than the diameter of the casing. This narrowing down is known technically as a venturi, and has the effect of speeding up the escaping gases. As a result all rockets, whether solid or liquid-propellent, have a venturi-shaped nozzle.

It should be obvious by now that the key to rocket performance is the speed with which the exhaust gases leave the nozzle. The best propellent, in theory, is that which produces the greatest volume of gas at the highest possible speed. As a rough guide, doubling the speed at which the gases are ejected (the exhaust velocity) will double the speed of the rocket: and the faster a rocket travels the farther it will continue to coast along (or 'freewheel') after its fuel is burned. Distance travelled is, therefore, directly proportional to speed.

This explains why Robert Goddard turned to liquid propellents in 1923, and why almost all of the big space rockets launched so far have had liquid-propellent motors, because such propellents produce far more energy in the form of fast-moving exhaust gases than did the old-fashioned gunpowder type of solid propellents. So great is this increase in performance that it often outweighs the vastly increased complexity and cost of liquid-propellent designs.

Before going further, let us take a look at the propellents that are used in present-day rockets. The essentials are a fuel and an oxidant to supply the oxygen in which the fuel is burned. Goddard began with petrol as his fuel and liquid oxygen as his oxident. The V-2 used alcohol fuel, again with liquid oxygen; the Atlas rocket which launched America's Mercury manned spacecraft into orbit used kerosene and liquid oxygen. Saturn V, which is used to send U.S. astronauts on their long journey to the Moon, uses in its upper stages a newer 'super fuel', liquid hydrogen, which gives far higher performance than petrol or kerosene.

There is, however, an increasing return to solid propellents in smaller rockets, following the development of new plastic-base compounds of high efficiency. The advantages are obvious, because liquid hydrogen, liquid oxygen, and alternative oxidants such as nitric acid and H.T.P. (hydrogen peroxide) are all comparatively difficult and unpleasant to store and handle, whereas solid-propellent motors can be treated in much the same way as other inflammable stores. They are particularly attractive to the armed services, for their use makes a missile available at a moment's notice—unlike liquid-propellent rockets, which usually require anything from fifteen minutes to several hours for fuelling and checking before they can be fired. What is more, solid-propellent motors can now be stopped instantly when required.

Designers of liquid-propellent engines have offered an alternative to solid propellents in the form of the pre-packaged or storable liquid-propellent engine. As the name implies, this is a self-contained power plant with fuel tanks and engine in a single, sealed 'package' which can be left in place in the missile, fully fuelled, giving the same instant readiness as a solid motor. Such engines are used in many of the smaller American air-to-surface and air-to-air weapons, giving higher performance than solid motors of similar size.

Nor is this the only way in which rocket designers are using existing forms of propellent in a new 'package'. Several companies are experimenting with hybrid engines, using a combination of solid and liquid propellents, and claim that these offer the advantages of both without most of the disadvantages.

A typical hybrid engine, built and tested at the United Technology Center, California, is 15½ feet tall and consists of a spherical tank of liquid fluorine/oxygen oxidant mounted above a cylinder of lithium/lithium hydride/polybutadiene solid propellent carrying the combustion chamber at its lower end. Because the fuel and oxidant are separated, and neither will burn by itself, this arrangement permits the use of high-energy propellents with complete safety during long periods of storage. Also, it is simple to provide stop and re-start capability and variation of thrust by using a throttle to control the supply of oxidant flowing from the tank into the cylinder of solid propellent.

This particular UTC hybrid engine gives 8,000 lb. of thrust for 35 seconds. It has shown that the use of such engines would more than triple the payload that can be put into orbit by several of America's standard space launch vehicles, such as Delta, Atlas-Centaur and Titan-Centaur.

War head

| Combustion chamber | Pumps and pump propellents | Liquid oxygen tank | Alcohol tank | Control compartment |

Diagram showing main components of V-2

The same basic principles govern the performance of a rocket whether it uses solid or liquid propellents. So, to find out more about these principles, let us take a closer look at the first large modern rocket, the German V-2.

In the extreme nose was the fuse and payload, consisting of a ton of explosive. Then came the control compartment, containing gyroscopes to turn the missile towards the target after vertical take-off and to keep it steady during flight, and a device to switch off the propellent supply when the rocket had built up sufficient speed to carry it to its target. Immediately behind the control compartment was the first of the two huge propellent tanks, containing about 3½ tons of alcohol (the fuel), followed by a second tank for five tons of liquid oxygen (the oxidant).

Level with the leading-edge of the tail-fins was the turbine and fuel pump assembly, which pumped the propellents into the combustion

chamber in the correct proportions. The turbine was driven by the reaction of two additional fluids—hydrogen peroxide and calcium per-
manganate—stored in small tanks to one side of it, and in turn drove
the fuel pumps. Finally, in the tail of the rocket was the combustion
chamber, in which the alcohol and liquid oxygen were mixed and burned
at a temperature of about 2,700 deg. C., producing an exhaust velocity of
4,500 m.p.h. through the venturi nozzle.

To prevent the chamber from being melted by the fierce heat it was
double-walled, and the alcohol was circulated between the walls on its
way to the interior of the chamber. This method of using the propellents
to cool the chamber is known as regenerative cooling.

Without its 8½ tons of propellents, V-2 weighed about 4 tons. Each ton
of rocket, including payload, carried therefore approximately 2·2 tons of
propellent, and this weight ratio between rocket and propellent is of great
importance, because the more propellent and payload it can carry in relation to its own structure weight, the more efficient it is. The Boeing-built
S-IC liquid-propellent first stage of the Saturn V Moon rocket has a structure weight of 135 tons yet carries nearly 2,045 tons of propellents, more
than 15 tons of propellent for each ton of rocket.

One of the ways in which designers save weight is to let the walls of the
propellent tanks form the outside skin of the rocket, so avoiding the need
for a separate skin. This is easy in the case of solid-propellent and storable
liquid-propellent rocket motors, as they are usually simple cylinders with
a nozzle at one end. All the designer need do is attach wings or fins to the
cylinder and bolt on a pointed nose section containing the payload,
guidance and control equipment, and he has a rocket.

Exhaust velocity is another measure of efficiency and is of the order of
5,500 m.p.h. in modern liquid-propellent rockets. However, a better yard-
stick is specific impulse, which has the same meaning for rocket engineers
as miles-per-gallon has for a motorist. It is simply a figure indicating the
amount of thrust derived from each pound of propellent in one second of
engine operation. In the case of the liquid hydrogen-fuelled upper stages
of the Saturn V launch rocket it works out at 424 at sea level; the specific
impulse of V-2 was 215.

Even with our present know-how, it would be impossible to attain the
speeds, heights, and ranges needed by ICBMs and space-rockets but for
the use of the step-rocket principle that was pioneered by Colonel Boxer
for his life-line rockets over a hundred years ago.

It is easy to understand how a step-rocket works if we think of the
similar technique used by mountaineers to climb a high peak.

When Sir John Hunt's party set out to conquer Everest in the spring of
1953, it consisted of thirteen climbers and a large party of porters to carry
all the food and supplies needed for the attempt. In this way, it was pos-

sible to set up a fairly large, well-provided camp at a height of 24,000 feet. From there, three men carried a small load of food and equipment up to 27,900 feet and then turned back. Hillary and Tensing were able to make use of this, without tiring themselves by hauling it up, and so were fresh enough to reach the summit of Everest. This would never have been possible if they had had to carry their own food and equipment all the way.

In just the same manner, a step-rocket consists of a small rocket carried by a larger rocket, which in turn can be carried by a still-larger one—and so on, depending on the number of steps, or stages, required. Theoretically, there is no limit to the number of stages that can be used, but the size of even a three-stage long-range rocket begins to get a little frightening.

We can see why when we remember that in the V-2 more than eleven tons of structure and propellents were needed to carry a one-ton warhead for 150 miles at 3,600 m.p.h. When the Germans wanted to extend its range to make possible attacks on America, they calculated they would need to attain a peak speed of 6,200 m.p.h. This required the use of a first-stage 'booster' rocket weighing no less than 78 tons to carry the V-2 on the first part of its journey.

If this step-rocket, the A-9/A-10, had ever been fired, the booster would have carried an improved V-2, with its propellents intact, high above the atmosphere at 2,600 m.p.h. When the booster's propellents were exhausted, it would have dropped away to save weight, automatically starting the engine of the V-2 which would have added its own 3,600 m.p.h. to that of the complete rocket, to give the required 6,200 m.p.h.

Use of a two-stage rocket weighing 90 tons to carry a one-ton warhead may seem an awfully expensive way of doing things; but it was the only way in which Germany could have attacked America in 1945, and the use of step-rockets is still the only way in which we can give a missile intercontinental range or put a satellite into orbit around the Earth.

The Missile Family

AT FIRST, rockets like the German V-2 were regarded mainly as a form of artillery, offering a longer range and greater accuracy than guns for the bombardment of distant targets. Then came anti-aircraft missiles, which replaced guns for air defence duties, and small air-launched missiles which began to take the place of cannon and machine-guns on fighter-planes.

Now the fighters themselves, and piloted bombers, are being replaced or supplemented by guided weapons for certain duties. The result is an immense variety of missiles of all shapes and sizes; but they can be divided into seven basic categories, according to the job they do. Before learning how they work, we must know something about these different jobs.

Air-to-air missile. Usually quite small, this type is fired from an aeroplane to shoot down other aircraft. It can be carried on pylons under the

Firestreak air-to-air missiles on a Lightning interceptor

aeroplane's wings or externally on the fuselage, on wing-tip launchers or in an internal weapons-bay in the bottom of the fuselage. Often it is fired automatically by the fighter's radar when the target comes within range.

Air-to-surface missile. A rocket or jet-propelled missile which is launched from an aircraft to destroy a target on the ground or at sea. Smallest are tiny guided anti-tank rockets fired from helicopters and light aircraft. Largest are the stand-off bombs which are launched by bombers many miles from the target and complete the attack under their own power. In this way, the bombers themselves do not need to battle past the final ring

The American Quail is unique. Launched in flight from a B-52 bomber, it is packed with electronic equipment designed to protect the bomber by confusing the enemy defences. Although under 13 feet long it is indistinguishable from the 157-foot bomber on radar screens

of defending fighters and anti-aircraft batteries. Stand-off bombs are usually carried under the wings of the launching aircraft, or half-inside a special cutaway bomb-bay in the bottom of the fuselage.

Hound Dog air-to-surface missile

Surface-to-air missile. Anti-aircraft weapon, usually launched from a ramp on the ground or on a ship. All those at present in use, except the Boeing Bomarc (see page 44), have a range of under 100 miles and are for 'last-

Bloodhound surface-to-air missile, showing the boosters falling away

ditch' defence of vital targets against aircraft that have slipped past the fighter defences. Both America and Russia are building surface-to-air rocket missiles able to locate and destroy an incoming ICBM at a distance or height of several hundred miles. These are known usually as anti-ballistic missiles (ABMs), and the way in which they work is described on pages 46 and 47.

Surface-to-surface missile. This type of missile takes the place of guns or piloted ground attack aircraft, and is fired from the ground or a ship against every kind of target on land or at sea. It includes tiny rockets that can be carried and fired by a single soldier against tanks and enemy strong-points, larger tactical missiles with ranges of from 10 to 1,000 miles, IRBMs (intermediate range ballistic missiles) with a range of at least

Bomarc long-range surface-to-air missile

1,500 miles, and ICBMs (intercontinental ballistic missiles) with a range of up to 9,000 miles.

Many Russian IRBMs, like 'Scapegoat', are carried on tracked launch vehicles which give them great mobility and increase their effective range by transporting them closer to their targets.

Another interesting Russian surface-to-surface rocket is the mighty SS-9 ('Scarp'), which serves in two forms. The standard ICBM is stored in and fired from an underground launcher and can be fitted with either

Nord SS.10 surface-to-surface anti-tank missiles
on a Jeep launcher

28

Russian rocket-powered 'flying bomb' missile (NATO code-name 'Styx'),
launched from containers on fast patrol boats like that shown beneath it. The
under-fuselage booster motor falls away when its fuel is all burned. Missiles of
this type were used by the Egyptians to sink the Israeli destroyer *Eilat* on
21 October 1967

Russia's 'Scamp' weapon system
consists of a tracked transporter-
launch vehicle which carries inside a hinged container the two-
stage 'Scapegoat' rocket. It is
highly mobile, and 'Scapegoat'
has a range of 2,500 miles. The
container has been omitted from
this drawing, for clarity

Known to NATO as 'Scarp', the huge Russian liquid-propellent SS–9 rocket is used both as an ICBM and as a launcher for the FOBS 'space bomb'

a 20/25-megaton H-bomb warhead or a special type containing three multiple independently-targeted re-entry vehicles (MIRV). These can be so arranged that they fall in a pattern that corresponds precisely with the locations of a flight of three American Minuteman ICBM underground launchers.

Instead of a single warhead, ICBM's can now be fitted with smaller multiple independently-targeted re-entry vehicles (MIRV) for precision attacks on several targets at once

In its second form, 'Scarp' is used to launch Russia's 'space bomb', known in America as the 'fractional orbital bombardment system' (FOBS). This has been described as a warhead which can be launched into an orbit about 100 miles above the Earth. At a given point, before completion of the first orbit, a retro-rocket slows the warhead and causes it to drop on the target. Intended primarily to attack U.S. missile and bomber bases, FOBS offers the advantages of a much reduced warning time and the ability to approach the targets from the south instead of the heavily-defended north. Main disadvantage is that FOBS would be less accurate than a normal ICBM.

Some surface-to-surface missiles are not rockets, but 'flying bombs', which look like pilotless aeroplanes and are powered by rocket or jet-engines. The jet-propelled types are often referred to as 'cruise missiles' or 'air-breathing missiles', because they have to cruise in the atmosphere below 65,000 feet instead of following a ballistic trajectory like a shell.

Surface-to-underwater missile. Fired from a ship, to attack another ship or submarine. A weapon of this type is the French Malafon, which is launched from a ship with the aid of two solid-propellent rocket motors that fall

Malafon surface-to-underwater missile

away when their fuel is burned. It then glides towards the target at about 500 m.p.h. A half a mile from the target a parachute opens, slowing Malafon so abruptly that its homing torpedo payload is shot out of the front by inertia and enters the water, finally homing on to the target.

Underwater-to-surface missile. Best-known missile of this type is the two-stage Lockheed Polaris, which is carried by a class of special nuclear-powered submarines. Sixteen of the missiles are carried by each submarine.

To launch one, a small rocket motor is fired so that the exhaust gases enter the launch-tube and 'pop' Polaris to the surface, after which the first-stage rocket motor ignites and Polaris travels through the air like an

Polaris underwater-to-surface missile being fired from a submerged submarine

ordinary surface-to-surface IRBM. Polaris sets the defences a tremendous problem, because, unlike its land-based counterparts, it comes from a mobile, difficult-to-locate base.

Underwater-to-underwater missile. A weapon in this category is the Subroc (submarine rocket) developed by Goodyear to enable U.S. submarines to attack enemy submarines and ships over long ranges. It consists of a supersonic ballistic rocket missile which is fired from the torpedo tubes of a submerged submarine. After rising to the surface, it is propelled through the air by a large solid-propellent booster, which falls away after burn-out, leaving the missile and its nuclear depth charge warhead to complete the trajectory, under continued guidance, and re-enter the water near the target.

(1) Horizontally launched

(2) Rocket motor ignites

(3) Missile climbs vertically out of the sea

(4) Booster separates

(5) Trajectory under guidance

(6) Supersonic re-entry into sea

(7) Nuclear warhead explodes

Subroc

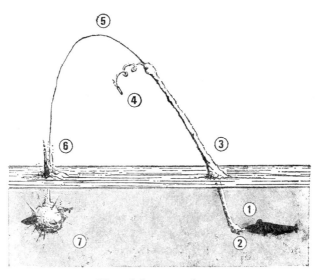

How Subroc works

An important point to remember is that the missile itself is usually only one component of a complete weapon system. Even a comparatively simple solid-propellent surface-to-surface artillery rocket like the American 460-mile-range Pershing needs a convoy of four tracked vehicles to get it on its way. They consist of the missile's transporter, with built-in erector-launcher; a vehicle to carry the nuclear warhead; another to generate and supply the power required by the complete weapon system; and a fourth to house the complex fire control and communications equipment. To add to the designer's problems, the U.S. Army insisted that all units must be small and light enough to be carried to far-off combat areas inside the U.S.A.F.'s C-133 Cargomaster freight-planes.

To get some idea of why all this ground equipment is needed, we must take a look under the smooth skin of the missiles at the maze of equipment which enables them to track down and destroy their target.

Guided Weapons

SOME people, who ought to know better, regard guided missiles as being merely super fireworks which carry chunks of high explosive for long distances. After experiencing attacks by the V-2 rocket in 1945, they predicted that the era of so-called push-button warfare was just around the corner. Yet the best bombardment missiles available in America fifteen years later were still no more than improved versions of the V-2, and the newspapers which forecast the imminent replacement of piloted fighter and bomber aircraft by missiles were beginning to regret their haste.

The fact is that V-2, although a tremendous achievement, was primitive by comparison with many of the guided weapons now entering production. This is no criticism of V-2, any more than one would criticize the Wright biplane of 1903 for not flying as fast and far as a jet airliner; but it must be understood that perfection of the first ICBMs represented per-

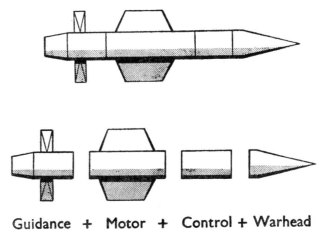

Guidance + Motor + Control + Warhead

Main parts of a guided weapon

haps the most difficult single engineering project ever undertaken by man. It would be the most tragic waste of genius and skill imaginable if it had no ultimate value except to destroy: but we know already that a rocket built to carry a hydrogen-bomb warhead from one place on Earth's surface to another, can just as easily lift a satellite or manned spacecraft right out into space.

Whatever its size and job, a guided missile is the product of a dozen advanced sciences. Except for its nose, its outside shape is far less important than that of an aeroplane and, more often than not, is basically a simple cylinder. Many of the latest long-range bombardment missiles do not even have tail-fins, because these would be effective for so short a period, as the rocket streaked through the atmosphere, that their weight is not justified. Instead, they are steered by pivoting the rocket nozzle.

Almost all of the problems and complexities are packed inside the missile's smooth skin, and they can be divided into four main groups—motor, guidance, control, and warhead.

So many variations of these four groups are available to the designer that his task in choosing the best combination is rather like trying to forecast the correct results on a football pool.

Should he power his missile by a ramjet engine, which will give it a longer range, or a rocket motor, which will enable it to fly higher and possibly faster? If he chooses a rocket, should it be of the solid or liquid-propellent type?

Should he rely on a simple, relatively cheap radio control system, or must he use one of the more complicated guidance systems which cannot be jammed by enemy countermeasures? Does he, in fact, need any guidance system at all? Why not point the missile in the right direction and keep it on a straight course by spin stabilization?

What kind of warhead is needed? Not every target justifies a nuclear warhead. If he fits the high-explosive kind, should it be of the fragmentation type which flings jagged pieces of metal in all directions, with the object of shattering or severing some vital part of the target, or should it destroy by sheer blast, or even by fire?

The answers usually are dictated by the precise job the weapon will have to do and whether or not it is needed in a hurry.

When, for example, the U.S. Air Force ordered its first guided missile there was no time to be too clever. It wanted a bombardment weapon with a range of about 500 miles, and the Martin Company produced a straightforward pilotless bomber, or 'flying bomb', to do the job. Named the Matador, it had a conventional aeroplane shape and was powered by an Allison turbojet engine of the same basic type that was fitted in thousands of Shooting Star jet-fighters and trainers.

Use of this jet-engine meant that the Matador would be able to fly no higher and faster than ordinary aeroplanes. Against this, its small size promised to make it a difficult target for the defences and its designers knew that at least they would encounter no power plant problems if they used such a well-proven and immediately available engine.

The guidance system was chosen in the same practical way. U.S. piloted aircraft in the Korean war had been controlled by a radar system known as MSQ, and it was decided to utilize this for the Matador. The chief disadvantage was that it required a network of ground radar stations to keep the missile continuously in view throughout its flight, which meant that accurate control was possible only while the missile was still within line-of-sight range of the last station. But it was a battle-tested system and would clearly suffice until something better could be devised.

As a result, the U.S.A.F. was able to rush the original TM–61A Matador into service by 1954, and improved versions of this weapon, known as the MGM–13C Mace, continue to form part of America's military machine, because advantage has been taken in the intervening years to fit them with much more advanced, self-contained guidance systems.

Matador, therefore, was an example of a guided weapon which began as little more than an aeroplane, with a few 'black boxes' replacing the human crew. At the other extreme was the Atlas ICBM, in which no considerations of cost or complexity could be allowed to influence the primary requirement of carrying a hydrogen-bomb warhead for at least 5,000 miles, with a high degree of accuracy and resistance to any counter-measures attempted by the enemy.

America had to be prepared to spend about £3,700 million in order to put twenty-five squadrons of Atlas and Titan liquid-propellent ICBMs into service, but in return for this vast expenditure, the U.S.A.F. knew that it would get a weapon force of terrifying power against which no defence would be possible.

Almost one-third of the entire cost of the Atlas development programme went in designing, perfecting and testing its oddly-shaped nose-cone. The reason is known technically as the re-entry problem, which means simply the problem of getting the nose-cone, containing the H-bomb warhead, back into the atmosphere over the

Atlas ICBM

target in one piece. It was the only part of Atlas that had to be brought back, and was separated from the rest of the airframe while still in space.

Anything that enters the atmosphere at high speed from space usually encounters so much friction from the air that it is burned up. That is why meteorites end their life as shooting stars and why Russia's early *Sputnik* satellites finished up as glowing streaks of molten metal.

Obviously, there is no point in carrying an H-bomb 5,000 miles on the nose of an ICBM if it is to be destroyed by heat as soon as it attempts to re-enter the atmosphere, and that is why so much time and effort have been devoted to the re-entry problem. All kinds of ideas have been tried out. The type of long narrow nose-cone that was developed for Atlas and is still used on the A2 version of Polaris (see page 32) is coated with special plastic materials that burn away, absorbing the heat and leaving the warhead unaffected. It has also been found that certain shapes of blunt nose-cone shed most of their heat into a strong shock-wave which protects them.

It took years of research before the Americans could be sure of recovering nose-cones that had re-entered the atmosphere at speeds of up to 17,000 m.p.h. (twenty-six times the speed of sound). Having done so they (and the Russians) were able to use similar techniques in designing their manned spacecraft. So techniques worked out for missile warheads have made it possible to get men back safely into the atmosphere after flights into space.

Nor is the re-entry of space vehicles the only additional benefit that is resulting from the ICBM programme. When the U.S. submarines *Nautilus* and *Skate* made their first historic underwater journeys beneath the north polar ice cap in the summer of 1958, they found their way with the help of a navigation system that had been developed originally for an intercontinental missile. Known as an inertial guidance system, it is only one of many interesting methods used to steer missiles unerringly to their target, as we shall see in the next chapter.

Guidance Systems

THE best, most versatile, and lightest guidance system in the world is the human brain. If the pilot of a fighter 'plane finds that the bomber he has been sent to attack is friendly, he can turn back. If something goes wrong with his aircraft in flight, he can usually discover for himself the cause and put it right. If his controls are damaged by enemy fire, or his radio packs up, or half his fuel is lost through a holed tank, he can work out what to do for the best and then do it.

In a missile, the guidance system takes the place of a pilot, and the better the system the more nearly it approaches the efficiency of a human brain.

No guidance system will ever be as good as a man in every way, because it cannot discriminate, change its mind, or put right mishaps that may occur once it has been launched. However, some of the more advanced systems come remarkably near to these ideals. They can be made to turn away from any friendly aircraft against which they have been fired accidentally, provided the aircraft is fitted with I.F.F. (Identification, Friend or Foe) radar. They can be so designed that any slight deviation from course, resulting from bad weather or damage, is corrected immediately; and they can ignore enemy radio or radar devices that try to jam their electronics.

In addition, many guidance systems can withstand accelerations, extremes of heat and cold, and other conditions that would kill a human pilot. Most important of all, they can be sent on missions from which there is no possibility of return.

The basic job of a guidance system is to ensure that a missile goes where it is meant to go. Obviously a missile designed to attack an aeroplane, which might change direction while it is on the way up, must have a different type of guidance from that fitted in a bombardment missile aimed at a large city, the position of which is known precisely and never changes. Similarly, an air-to-air weapon, fired from one aeroplane at another, is far too small to contain the sort of guidance system that a 120-foot-long ICBM uses to find its way to a target more than 5,000 miles away.

As a result, no fewer than eleven basic types of guidance system have been widely used, and some missiles utilize two different systems during successive stages of their flight.

Magnetic Heading Guidance. This is an extremely simple system for surface-to-surface missiles, needing no ground equipment, and was used in versions of the V-1 'flying bomb' launched against England in 1944–5. Before launching, the missile is set to follow a precise compass course to the target and is kept on this course by an automatic pilot. To make interception more difficult, a 'programming' device can be included, so that instead of flying in a straight line the heading is changed one or more times during flight. After a pre-calculated time, a clockwork mechanism cuts off the missile's fuel supply and it dives to the ground.

Wire Command Guidance. Simplest of all guidance systems, wire command is used nowadays only on the smallest types of surface-to-surface or air-to-surface anti-tank weapons. As the missile leaves its launcher and travels towards the target, it trails behind it one or two fine wires, which unwind from bobbins and continue to link it with the operator's control box.

By means of a simple thumbstick or joystick control, the operator can pass electrical signals through the wires to steer the missile into its target. This type of guidance is limited to a range of about two miles, because of the difficulty of packing greater lengths of wire into a small missile, and can normally be used only when the target is visible. Within its limits, it is efficient and almost immune to jamming, and the average operator can usually achieve 80 per cent direct hits against static or moving targets after very little practice.

Radio Command Guidance. This is similar to wire command guidance, except that the signals are transmitted by radio instead of through wires, so that the system can be used over longer ranges. The operator need not be near the launching point, which could be behind the combat area. Normally he would be in a front-line position, and would fire and control the missile remotely. He need not even be able to see the target if he knows its precise position, because he can keep track of the missile's position on a radar screen and so steer it into the target.

Radio command is susceptible to jamming, and missiles using it are designed to operate on a variety of different radio frequencies. By setting a frequency on the transmitter and on the receiver in the missile immediately before firing, the operator gives the enemy very little time to discover the chosen frequency, which he must do before he can jam the guidance system.

Radar Command Guidance

Some missiles equipped with radio command guidance carry a small television camera in their nose. This transmits a picture of the scene ahead of the missile to a screen on the ground. By keeping the target centred on the screen, the operator can steer the missile even when it is out of sight, enabling the system to be used over longer ranges.

Radar Command Guidance. Radar command requires very little equipment in the missile, but a great deal on the ground. It involves the use of two radar transmitters. One picks up the target, 'locks' on it, and works out its speed and position. The other 'locks' onto the missile after it has been fired and keeps track of its speed and position. Data from the two radar sets are fed into a computer, which calculates rapidly the correct course for the missile to follow, so that it will intercept and destroy the target. The computer then transmits the appropriate signals by radio command, to steer the missile on an interception course.

This type of guidance is used for the American Nike-Ajax surface-to-air anti-aircraft missile, the ground equipment for which is said to contain $1\frac{1}{2}$ million individual parts.

Radio Navigation. This is another system requiring two transmitters at known positions on the ground, but is much simpler than radar command guidance. A receiver in the missile picks up radio signals transmitted at regular intervals by the two ground stations and, by measuring the difference in time of reception of the two signals, can work out its distance from the transmitters. It can then use this information, in conjunction with the length of time it has been airborne, to work out its precise position. If this does not lie along the correct course to the target, it is steered automatically back onto course.

Beam Riding Guidance. In this system, the missile flies along a narrow 'pencil beam' of light or radio signals 'locked' onto the target. It is used mainly for air-to-air or surface-to-air weapons and has the advantage of requiring less equipment than radar command and of being able to control more than one missile at a time. As the width of the beam increases with distance, it has to be kept as narrow as possible at the transmitter, and a much wider 'gathering' beam is usually transmitted simultaneously to pick up the missile after firing and direct it into the main beam, in which it is kept by its radio equipment.

In a typical air-to-air system, the fighter 'plane carries in its nose a radar scanner which sweeps the sky ahead until it picks up the target and 'locks' onto it. As soon as the fighter is within range, the missile is fired and centred into the radar beam, down which it flies to the target. Its warhead is exploded by a proximity-fuse as soon as it is near enough to destroy the enemy.

Semi-Active Homing. This is the system used for two of Britain's land-based surface-to-air guided weapons—the Royal Air Force's Bloodhound

Target
Radar

Target Tracking Radar

Servo Link   Link from Early Warning Radar

Beam Riding Guidance

LOCK-ON 'LAMP'
RADAR

RADAR
REFLECTIONS

MISSILE HOMES ON
SOURCE OF REFLECTIONS

Semi-Active Homing

41

and the Army's Thunderbird. It uses a powerful ground radar which picks up the target, 'locks' onto it, and 'illuminates' it with very strong radar beams. These radar beams bounce back off the target and are picked up by a receiver in the nose of the missile. By flying towards the source of the reflections, it 'homes' onto the target and destroys it either by impact or through the use of a proximity-fuse.

Active Homing. Unlike most of the systems described so far, this one is self-contained in the missile. It dispenses with most of the ground equipment, making the weapon more mobile, but adds to the complexity and size of the missile itself.

Active homing works in the same way as semi-active homing, except that the missile carries its own radar transmitter, as well as a receiver.

Active Homing

When it is fired, its transmitter sends out signals which bounce back from the target and are picked up by the receiver, which tells the control system how to steer the missile towards the source of the reflections.

Passive Homing. This system gets its name from the fact that no signals of any kind are transmitted by the weapon system. Instead, the missile is fitted with a device which homes onto some type of energy or disturbance caused by, or emitted from, the target. The acoustic system fitted to homing torpedoes is one example, because it picks up the noise of a ship's engines and homes on the source of the noise.

The most common passive homing system used in missiles is an infra-red or heat-seeking unit. This consists of a quite small unit mounted behind a glass dome or panels in the nose of the missile, which homes on heat emitted by the target and particularly the hot exhaust from the engines. It is so sensitive that it could detect the heat of an ordinary household electric fire from a distance of more than a mile away, and is immune from jamming. Main disadvantage is that its infra-red 'eye' cannot see through

Passive Homing

dense cloud, so that a fighter armed with infra-red missiles often carries also batteries of unguided or radar-homing missiles.

A very advanced passive homing system is under consideration for one of the anti-ballistic missiles designed to provide a defence against the ICBM. Success would depend on detecting the firing of the ICBM, so that its trajectory could be predicted quickly by a computer. A surface-to-air missile would then be launched automatically on an interception course, fitted with a passive homing device which would steer towards the electro-magnetic disturbances caused by the missile's warhead as it re-entered the atmosphere.

Celestial Guidance. Known also as 'star-tracking', this system is an automatic version of the astro-navigation which has enabled sailors and airmen to find their way for centuries. There are two or three variations of the same idea, but what happens basically is that a telescope in the missile 'locks' onto a chosen star and holds the missile at a pre-calculated angle to the star throughout its flight. The angle will of course change constantly, but it is comparatively easy to work out what it should be as the missile approaches the target. As a result, the guidance system can be set to put the missile into a dive when the telescope shows the star to be in this angular position relative to the missile.

Inertial Guidance. This is the most advanced system of all, being self-contained in the missile, unjammable, and extremely accurate. It was used in a simple form in one version of the wartime V-2, and has been chosen for the most modern long-range bombardment missiles.

The basic idea is simple, involving the use of accelerometers or gyroscopes to measure every slight change of direction of the missile during its flight. If any change of direction would carry it off its pre-determined course to the target, the guidance system moves the controls automatically to put it right. The mechanism needed to do this is too complex to describe in detail in this book.

By now, it should be clear that there is much more to a guided missile than is apparent at first glance. So, before passing on to more exciting types of rocket, it might be best to see quickly how all the different systems and components work together to enable some typical missiles to reach their target.

Missiles in Action

FIRST OF ALL, let us imagine we have just taken off in a Lightning fighter 'plane of the R.A.F. to intercept one of the Jindivik pilotless radio-controlled jet-propelled targets that are being used to test British missiles in a realistic way. Over our radio we hear the voice of the ground controller telling us to climb to 50,000 feet on a bearing of 87 deg., which will take us towards the target. In the pointed nose-cone of the Lightning, the scanner of the Airpass (Airborne Interception Radar and Pilot's Attack Sight System) searches a wide area of the sky ahead. Soon its signals bounce back from an object off to the left of our line of flight. The Jindivik has been found, and a slight pressure on the control column turns the fighter towards it.

There is no need even to see the target because Airpass measures the range, works out the deflection, and tells us automatically when to fire the Firestreak missiles that are carried on pylons on each side of the fuselage. Once they have been launched the Jindivik is doomed. No matter how it twists and turns, the missiles' infra-red 'eyes' will home on the heat of its jet-engine; so we can break off our attack and turn for our base even before the target disintegrates.

Now we will go over to America to see a Bomarc surface-to-air missile under test. It stands on its tail for take-off, but otherwise looks very much like an aeroplane. Inside its rear fuselage is a rocket motor, to thrust it off the ground and accelerate it to a speed where the two ramjet engines slung under its body can take over for cruising flight.

Like all other anti-aircraft missiles and fighter 'planes in the United States and Canada, Bomarc is controlled by a vast electronic network known as SAGE (semi-automatic ground environment). This receives signals from the radar chains whenever an aircraft or missile approaches North America and, in wartime, would decide whether the target should be intercepted by piloted aircraft or missiles. No target would be overlooked and no attack duplicated. Nor is there any need for each fighter station and missile base to have its own control centre, because SAGE direction centres can control the entire defence system.

The firing button that launches our test Bomarc might be hundreds of miles from where it takes off, trailing behind it the diamond shock-wave

44

pattern of its exhaust, and the missile is guided entirely automatically. Radar signals showing the position of the target—in this case a pilotless bomber —are fed into a computer which in turn transmits guidance signals to Bomarc, now cruising 60,000 feet above the ground at more than twice the speed of sound. Each signal is picked up by the receiver inside the missile and passed on to the control system, which makes tiny movements of the pivoted wing-tip control surfaces to steer the missile to the target.

After a flight of anything up to 400 miles, Bomarc's own active radar homing takes over, locking onto the bomber and steering the missile into it with merciless precision.

Next, we will watch a trial firing of a Minuteman ICBM, over the range that stretches thousands of miles across the Pacific from Vandenberg Air Force Base, California. The scene is very different from that prior to launching one of the Atlas missiles which Minuteman replaced. The change to solid-propellent motors made possible a range of more than 7,000 miles with a weapon only 60 feet long, weighing less than one-third as much as Atlas. Nor is it so vulnerable to enemy surprise attack, for Minuteman is stored in and fired from a concrete hole in the ground, known as a 'silo'. Even its fire-control and servicing crews work in underground rooms, safe from nuclear attack.

Nevertheless, even with such a reliable and comparatively simple missile, things go wrong sometimes. So not until the firing button has been pressed and Minuteman climbs away on the brilliant exhaust flames from its four first-stage nozzles does anyone relax. Even then there is much to do, for its flight must be tracked continuously by radar to make sure that everything works perfectly.

As the missile climbs higher and higher its inertial guidance system follows a pre-set flight programme, tilting the four nozzles to steer the missile away from the vertical in a curving ballistic trajectory that will take it to a height of many hundreds of miles. Soon, the first stage burns out and falls away. The second stage ignites, thrusting the missile ever faster and higher. It, too, burns out and drops away, its job done. Now it is the smaller third stage that accelerates the warhead to 22 times the speed of sound. When its motor dies, the warhead continues to climb, to more than 700 miles above the Earth, slowing only gradually as gravity tries to pull it back.

At last, gravity wins and it can climb no farther through the black almost air-less emptiness of space. It begins curving back towards the Earth, at ever faster speed, not necessarily nose-first, because there is insufficient atmosphere to straighten it at first. As it nears the denser atmosphere the nose-cone which would house an H-bomb warhead or multiple warheads if this were a wartime flight, falls away. The rest of the rocket melts in a streak of white-hot metal, but the nose-cone goes on—

glowing, but protected by its strange shape and secret design. And, little more than 20 minutes after the firing button was pressed, the warhead slams into the sea with a searing, sizzling splash that flings a column of water high into the air.

From scattered points all around the target area, ships and aircraft begin moving in to retrieve the nose-cone. At Vandenberg AFB, the firing officer writes 'Launching entirely successful' at the end of his report.

Finally, let us imagine what would happen at one of America's Safeguard anti-ballistic missile (ABM) sites if it ever had to go into action against an enemy ICBM attack. Equipment at the site, protecting a Minuteman missile base, comprises a missile site radar (MSR), a perimeter

A Spartan missile leaves its underground launcher

acquisition radar (PAR) and a number of Spartan and Sprint missiles on underground launchers. Spartan is a long-range three-stage missile designed to destroy an incoming warhead above the atmosphere, at a range of several hundred miles. The strange, conical Sprint is an extremely high-speed rocket able to destroy at low altitude any warhead that slipped past the Spartans.

An attack would first be detected by the PAR, which would alert the Safeguard site and give the general track of the enemy warhead. The MSR would then work out the precise position of the warhead and guide a Spartan or Sprint missile to intercept and destroy it by means of a nuclear explosion. The entire operation would normally be automatic, but human intervention would be possible at any stage, to ensure the safety of people on the ground or of 'friendly' aircraft and missiles in flight.

Test firings of ABMs from Kwajalein atoll in the Pacific have proved the ability of the weapons to intercept ICBM warheads. However, the cost of protecting all targets in the U.S.A. or Russia against ICBM attack would be so great that neither country can afford a full deployment of ABMs to defend major cities and factory areas. That is why America is concentrating at present only on defence of its Minuteman sites, and why the ICBM forces of East and West remain a major deterrent to any future world war.

Learning About Space

SPACE FLIGHT is no longer a dream of the distant future, but something that happens every day of the year. This does not mean that men with 'goldfish bowls' on their heads are strapping themselves into space-ships daily and setting out for the Moon and Mars. Space begins much nearer to the Earth than most people realize, and within a few years even airline passengers will travel on the fringe of space without considering it at all out of the ordinary.

If we look back a mere twenty-five years we find that the average airliner then cruised at heights between 1,000 and 10,000 feet. Today turbo-prop airliners fly at 20,000 to 35,000 feet, whilst the jets may cruise above 40,000 feet.

Inside their cabins, in armchair seats, passengers are more comfortable than ever before. Yet if the cabins were not pumped full of warm air, everyone would soon be in a very sorry state because, in terms of air density, they are already three-quarters of the way to space when flying at 40,000 feet.

On the other side of the thin metal walls of the cabin, the outside air is only 24 per cent as dense as at ground level, and its temperature is more than 100° Fahrenheit below freezing. This temperature remains the same at much greater heights, but air density decreases steadily and a pilot flying at 100,000 feet is above 98·6 per cent of the atmosphere. The odd 1·4 per cent would make so little difference that he can consider himself in space.

Rocket-planes have flown often at such heights, and it will not be many years before passengers cruise at 60,000 feet or more in supersonic airliners, above 91 per cent of the atmosphere. As a result, designers and scientists had to solve many of the problems of flight in space long before anyone was ready to make the first journey to the Moon.

Our bodies are designed to work at ground level, where there is plenty of air for them to breathe and where the weight of all the air above us in the atmosphere exerts a pressure of about 14·7 lb. on every square inch of our skin. At a height of 20,000 feet, the atmosphere is so 'thin' that an airman begins to need a supply of oxygen. Above 30,000 feet oxygen equipment is essential.

Higher still, even this is not enough. The decrease in air density results in a corresponding decrease of air pressure, and the airman's body rebels against having to work in a pressure only one-tenth of the customary 14·7 lb. per square inch. First, the nitrogen gas in the blood-stream begins to form bubbles, resulting in the painful condition that deep-sea divers call 'the bends'. Even worse, above about 62,000 feet, the pressure is so low that the blood would start to boil if nothing were done to prevent it.

What designers have to do is provide not only the oxygen missing from the atmosphere but the pressure as well. As already mentioned, they do this in airliners by pumping the cabin full of air, which does both jobs at once. The higher an airliner flies, the more it has to be pressurized and

North American X-15

the stronger its structure has to be to prevent its bursting like an over-filled balloon. In supersonic airliners, flying above 60,000 feet, the pressure will have to be so high that some designers would like to make the cabins window-less, to avoid weakening their structure with cut-outs.

There is an alternative to pressurization which is used in military aircraft, to avoid the excessive weight of thick cabin walls and to protect the pilot if the cabin is suddenly holed in combat, or if he has to escape by parachute at great heights.

48

It consists of clothing him in a pressure-suit, so designed that, when necessary, it fills automatically with compressed air, exerting a pressure on the pilot's body sufficient to enable him to breathe and to stop his blood from misbehaving. It is, in fact, a space-suit, complete with a large, strongly built pressurized helmet.

The ordinary pace of aviation progress, therefore, perfected the pressurized cabins and space-suits that are needed for journeying into space. The first of such journeys were made by rocket-planes like the North American X-15, fastest, highest-climbing aeroplane ever built, which flew at 4,534 m.p.h. and reached a height of 67 miles.

At even greater heights, there are many problems besides lack of air. For example, science-fiction writers have told us for years about the terrifying showers of meteorites that sweep through space at fantastic speed and would smash to pieces any space-ship that got in their way.

We knew that they existed, because the shooting stars we see if we look long enough on any clear night are caused by meteorites burning up as they enter Earth's atmosphere. What we had to find out was just how serious a danger they represent. Equally, we wanted to know if, when we left the protective shield of our atmosphere, cosmic rays and other radiation would be so intense that they would kill any living creature exposed to them.

To find the answers to these questions, and many others, vast sums of money were spent on research rockets. The first, fired in America after the war, were captured V-2s, carrying instruments instead of a warhead. The Martin Company produced an improved liquid-propellent rocket named the Viking, one of which reached a record height of 158 miles, and this has been followed by a host of other rockets.

The earliest experiments were not very ambitious. The data collected by instruments and telemetered (sent by radio sets in the rocket) back to recorders on the ground were concerned with simple measurements of air density, pressure, and temperature at varying heights. In some cases the nose-cone containing the instruments was retrieved by parachute, and soon we were able to see wonderful ciné-films of the Earth taken from rockets as they climbed to heights of more than 100 miles. If anyone still refused to believe that the world is round, these films should have made him change his ideas, because in many of them the curvature of the Earth could be seen clearly.

One film was of particular interest to meteorologists, because it showed for the first time what a hurricane looks like when seen from a height of 100 miles, and it was soon apparent that rockets might one day make possible far more accurate weather forecasts, by providing pictures of cloud formations and movements over immense areas.

As more rockets became available, the scope of the experiments grew.

D   49

New instruments and equipment were designed and fitted into the rocket nose-cones to measure and study such things as the humidity and composition of the atmosphere, the varying pull of gravity at different heights and in different places, changes in the Earth's magnetic field, the polar aurora, and cosmic radiation. Strips of metal-coated paper were flung out of some rockets at successive altitudes and then tracked by radar to show the strength and direction of high-altitude winds and air currents.

With the approach of the 1957–58 International Geophysical Year, the research was intensified. The object of the Year was for scientists of every nation to work together to find out more about the Earth, its weather, its magnetism, its shape, and conditions in the upper atmosphere and space around it.

Britain, France, and Japan announced plans to build new research rockets as part of their contribution. The United States told an excited world that it hoped to overcome the main drawback of rockets—the short duration of their flight—by putting a series of instrumented satellites into orbit around the Earth.

Russia said very little, and the surprise announcement by Moscow Radio on 4 October 1957 that *Sputnik I* was at that moment circling silently and unseen over our heads at 18,000 m.p.h. was one of the most dramatic in history. Man had taken another major stride into the dark emptiness of space—admittedly with only a 23-inch sphere, but few people were able to doubt any longer that spaceflight would be possible one day.

Skylark upper atmosphere research rocket

Sputniks and Explorers

THE Russians chose well when they named their first satellite the *Sputnik*, meaning 'fellow-traveller'. For millions of years the Earth had been accompanied on its voyaging through space by nature's satellite, the Moon. After 4 October 1957 it had two moons, for *Sputnik I* continued to weave its cat's-cradle orbit around the globe day after day, week after week.

Until that date, no man-made object had ever travelled faster than about 6,800 m.p.h. Yet there was the little satellite, clearly visible to the naked eye when the sun glinted on its polished shell after sunset or before dawn, streaking along at 18,000 m.p.h. without any engine to power it.

How did it get there, and what kept it up?

No pictures of the launching were published, but the Russians said they had used a three-stage rocket, which was logical, since the rocket with

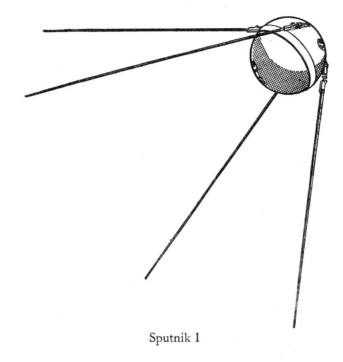

Sputnik I

which the Americans planned to put their Vanguard satellite into space was also a three-stage design.

After firing, they said that it climbed vertically for about a mile and a

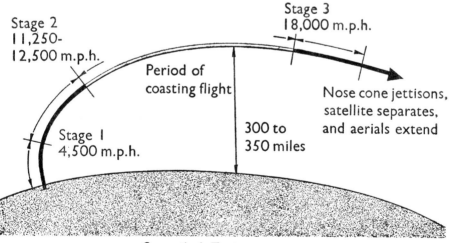

Sputnik I Trajectory

quarter and then, controlled by a 'programmed' guidance system (probably inertial), began tilting over. Soon afterwards, with the rocket travelling at around 4,500 m.p.h., at an angle of 45 deg. to the Earth's surface, the first-stage motor stopped and fell away.

With little atmosphere to slow it, stage two then took over, accelerating quickly to between 11,250 and 12,500 m.p.h. before it too fell away, its job done. After that, the last stage carrying on its nose the little *Sputnik*, coasted along in a powerless curving trajectory—on and on until it was hundreds of miles high, its path parallel with the surface of the Earth.

Six hundred miles from where the rocket was launched, the critical moment arrived. It was at the right altitude to enter an orbit, but was travelling nowhere near fast enough. Unless the third-stage motor, which burst into life at this point, could accelerate it to 18,000 m.p.h., it would start falling back towards the Earth on the downward half of the gigantic ellipse it had traced through space.

Stage three did work, and when its motor died it flung the *Sputnik* free

of the empty casing to continue its swift, silent flight alone, far above the atmosphere.

From that moment there was no reason why the little satellite should fall quickly to the Earth, any more than we should expect the Moon to drop on our heads one night. You can get some idea why if you half-fill a bucket with water and swing it round in a circle in the air. Provided you swing it quickly enough and hold the handle tightly the water will stay in the bottom of the bucket, even when it is upside down. If you slow down too much you will probably get a good wetting, and if you let go of the handle both bucket and water will fly away.

The water represents the *Sputnik*; the speed at which you swing it represents the speed of the *Sputnik's* orbit around the Earth, and your arm and hand represent the pull of gravity. Provided the *Sputnik* travels fast enough the centrifugal force trying to carry it off into space (the force that makes the bucket fly away if you release the handle) will always balance gravity and keep it in orbit.

At the orbital height of the Moon, about 238,000 miles above the Earth, a speed of something over 2,000 m.p.h. is sufficient to offset the pull of Earth's gravity. At the sort of height at which most satellites travel, a speed of around 18,000 m.p.h. is necessary because gravity becomes much more powerful as one approaches the Earth.

Obviously, the farther out into space we can send our satellites the more useful they are. Even before *Sputnik I*, we knew quite a lot about conditions near the Earth, but very little about what it is like beyond the atmosphere. What is more, if we send satellites far enough, they will stay up for ever; whereas even at a height of 400 miles there are still sufficient traces of atmosphere to slow them gradually. And as they slow down, the pull of gravity begins to make them lose height, so that they gradually get nearer and nearer to the Earth, until finally they burn up in the atmosphere.

One snag at first was the difficulty of putting the satellites into a perfectly circular path. *Sputnik I*, for example, was 588 miles above the Earth at the farthest point of its orbit (known technically as its apogee), but only 142 miles away at its nearest point (its perigee). This brought it within the last traces of the atmosphere on each revolution and it stayed up for only three months.

By comparison, although America's little Vanguard I satellite entered an elliptical orbit with an apogee of 2,453 miles and perigee of 409 miles, the perigee is high enough to ensure that it is being slowed at a negligible rate and it is expected to stay up for about one thousand years.

The satellites sent up by America and Russia have varied greatly in size and purpose. Vanguard I was the smallest, consisting of a tiny sphere only $6\frac{1}{2}$ inches in diameter and weighing less than 4 lb. But it was no toy. Brilliant engineering produced tiny radio transmitters weighing only $6\frac{1}{4}$ ounces, a device to measure solar radiation that weighs only $2\frac{1}{2}$ ounces, and a whole range of other tiny instruments. In glass-walled housings on the shell of the satellite is a series of solar batteries which absorb the sun's light and turn it into power to recharge the normal batteries, so that Vanguard I is continuing to radio data down to the Earth long after it would otherwise have become silent.

Sputnik II attracted far more publicity because it carried a living passenger, the dog Laika. The object was to find out if life could survive in space, and measurements of Laika's heart-beats, temperature, and other conditions as she made her 18,000 m.p.h. journey in a little pressurized cabin, showed that she appeared to be unaffected. Unfortunately, the Russians had not then devised a way of enabling her cabin to re-enter the atmosphere safely and she had to be put to death painlessly after eight days.

Because of this, there was no way of telling if she would have died later

Sputnik II mounted on the third-stage rocket

Explorer satellite

from the effects of radiation; and any optimism that might have been felt when she survived so long was dampened when signals transmitted by America's torpedo-shaped Explorer satellites revealed a layer of intense radiation only a few hundred miles above the Earth.

The existence of this mysterious radiation was only one of the things we learned from the first satellites: and it became clear that we should receive many surprises as we began to explore still further the secrets of space.

Man in Space

IT WAS EASY to be depressed by discoveries such as the radiation belt reported by America's Explorer satellites, and doubt that men would ever be able to reach the Moon. Yet this was silly, because every worthwhile achievement presents problems that must be overcome. It cost years of research, millions of pounds, and many lives before we learned how to fly safely through the 'sound barrier' at only 660–760 m.p.h. near the Earth; so we could hardly have expected to reach the Moon easily.

On the other hand, the fact that we had a satellite orbiting in space a mere fifteen years after the first successful firing of a V-2 rocket, and that both the Russians and the Americans had put men into orbit within a further $3\frac{1}{2}$–$4\frac{1}{2}$ years, showed how fast was the pace of progress in the new science of space flight, or astronautics.

Before new 'super-propellents' were developed, it was usually reckoned that rockets designed for flight into space would weigh 1,000 lb. for every 1 lb. of payload that they carried. That is why American scientists took such pains to design tiny lightweight instruments, so that a vast amount of information could be gained from a 21 lb. Vanguard satellite carried by a specially built three-stage rocket weighing only 22,600 lb.

Russian scientists, on the other hand, decided to use relatively huge rockets as the first and second stages for their *Sputniks*. This enabled them to put into orbit satellites of surprising size and bulk.

Rocket experts in the west received a shock when they learned that *Sputnik I* weighed 184·3 lb. Yet *Sputnik II* weighed an even more startling half a ton; while the great cone-shaped *Sputnik III*, launched on 15 May 1958, weighed no less than 1 ton 6 cwt. It was impossible to believe that it was launched by a rocket weighing 1,300 tons, which would have made the 120-ton Atlas launch rocket look like a squib, so it was clear that the Russians, too, must have made major advances in rocket design and construction. The subsequent achievements resulting from such advances, and from progress in America, still seem hard to believe.

Both countries decided in 1958 to try to put a satellite in orbit around the Moon. Such a leap forward, from 2,453 miles into space with Vanguard I to 238,000 miles for the Moon-satellite, was not over-ambitious. A speed of 18,000 m.p.h. is needed to put an Earth satellite into orbit; the addition of only 7,000 m.p.h. enables a rocket to reach the 'escape velocity' required to overcome the pull of gravity and head for the Moon. What is more, a further 1,000 m.p.h., giving a final speed of 26,000 m.p.h., makes possible a flight to Venus, 26 *million* miles away.

America shot for the Moon first with Thor-Able, an 88-foot high three-stage rocket which used a Thor IRBM as the first stage. The payload, known as Pioneer I, was an instrument container with a diameter of 30 inches and weight of 85 lb., and with a forward-firing solid-propellent rocket intended to slow it down as it neared the end of its journey, so that it would enter an orbit round the Moon. Launched on 11 October 1958, Pioneer I deviated from its course but travelled 70,700 miles out into space before gravity pulled it back into Earth's atmosphere. Russian scientists

Lunik III, which photographed the other side of the Moon

were more successful when they fired their 796 lb. *Lunik I* satellite on such an accurate course that it passed within some 4,600 miles of the Moon before going on to enter an orbit round the Sun.

America's Pioneer IV followed into a solar orbit, but after that Russia set a fantastic pace. On 14 September 1959, after a 34-hour flight, *Lunik II* slammed into the Moon and scattered over its surface tiny pennants bearing the 'hammer and sickle' badge. For the first time man had made physical contact with another body in space. On 4 October *Lunik III* was launched into a wide orbit which took it right round the Moon. On the way past it took photographs automatically, developed them, and sent them back to Earth by television, over a distance of 300,000 miles. This tremendous achievement gave us our first exciting glimpse of the side of the Moon that is always hidden from Earth.

On 15 May 1960 *Sputnik IV* went into orbit. Bigger than ever, it was described by Moscow as a space-ship, similar to the kind being prepared

Vostok spacecraft in orbit. Only the spherical cabin, containing the cosmonaut, returned to Earth

for the first orbital flight by a man. Something went wrong and the Russians failed to get it back into the atmosphere. America did score an important 'first' on 10 August by retrieving from orbit the small Discoverer XIII satellite capsule; Russia got back *Sputnik V*, its second space-ship, only nine days later, complete with its living occupants—two dogs, Belka and Strelka, forty mice, two rats, flies, and even microbes.

From that moment it was clearly only a matter of time before the first space-man was put into orbit around the world. America was well in the running with its Mercury manned satellite programme. On 31 January 1961, a chimpanzee named Ham was recovered safely after a flight to a

The huge launch vehicle used to put Yuri Gagarin's *Vostok* spacecraft into orbit. The first stage consisted of a central rocket and four 'wrap-round' boosters, each powered by a four-chamber engine, to give a total first-stage thrust of 1,125,000 lb.

height of 155 miles in a Mercury satellite, during which it travelled 420 miles down the Atlantic missile range. The men in charge of the Mercury programme were urged by some people to by-pass their plan to send men on similar up-and-down ballistic flights and to progress straight to an orbital attempt. Wisely, they refused, for it is far better to get men back safely from space, and to obtain as much scientific data as possible from a well-planned programme, than simply trying to be first.

So, on 12 April 1961, it was Major Yuri Gagarin of Russia who made one of the most momentous and daring voyages in history, by encircling the Earth in 108 minutes in the $4\frac{1}{2}$-ton spacecraft *Vostok* 1. Within less than a month, on 5 May, Cdr. Alan Shepard of the U.S. Navy completed a ballistic flight, like that of Ham, in a Mercury capsule. Nine months later, on 20 February, the Mercury programme reached fulfilment with the first orbital flight by an American, Lt.-Col. John Glenn.

Since then, many more Russian cosmonauts and American astronauts have returned successfully after orbiting the Earth. Manned space-flight is becoming almost routine. Nothing made this more apparent than the fact that the sixth Russian cosmonaut was a woman, Valentina Tereshkova.

Gemini two-man spacecraft, with hatches open to show the crew on their ejection seats

The Russians were first to put into orbit a spacecraft carrying more than one person—the three-man *Voskhod I*—on 12 October 1964. A Soviet cosmonaut, Alexi Leonov, was also first to step outside his space-craft and 'walk in space', on 18 March 1965. America was never far be-hind: on 23 March 1965 it began launching its highly successful series of

Gemini two-man space-
craft docked in a satellite
in orbit

Gemini two-man spacecraft, similar in shape to the Mercury 'TV tube'
capsule, but larger. Within three months, on 3 June, astronaut Edward
White became the first American to walk in space. In December Frank
Borman and James Lovell broke all endurance records by staying in orbit
nearly 14 days in Gemini-7, during which they made the first-ever rendezvous with another spacecraft, orbiting in close formation with Gemini-6
for long periods at a height of 160 miles above the Earth on 15 December.

Next stage was to dock a Gemini into an orbiting satellite, and this went
less smoothly at first. On 16 March 1966 the Agena-8 target satellite was
put into Earth orbit, with an adaptor at one end into which the crew of
Gemini-8 were to attempt to dock their spacecraft. When they blasted off
the launch-pad, entered the same orbit as the Agena and began to close the
gap between the two craft, it seemed almost too easy. Slowly, the command pilot, Neil Armstrong, nosed Gemini-8 into the adaptor; but the
feeling of triumph that his radio reports produced in the control centre at
Cape Kennedy was short-lived.

No sooner were the two craft 'locked' together than all hell seemed to
break loose. For no apparent reason, the Gemini began to spin violently,
as if it was completely out of control. Armstrong reacted immediately and
correctly, disengaging from the Agena and switching on the emergency
control system which would be able to bring the spacecraft back to Earth
automatically in the absence of any normal control. In fact, it not only
re-entered the atmosphere safely but landed 'on target' in the Pacific recovery area.

The spinning had been caused by one of Gemini-8's control rockets
jamming open. Gemini-9 was robbed of success by an even more frustrat-
ing snag. When it neared its target, it could not be docked as the fairings
that covered the docking adaptor during launch had not jettisoned. So, it
was not until 18 July 1966 that complete success was finally achieved. On
that date, astronauts John Young and Michael Collins not only docked

Gemini-10 in the Agena-10 target satellite, but used the fuel which remained in the Agena's tanks to take the two locked-together craft to a second rendezvous with the Agena-8 into which Neil Armstrong had docked so briefly four months earlier. Collins then 'space-walked' over to Agena-8 and removed from it an experiment for study back on Earth.

In the two remaining flights, Gemini recorded spectacular successes. On 12 September 1966, Gemini-11 docked in Agena-11 and then used the target satellite's engine to carry astronauts Charles Conrad and Richard Gordon into a new orbit which took them to an unprecedented height of 850 miles above Earth. Gordon spent 44 minutes in space, and the only cause for concern was that the work he did made him perspire so heavily that moisture clouded the window of his helmet and overloaded the life-support system of his suit.

It was left to 'Buzz' Aldrin, on the final mission two months later, to show that it was possible to work in space for long periods without encountering such problems, by introducing two-minute rest periods and making full use of hand-holds and restraint straps when moving between and on spacecraft in orbit.

There was no longer any doubt that man could work in space. Even more important, Project Gemini had perfected the technique of rendezvous between one spacecraft and another. The next step for America required this kind of get-together whilst two spacecraft were in orbit around the Moon.

To the Moon

A GOOD SCIENTIST is never satisfied, but must always look forward to doing further research and making even more exciting discoveries. That is why the photographs of the hidden side of the Moon sent back by *Lunik III* only whetted the scientists' appetite for more. Better photographs would be helpful as a first step. After that, it was essential to find out, as accurately as possible, what the Moon was made of, and whether its surface was firm enough to support the weight of a spacecraft.

America was too ambitious at first. The National Aeronautics and Space Administration (NASA), which controls its space programmes, ordered a series of Ranger spacecraft which were designed to take TV pictures of the lunar surface and investigate the composition of the soil as they neared the Moon, and then eject a container of instruments which would be slowed sufficiently by retro-rockets to make a gentle landing.

None of the first five Rangers that were launched succeeded in performing so complex a mission. It was decided to simplify Ranger-7 so that it would be expected only to take photographs as it crashed down onto the

Moon's surface. At once, the whole situation changed. Launched on 28 July 1964, this conical spacecraft, with its two wing-like panels of solar cells, transmitted 4,316 photographs, some of which showed craters only a few feet in diameter.

Ranger-8, launched on 17 February 1965, did even better with 7,137 close-up photographs of the Sea of Tranquillity that were hundreds of times better than anything that had ever been taken through a telescope. NASA were so pleased that they decided to transmit live, through public television circuits, the pictures taken as Ranger-9, last of the series, neared the end of its journey. As a result, countless viewers shared the excitement of scientists and technicians at Cape Kennedy as the spacecraft hurtled towards the now-familiar craters, a quarter of a million miles away.

After Ranger came a really massive unmanned assault on the Moon by both the U.S.A. and Russia. Back on 25 May 1961, the late President Kennedy had told Congress: 'I believe that this nation should commit itself to achieving the goal, before the decade is out, of landing a man on the Moon and returning him safely to Earth. No single space project in this period will be so difficult or so expensive to accomplish.'

It seemed unlikely that Russia would sit back and let America pull off such a tremendous achievement without any attempt to match it. In fact, there was good reason to believe that the five *Luna* spacecraft sent from Russian launch-sites to the Moon between 2 April 1963 and 3 December 1965 had been intended to make soft landings with instruments but had failed to do so. Success was unlikely to be delayed much longer. Meanwhile, America prepared to send two different kinds of robot spacecraft to the Moon.

One of them, known as Lunar Orbiter, was designed to go into orbit around the Moon and photograph the lunar surface from a height of under 30 miles. Five launches were made, using Atlas-Agena rockets, between 10 August 1966 and 2 August 1967. All were successful, and by the time Lunar Orbiter 5 was crashed into the Moon, to prevent it from becoming a menace to later manned flights, these automatic explorers had photographed more than 99 per cent of the entire lunar surface, totalling some 14 million square miles.

Some of the scenery photographed by the Lunar Orbiters was truly awe-inspiring, with great ranges of barren mountains and deep forbidding craters. These were clearly areas for future spacemen to avoid in their first journeys to the Moon, and the scientists of NASA spent day after day studying the thousands of photographs sent back by the Orbiters and pinpointing more promising landing areas.

By then, the other type of American unmanned lunar spacecraft, Surveyor, had confirmed that the surface of the Moon was firm enough to support man-made objects . . . but it had not been the first to do so.

Lunar Orbiter near the Moon

On 4 February 1966, Britain's radio observatory at Jodrell Bank issued to the press photographs which its director, Sir Bernard Lovell, claimed had been transmitted by a Russian spacecraft that had soft-landed on the Moon on the previous day. It transpired later that the prints were distorted, as their scale had been compressed in width. Nonetheless, it represented an achievement for Jodrell Bank, as the Soviet Union had maintained its customary silence about the purpose of *Luna-9* and did not itself distribute correct prints until some time later, by which time the British photographs had been seized upon by almost the entire world press.

Putting aside politics and press tactics, the soft landing of *Luna-9* on the lunar surface, a quarter of a million miles from Earth, represented a great advance in the exploration of the Moon. The complete spacecraft weighed 3,269 lb., including equipment that enabled its course to be corrected *en route* between Earth and the Moon, and orientation devices which ensured that it was vertical to the lunar surface when its retro-rocket fired at a height of around 46 miles.

Just before the complete spacecraft touched down on the Moon, it ejected a spherical instrument container, the top half of which was covered with four panels that opened like the petals of a flower to put the whole

Luna-9, which sent back the first photographs from the surface of the Moon

package in an upright position on the ground. Four aerial rods then extended automatically and the TV camera carried by the instrument package began photographing the scenery around it and transmitting the pictures to Earth. It was these first historic pictures of the Moon that had been intercepted by Jodrell Bank.

Six and a half years earlier, *Lunik III* had taken the first photographs of the hidden side of the Moon; but it had been left to America to produce top-quality, comprehensive photographs of the whole vast area. This time, too, it was America which eventually achieved better scientific results from its more advanced equipment, after losing the political prestige of being first.

Its Surveyor spacecraft was a gawky, surrealistic contraption by comparison with the compact cylindrical *Lunas*. Ten feet tall and with a 'diameter' of 14 feet, it consisted of a triangular metal-tube framework, packed with equipment in a seemingly haphazard fashion and with legs and aerials extending in all directions. In fact, of course, it was extremely carefully designed to combine minimum weight with maximum usefulness and reliability.

Each of the three legs carried at its tip a crushable honeycomb pad to absorb landing shocks. What looked like a droopy sunshade on top of the central mast was a pair of flat panels, one carrying 3,960 solar cells to power the Surveyor's equipment and the other an aerial. Two more small antennae were fixed at the ends of booms which extended to each side of

Surveyor soft-landing on the Moon

the spacecraft and, to one side of the central mast, a small TV camera was mounted in such a way that it would photograph the lunar terrain up to a distance of about one mile around the craft as well as two of the crushable 'feet', to show how far they had sunk into the surface.

To ensure a safe and soft touch-down, Surveyor carried a flight programmer and analogue computer, radars to check its height and rate of descent, and no fewer than four rocket-engines. These last included a solid-propellent main retro-rocket and three throttleable liquid-propellent vernier engines to 'trim' the spacecraft's direction and speed. The whole thing weighed 2,194 lb. at launch but only 620 lb. at touch-down, after the propellents had been burned and the retro-rocket jettisoned.

Surveyor-1 was launched from Cape Kennedy on 30 May 1966 by an Atlas-Centaur booster. It is worth noting that the Centaur stage was powered by two Pratt & Whitney RL10A-3 engines burning liquid hydrogen fuel, as the availability of these new high-energy power plants gave fresh impetus to NASA's space programmes at this important period.

After soft-landing successfully on 2 June, Surveyor-1 sent back over 10,000 photographs during the next two weeks. Shut-down preceded the cold two-week lunar night and that should have been the end of the spacecraft's usefulness. However, scientists at Cape Kennedy decided to see if its TV camera would still work after the long period of darkness, although such re-activation had not been planned. Surveyor-1 responded nobly to the signals it received, and the scientists were interested to see that its solar cell panel appeared to have suffered damage, presumably from meteorite bombardment.

Six more Surveyors were sent to the Moon between 20 September 1966 and 7 January 1968. Numbers two and four failed to soft-land; but the others expanded our knowledge of the Moon enormously, not only transmitting tens of thousands of photographs but also using a mechanical 'scratcher' to examine the surface and a radioactive 'bombardment' device to determine the constituents of the soil.

Biggest task carried out by the Surveyors had been to forewarn America's Apollo astronauts of the kind of conditions they could expect at selected landing sites. Thus, Surveyors 1 and 3 had been landed in the so-called Ocean of Storms, while Surveyor 5 investigated the Sea of Tranquillity and Surveyor 6 was put down in the Sinus Medii (Central Bay). This last spacecraft performed an important feat on 17 November 1967 when, eight days after touch-down, its rocket engines were restarted by a signal from Earth, to make it rise 10 feet and hop sideways 8 feet to a new position. Once again, valuable data were provided for the astronauts, this time on the practicability of taking off from the lunar surface.

All was now ready for the greatest adventure in history, for NASA no longer doubted that it was capable of sending men to the Moon and that they could land, survive there and take off again in reasonable safety.

Man on the Moon

IN the early years of space exploration, Russia tended to set the pace because its booster rockets were so much larger and more powerful than the launch vehicles available to NASA. Saturn changed all that.

Development of the Saturn family began in late 1958, only a few months after the first American satellite went into orbit and long before anything positive was known about the size and shape of Russian space rockets.

The series began with Saturn I, made up of an S-I first stage by Chrysler, powered by a cluster of eight Rocketdyne H-1 engines similar to that used in the Thor rocket, and an S-IV second stage by Douglas, powered by six RL10A-3 liquid-hydrogen engines of the kind used in Centaur. The complete vehicle stood 190 feet high at launch and weighed approximately 1,165,000 lb. (520 tons). Yet only four or five years earlier, America had almost decided to abandon development of the Atlas ICBM when it appeared that the missile would weigh 200 tons and need seven rocket engines in its first stage. It might have done so had not the evolution of a smaller H-bomb warhead made possible a rocket of only 115 tons, with three main engines.

Ten Saturn Is were launched successfully in 1961–5, two of them putting dummy Apollo spacecraft into Earth orbit. They were followed on 26 February 1966 by the first Saturn IB, with improved H-1 engines in the S-IB lower stage, and a single Rocketdyne J-2 liquid-hydrogen engine, rated at 200,000 lb. thrust, in the S-IVB second stage. But the real workhorse of the family was to be Saturn V, a three-stage rocket so immense that it would use the second stage of Saturn IB as its payload-carrying third stage (see *Frontispiece*).

Fully fuelled for take-off, Saturn V weighs an incredible 2,725 tons and stands 353 feet 5 inches tall—only 12 feet less than the height above ground of the tip of the cross on St Paul's Cathedral in London. The five Rocketdyne F-1 engines in its Boeing-built S-IC first stage each generate 1,500,000 lb. of thrust, burning liquid oxygen and kerosene propellents. The S-II second stage, built by North American Rockwell, contains five J-2 engines, with the result that both upper stages run on liquid hydrogen 'super-fuel'.

This was only the start, for everything about the Apollo programme had to be giant-size. Even the S-II second stage of the Saturn V rocket is so large that it has to travel by water from where it is built to Cape Kennedy, on a special barge. The S-IVB third stage makes the trip by air, but only the world's largest aeroplane, the outsize Aero Spacelines Super Guppy, has a cargo-hold big enough to accommodate it.

At Cape Kennedy, a metal skyscraper 552 feet high, known as the Vertical Assembly Building (VAB), had to be erected as an assembly hall for Saturn V rockets. It was the largest building in the world when first put into use. Furthermore, each Saturn it produces is then carried, with its servicing tower, $3\frac{1}{2}$ miles to the launch-pad on the largest land machine ever built, a 2,450-ton crawler-transporter half as big as a football pitch.

All of these huge structures, and others, were needed to put on the Moon a spider-like Lunar Module (LM) only 22 feet 11 inches high and with a fully-fuelled weight of 14 tons.

The LM is, however, only one of three component parts of the complete Apollo spacecraft, which includes also a conical Command Module (CM) housing the three-man crew and a cylindrical Service Module (SM) containing fuel, oxygen for breathing, electric power supplies and a 22,000 lb. thrust Aerojet rocket-engine.

The five-ton CM is 10 feet 7 inches high and consists of an inner pressure cabin of aluminium honeycomb and an outer shell of stainless steel honeycomb. It is covered with a plastic ablative (burn-away) heat shield of the kind that protects ICBM warheads during re-entry and has been used on all manned spacecraft. It carries on its nose a rocket tower which could lift the CM clear of the launch rocket if any serious emergency developed during count-down or lift-off.

On the launch-pad, the CM is mounted on the front of the 23-foot long,

66

24-ton SM, atop the Saturn V rocket, with the LM housed in the Saturn's nose fairing below the rocket-nozzle of the SM. This means that the astronauts have to transfer the LM from the burned-out Saturn third stage to the nose of the CM during their flight through space to the Moon, but the task has proved less difficult than it may have appeared initially.

The most serious setback that the Apollo programme encountered was on 27 January 1967 when the first men died inside a spacecraft, albeit on the ground. Astronauts Virgil Grissom, Edward White and Roger Chaffee, selected as the crew for the first orbital flight, were testing their spacecraft when an accidental fire broke out inside their CM and they were killed.

Not until 9 November of that year was the first Apollo spacecraft put into Earth orbit by a Saturn V rocket, and even then it was unmanned. Two more unmanned tests were made in January and April 1968. Then, on 11 October astronauts Walter Schirra, Walter Cunningham and Don Eisele were blasted off in Apollo-7 by a Saturn IB booster, on America's first manned space flight for nearly two years. They tested the SM propulsion engine in eight separate firings, sent back TV pictures that were broadcast live on commercial programmes and completed other tasks so satisfactorily that NASA decided to send Apollo-8 around the Moon.

So it was that astronauts Frank Borman, James Lovell and William Anders became the first men to see the cratered surface of the Moon from a height of only 70 miles during ten orbits on Christmas Eve, 1968. No attempt was made to land on the lunar surface; in fact, no LM was carried on this occasion, but the flight was highly successful and the pictures transmitted back to Earth were the most spectacular seen on a TV screen up to that time.

In March 1969, James McDivitt's crew took the complete Apollo-9 spacecraft into Earth orbit, transferred the LM from inside the S-IVB stage to the nose of the CM and then flew the LM 113 miles away from the parent craft to prove that separation and subsequent rendezvous were practical and safe.

About ten weeks later, Apollo-10, commanded by Thomas Stafford, repeated these manoeuvres in lunar orbit, during which the LM was taken down to within 9 miles of the surface of the Moon. Everything possible had now been done to prove the practicability of the Moon landing mission, and on 16 July 1969 Apollo-11 was launched from Cape Kennedy, carrying astronauts Neil Armstrong, Edwin Aldrin and Michael Collins on man's first journey onto another world.

Eleven minutes, 50 seconds after launch, the spacecraft was safely in orbit about 105 miles above the Earth. After 1½ orbits, the engine of the S-IVB stage was re-started to put it on course for the Moon. Thirty-six minutes later, the CM/SM assembly was separated from the burned-out

S-IVB, so that the LM could be extracted and attached to its nose. The complete Apollo spacecraft then continued its 73-hour trajectory towards the Moon, unpowered except for a brief three-second burst from the SM engine at one stage, to correct the course.

Astronaut inside LM in harness

Astronaut in Apollo suit setting up instruments on Moon

Apollo CM after descent into the sea

Apollo spacecraft, with Lunar Module on its nose, orbiting the Moon

Take-off from the Moon. The base of the Lunar Module serves as a launch-pad for the crew cabin as it leaves to rejoin the Apollo spacecraft in lunar orbit

At about mid-day on the 19th, the control room at Cape Kennedy fell strangely silent. Apollo-11 had disappeared from radio contact, behind the Moon. While out of sight, the crew had to fire the SM rocket to put them into lunar orbit. The whole success of the mission depended upon an

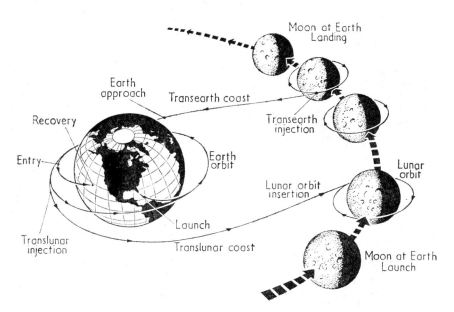

Diagram of Apollo mission

accurate burn—too much or too little and the spacecraft might either crash into the Moon or go racing towards the Sun and total destruction. But all was well. After entering an initial lunar orbit varying from 69 to 196 miles, a further burst of power put the spacecraft into what became a circular orbit 69 miles high.

Next day Armstrong and Aldrin clambered into the LM, strapped on the harness that served as a 'seat', separated their strange craft from the CM and, after Collins had checked that he could see nothing wrong, fired the LM's descent engine. From that moment, the CM/SM was known by the code-name *Columbia* and the LM as *Eagle*.

Descent of the *Eagle* took about 66½ minutes. In the last brief seconds, Armstrong had to take over control manually to avoid boulders and rocks and the LM eventually touched down with less than 2 per cent of its landing propellent left. At 2118 hrs BST, a radio message across a quarter of a million miles of space reported: 'Contact lights. O.K. engine stop. Tranquillity Base here. The *Eagle* has landed.' President Kennedy's pledge to put men on the Moon during the 1960s had been kept.

The two astronauts spent 2 hrs 16 mins on the lunar surface, leaving behind a number of experiments and bringing back to *Eagle* samples of lunar rock and soil. Then, after several hours' rest, they fired the ascent

Eagle's take-off from the Moon

engine and the top half of the LM took off to rendezvous with the still-circling *Columbia*, using the lower half as a launch-pad.

After that, all continued to go well. *Eagle* locked onto *Columbia* in orbit; Armstrong and Aldrin rejoined Collins and the LM was then jettisoned. Early on 22 July, the SM engine was fired to shoot Apollo-11 out of lunar orbit, on course for Earth. The SM was cast off before re-entry

Boeing vehicle for moon exploration

Lunar scooter

Mobile laboratory for later Moon exploration

and the CM finally splashed down in the Pacific during the afternoon of 24 July, just 30 seconds later than the time predicted at the start of the 195-hour mission and about 13 miles from the recovery aircraft carrier, USS *Hornet*.

It was not quite the end of the adventure, as the astronauts, after pick-up by helicopter, had to spend the next 18 days in isolation in a mobile quarantine coach, to avoid any possibility of contaminating Earth with germs or viruses from the Moon.

Since then, other astronauts in other spacecraft have visited the Moon and the Apollo landings will continue for some years. Already, Boeing have a contract to build lightweight lunar roving vehicles to transport future crews from their landing sites on journeys of discovery. Far from being at the end of a long road, *Eagle*'s Tranquillity Base was clearly only the beginning.

In Earth Orbit

WE must not let the excitement of manned flights to the Moon cause us to overlook the wonderful work that is still being done—and will always be done—nearer Earth by unmanned successors of the first *Sputniks* and Explorers. Who was not thrilled when the little Telstar communications

Telstar communications satellite

satellite relayed the first live TV pictures from across the Atlantic? Yet this was only a start. For example, when satellites of this kind are launched into an orbit 22,000 miles above the Earth, they take just 24 hours to make a circuit. If the orbit is parallel with the Equator the satellites stay permanently over a particular point on the surface (for the simple reason that the Earth also takes 24 hours to make one complete rotation on its axis).

First satellite to enter this kind of orbit (known as a synchronous orbit) was the American Syncom 2, launched on 26 July 1963. Many more satellites have since been put into synchronous orbit, and we now take for granted TV pictures passed to us by satellites from the other side of the world, so that we can watch great events anywhere, as they happen.

Russia's communications satellites have the name *Molniya* (Lightning) and are very large spacecraft, with a cylindrical centre structure and a number of large solar-cell panels. The Intelsats built in the West for the international Interim Telecommunications Satellite Consortium are drum-shaped, with most of the circumference covered by solar cells. Typical are the 608-lb., 56-inch diameter Intelsat 3s, positioned over the Atlantic,

Pacific and Indian Oceans and used commercially by more than 45 countries. Each can handle simultaneously 1,200 telephone channels or four TV channels.

Intelsat 4 satellite

Molniya satellite

Because of the Earth's rotation on its axis, a satellite that is not in synchronous orbit appears over different places during each successive orbit. In the case of the early *Sputniks*, launched in an orbit at an angle of 65 deg. to the Equator, each successive orbit was 1,000 miles west of the previous one at the latitude of London. As a result, over a period of time, the *Sputniks* passed over all the land areas lying approximately between the Arctic and Antarctic Circles. Since then both America and Russia have put increasing numbers of satellites into orbits that encircle the north and south poles and, hence, pass over every place on Earth over a period of time. Reconnaissance cameras in these satellites have brought back valuable information on military installations, such as airfields and rocket sites, making the possibility of surprise attack by any major nation upon another almost out of the question.

Nimbus weather satellite

Ultimately, though, the greatest value of satellites will be for science rather than war. The photographs taken by America's Tiros (*T*elevision and *I*nfra-*R*ed *O*bservation *S*atellite) series of satellites, and the later Nimbus, are intended to show not military installations but clouds,

77

Wernher von Braun's famous design for a large space-station containing laboratories, an observatory, and living quarters. Made of flexible nylon and plastic fabric it could be ferried out to its orbit in a collapsed condition and assembled in space. It would be 250 feet in diameter

enabling meteorologists to study weather formations over vast areas. In the future, such information will make possible far more accurate weather forecasts than those we get today.

Satellites can be used as manned or unmanned observatories, giving astronomers good clear pictures of the universe, undistorted by the atmosphere. They can be used to assist navigation, just as sailors have for centuries used stars in the sky to guide them—and, unlike the stars, they can be located precisely by radio and radar when the sky is cloudy.

They can also be used as refuelling stations for space-ships, using the rendezvous technique first proved practicable by Gemini. Obviously, if a space-ship could take on most of its propellents at a satellite, it could be much lighter in weight when it left the Earth, which would reduce tremendously the size and cost of its launching rockets.

It has often been claimed that Russia is far more interested in using this indirect method of getting to the Moon than in the direct landing techniques adopted by the Apollo astronauts. This may explain the pre-occupation of Russia's cosmonauts with their Earth-orbiting *Soyuz* spacecraft while their U.S. counterparts have been voyaging to and from the Moon.

Little was said about *Soyuz 1*, launched on 23 April 1967. This was, perhaps, understandable, for when it re-entered the atmosphere during the 18th orbit, its main parachute straps became entangled and it crashed to the ground killing its occupant, Colonel Vladimir Komarov. Veteran

Refuelling a space-rocket from an unmanned tanker placed in orbit for the purpose. Although apparently stationary, the vehicles are orbiting together at 18,000 m.p.h.

pilot of *Voskhod 1*, back in 1964, Komarov was the first person known to have been lost during a space flight and his death caused a delay in the *Soyuz* programme mere months after the death of astronauts Grissom, White and Chaffee led to redesign of parts of the Apollo Command Module.

Not until October 1968 was the *Soyuz* programme resumed; then Colonel Georgy Beregovoi, in *Soyuz 3*, gave a hint of future developments by making two successful rendezvous with the unmanned *Soyuz 2*, launched one day earlier.

In the following January, two members of the crew of *Soyuz 5* space-walked over to join Lt-Colonel Vladimir Shatalov in *Soyuz 4*, while the

A space-ship might look like this. Streamlining is unnecessary in airless space and could be left off to save weight. At the front is the crew's accommodation; then come the two large propellent tanks, followed by the rocket motor

two craft were docked in orbit. They landed in their new vehicle, leaving their original pilot, Lt-Cdr Boris Volynov, to re-enter alone.

Next stage was to send up three *Soyuz* spacecraft, containing seven cosmonauts, simultaneously in October 1969. Automatic vacuum welding experiments were made in *Soyuz 6* and new navigational techniques were tried out while the spacecraft orbited the Earth in pairs. The eventual plan may well be for two or three *Soyuz* craft to be joined together in orbit to form a proper space station. It can be no coincidence that each of these spacecraft carries on its nose a sizeable workshop, or that Russia has already demonstrated its perfection of docking techniques with unmanned satellites like *Cosmos 186* and *Cosmos 188*, which completed the first fully automatic rendezvous and docking in October 1967.

America, too, plans to put large workshops into orbit in the early 'seventies, under NASA's new Skylab Programme. Intended to capitalize on equipment developed under the Apollo project, the first step will be to put into Earth orbit an Apollo spacecraft and its three-man crew, using a Saturn IB launcher. A few days later, the S-IVB second stage of another Saturn IB will rendezvous with the orbiting Apollo. The astronauts will then space-walk to the empty S-IVB and fit it out as an orbiting workshop. Later, it is expected that a large solar telescope will be orbited by another Saturn and attached to the S-IVB workshop, turning it into a space observatory.

Soyuz cutaway

Automatic docking of *Cosmos* 186 and *Cosmos* 188

Skylab orbital workshop
with telescope in place

Such orbital laboratories and workshops are certain to grow in number, size and importance in the years ahead, until one day the old dream of hotels and terminals for interplanetary flights, anchored high above us in space, may come true.

Already, American designers are putting a great deal of effort into evolving craft that could ferry men, supplies and equipment between Earth and space stations of this kind. The most promising shape seems to be a wingless, or almost wingless, delta aircraft that can re-enter Earth's atmosphere safely at hypersonic speed and yet develop sufficient lift from its aerofoil-shape body to land normally at airfields on the ground. Tests with piloted aircraft of this kind, such as the NASA/Northrop HL-10, have confirmed the practicability of the idea, and designs for much larger space ferries are on the drawing board at some American factories.

Beyond the Moon

WHILE preparing to explore the Moon, America achieved its first immense successes much deeper into space. It began by sending the Mariner II spacecraft on a curving 180-million-mile journey to Venus. As it passed the planet, its instruments radioed back to Earth data that killed all hope of our ever finding life as we know it on Venus, for the surface temperature there is about 800 deg F., or well above the melting point of lead.

Hypothetical 10-seat space ferry

HL–10 lifting-body research
aircraft

Mariner II, the space probe that told
us so much about conditions on the
planet Venus

The news transmitted by Mariner IV as it passed Mars in the summer of 1965 was no happier. Dreams of canals and Martians seemed to fade as inspection of its photographs revealed a cratered, lifeless surface looking little different from the Moon; nor were later pictures taken by Mariners VI and VII in 1969 any more encouraging.

Even to consider human travel to these other planets of our solar system, or the stars beyond, may seem premature at a time when we have only just learned to reach the Moon: yet scientists are already studying types of engine that would make this possible.

There is no reason why chemical-propellent rocket space-ships should not carry explorers as far as Mars and Venus one day, and designs for such vehicles have already been produced by the dozen. Intended usually to start out from space-stations, to which the crews would be carried by

In this nuclear rocket, the propellent is heated by the reactor instead of being burned in the usual combustion chamber. It is first circulated around the chamber to cool the motor

ferry-rocket, they have fantastic open-girder structures, because stream-lining is unnecessary in airless space.

A promising alternative to chemical rockets is some form of nuclear power, in which an atomic reactor would be used to raise the temperature of the propellents instead of burning them in a combustion chamber. This type of motor could take men as far as Jupiter, (or even Saturn, which is 793 million miles from Earth), provided they could be certain of finding suitable frozen materials such as ammonia or methane on the planets' moons to make possible refuelling for the return trip.

One day, therefore, men may have travelled to all the planets of our solar system—although it is unlikely that they will be able to land on any but Mars and Mercury, because some outer planets have atmospheres which are poisonous to human life and continuous surface storms of indescribable ferocity. However, there seems hope of being able to land on the moons that exist round these planets.

Nuclear-powered space-ship, with the crew's compartment remote from the reactor to reduce radiation hazards. The large sphere contains hydrogen propellent

Yet that will be but the start, with a whole universe of other solar systems beckoning across outer space. From that moment on, chemical and nuclear rockets will no longer be good enough. Instead of engines producing tremendous thrust for short periods, designers will turn to types which produce a little thrust over very long periods, building up the rocket's speed gradually to velocities that we cannot even begin to consider seriously today.

One such engine is the ion rocket, which produces what can be called 'electric wind'. It is a principle that can be demonstrated easily in the physics laboratory, because if one pole of an electric generator or spark coil is connected to a pointed metal rod the air is pushed away from the point with sufficient force to blow out a candle.

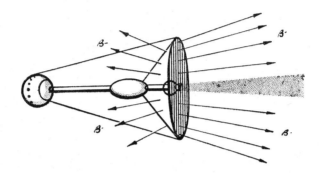

An ion rocket. The sphere contains the crew accommodation, with propellent in the oval container. A nuclear reactor drives powerful generators which discharge ions in much the same way that a television cathode-ray tube discharges electrons to form the picture. These ions are accelerated by beta particles (β) emitted by a large 'plate' made of waste material from atomic power stations

In a space-ship, electric current of enormous power could be generated by a nuclear power plant, to accelerate to very high speeds a liquid-propellent that had been stripped of electrons. This may be difficult to grasp but so long as you remember that ion propulsion is 'electric wind', working by reaction just like any other rocket, you will understand its basic principle.

Finally, there is the photon space-ship, driven by the pressure of light, although construction of such a vehicle would require scientific knowledge so far beyond our present attainments that it may be generations away. In brief, a photon rocket will send out waves of energy from a photo-sensitive surface, either when light falls upon it or when it is bombarded electronically. It might, in fact, be no more than a reflector of vast size, energized by the Sun's rays. The snag is that the thrust produced would probably be no more than one-tenth of one per cent of the reflected heat.

As a result, the acceleration of a photon rocket would be so small that it would require whole generations of human operators before it attained speeds representing a sufficiently high proportion of the speed of light to make possible flight through outer space to other star systems.

The idea that men and women might set out on a journey that would be

Impression by a Convair artist of an ion-rocket space-ship with un-limited interplanetary range

completed by their great-great-great-great-great-great-grandchildren—with perhaps even a few more 'greats' thrown in for good measure—may seem too much for anyone to believe today. But our descendants may think differently after they have seen the wonders of the planets of our own solar system.

Careers in Rocketry

BECAUSE it is a new industry, the prospects for any young person entering the guided missile business are tremendously exciting.

Guided missiles are so complex that they can be designed only by a large team of scientists and engineers from many branches of science. The first decision you must make, therefore, is which particular part of the job interests you. Engineers are needed for the airframes and power plants, electronics experts for the guidance equipment, chemists for the propellants, and men and women from almost every conceivable industry to produce the $1\frac{1}{2}$ million components that make up some weapon systems.

As in other careers, the greatest prospects await those who begin with the best qualifications; and for many jobs a university degree is essential. But even without university training a young person with a quick brain and the ability to work with the utmost precision can learn to operate the electronic computers, wind tunnel equipment, and telemetering receivers that play such a big part in rocket development.

In most cases, the people now working on rockets just drifted into the business when the companies for which they work added missile contracts to their normal manufacture of aeroplanes, aero-engines, radio and television sets, refrigerators and so on. This again emphasizes the immense variety of industries and trades that contribute to the new science of astronautics.

Even if you have no great technical skill or knowledge, there are openings in the most exciting side of the whole business—the actual launchings. More and more tradesmen in the Royal Air Force, the Army, and the Navy will be switched to missile operation as guided weapons take the place of guns, torpedoes, and some types of piloted aeroplanes. When they leave the Services, after a thorough training, there will be a multitude of jobs waiting for them.

In fact, about the only job that is not open is that of piloting the manned satellites and space aircraft of the future. Their crews will be the finest test pilots that the aircraft industry and air forces have available—men with vast experience of flying high-speed aeroplanes and, in many cases, with university degrees as well as flying skill. It seems certain that the men who fly space vehicles will continue to be chosen in this way for many years, and so the best way to become a 'space-man' is probably to join the Royal Air Force and work very, very hard.

A Soviet scientist has said that somewhere in Russia there lives today the boy who will one day be the first man to build a home on the Moon. He may be wrong. The boy may live in Britain or America. In fact, he might even be you.

Index

MSQ radar guidance, 36
MSR, 46-7
Multiple independently-targeted re-entry vehicle (*see* MIRV)

Newton, Sir Isaac, 9, 10
Nike-Ajax missile, 40
Nimbus satellite, 77
Nitric acid oxidant, 22
Nord SS. 10 missile, 28
North American X-15 aircraft, 48-9
Nose-cone, 36-7, 45-6, 49, 51
Nozzle design, 21, 35, 45
Nuclear propulsion, 84-5

Oberth, Prof. Hermann, 18
Observatory in space, 78
Orbits, 50-82
Oxidants, 22-24

PAR, 47
Passive homing guidance, 42-3
Peenemunde Experimental Station, 19, 20
Perigee, 53
Perimeter acquisition radar (*see* PAR)
Pershing missile, 33
Photon propulsion, 86-7
Pioneer satellites, 56
Polaris missile, 31-2, 37
Powder rocket, 12-16, 20-1
Power, 9-11
Pressurization, 47-9, 53
Pressure-suit, 49
Programmed guidance, 38, 52
Propellents, 9-12, 17-19, 20-5, 45, 84-7
Proximity-fuse, 40, 42

Quail missile, 26

Radar command guidance, 39, 40
Radio command guidance, 39-40
Radio navigation guidance, 40
Ramjet propulsion, 9, 35, 44
Ranger spacecraft, 60-1
Reaction, 9, 10
Reactor, atomic, 84-6
Reconnaissance satellites, 77
Re-entry, 36-7, 53, 57, 66, 72-4, 78, 82

Refuelling in space, 60, 61
Regenerative cooling, 24
Rendezvous in space, 59, 60, 67-72, 78-82
Research rockets, 49, 50
Rocket Brigade, 14
Royal Air Force, 40, 89-90

Safeguard ABM system, 46-7
SAGE (semi-automatic ground environment), 44
Satellites, 25, 35, 50-60, 75-82
Saturn, 84
Saturn rocket, 2, 7, 22, 24, 65-7, 81
'Scamp' weapon system, 29
'Scarp', 28, 30
Schirra, Walter, 67
Semi-active homing guidance, 40-2
Service module, (SM), 66-72
Shatalov, Lt.-Col. V, 79
Shepard, Cdr. Alan, 58
Signal rockets, 15
'Silo' launcher, 4-
Skylab programme, 80-2
Skylark Rocket, 50
Solar battery, 53
Solid propellents (*see* Propellents)
Soyuz spacecraft, 78-81
Spacecraft, 9, 12, 17, 37, 49, 56-74, 78-88
Space station, 78-82
Space-suit, 49
Spartan missile, 46-7
Specific impulse, 24
Spin stabilization, 14, 35
Sprint missile, 47
Sputnik I, 37, 50-3, 55, 75, 77
Sputnik II, 53, 54, 55
Sputnik III, 55
Sputnik IV, 56-7
Sputnik V, 57
SS-9 'Scarp', 28, 30
SS. 10 missile, 28
Stafford, Thomas, 67
Stage (multi-stage rocket), 16, 24-5, 45, 51-7, 65-6
Stand-off bomb, 26-7
Star-tracking guidance, 43
Step-rocket, 16, 24-5, 45, 51-7, 65-6
Strelka, 57

93

'Styx' missile, 29
Submarines, 31–3, 37
Subroc missile, 33
Super-propellents, 55
Surface-to-air missile, 27, 40, 42, 43, 44–5
Surface-to-surface missile, 28–31, 36, 43, 44
Surface-to-underwater missile, 31
Surveyor spacecraft, 62, 64–5
Syncom satellite, 75
Synchronous orbit, 75

Telemetry, 49
Television, 7, 40, 56, 61, 63, 67, 75–6
Telstar satellite, 75
Tereshkova, Valentina, 58
Thor-Able rocket, 55
Thrust, 10, 11, 24, 57
Thunderbird missile, 42
Tiny Tim rocket, 21
Tiros satellites, 77
Titan missile, 36
Trengrouse, Henry, 15
Tsiolkovsky, Konstantin, 17

Underwater-to-surface missile, 31–2
Underwater-to-underwater missile, 33
United Technology Center, 23
Upper atmosphere research, 49–50

V-1 flying bomb, 38
V-2 rocket, 20, 22–3, 24–5, 34, 43, 49, 55
Vandenburg Air Force Base, 45, 46
Vanguard satellite, 51, 53, 55
Venturi nozzle, 21, 24
Venus, 55, 82–4
Verein für Raumschiffahrt (VfR), 18, 19
Viking rocket, 49
Volynov, Lt.-Cdr. Boris, 80
von Braun, Dr. Wernher, 19, 78
Voskhod I, 58, 79
Vostok space-ships, 57, 58

Weight ratio, 24, 55
White, Edward, 59, 67
Wire command guidance, 38–9

X-15 aircraft, 48–9

Young, John, 59

World History

50 key milestones

you really need to know

Ian Crofton

Quercus

Contents

Introduction

Many will no doubt regard it as insufferably presumptuous to claim that the history of the world can be compressed into so short a book as this. Even 'short' histories of the world are usually much longer. But the aim here is not to provide an overarching survey of the story of humanity, but to focus on certain key developments and events, so providing some very basic foundations for the reader to build on if he or she so wishes.

It is a common complaint that children are only taught a handful of historical topics at school – the Romans, the Tudors, the Nazis, for example – and have no idea about all the bits in between. This book does not claim to fill in all those bits in between, but it does aim to broaden horizons and to introduce the reader to topics of which he or she may only have had the littlest inkling.

There are many lenses through which one can examine the past. Recent decades have seen a blossoming of a variety of approaches that cut across the stories we traditionally told ourselves about how we got to where we are – social history, economic history, black history, the histories of labour, of women, of ideas, to name but a few. To exponents of these disciplines, the present volume will no doubt appear terribly old-fashioned, with its chronicles of wars, empires, conquerors, discoveries, and so on. But this book aspires to be more than a bald and unconsidered account in which one event simply follows another, without explanation. Economic, social, geographic, cultural and other factors are all considered, and it is hoped that the reader will come away with some flavour of the complexities and uncertainties involved in attempting to understand the past, and how it might or might not colour the way we live now.

Ian Crofton

01 The beginnings of agriculture

None of the things that we take today as marks of our civilization – our great cities, our art, music and literature, our commerce and industry, our scientific and technological achievements – would be possible without agriculture.

It was only after we human beings learned how to farm that we could produce sufficient food surpluses to allow some of us to follow pursuits other than hunting and gathering. With some people specializing in food production, others could become full-time priests or soldiers or artisans or scribes or scholars. Thus more complex, and less egalitarian, societies began to emerge. But these developments only came very late in the story of humankind.

The dawn of humanity The earliest of our ancestors that we might recognize as human emerged some 4 million years ago. Over the ages a variety of human species evolved – *Homo habilis*, *Homo erectus*, the Neanderthals – but it was not until around 100,000 years ago that modern humans began to spread out of Africa and started to colonize the rest of the world.

Humans had started to use stone tools around 2 million years previously, but the rate of technological progress was extremely slow. Gradually tools and weapons – of wood, stone, bone and antler – became more refined, and humans learned how to use fire. People sustained themselves by fishing,

timeline

10,000–8000 BC	8000 BC	7500 BC	6500 BC
Last Ice Age draws to a close	Barley and wheat grown in Middle East	Sheep and goats domesticated in western Iran	Millet and rice grown in China; beans, squash and peppers in highland Peru

hunting and gathering fruits, seeds, nuts and berries – a way of life that can support small groups, but which requires that the hunter-gatherers must move on once the resources of one area are temporarily exhausted.

Then around 8000 BC something extraordinary happened in the Fertile Crescent, an area of the Middle East that extends from the valleys of the Tigris and Euphrates rivers westward through Syria and then south through the Levant. It was here that people first began to cultivate crops, kick-starting a global revolution in the way that humans live. The Fertile Crescent was the first but not the only area to experience an agricultural revolution: farming independently began in various other parts of the world, including Mesoamerica, the Andean region of South America, China, south-east Asia and sub-Saharan Africa.

The first crops It is probably no coincidence that the beginnings of agriculture 10,000 years ago coincided with the end of the last Ice Age. As the earth warmed, the ice sheets covering much of northern Eurasia and North America melted, releasing vast amounts of fresh water. In these conditions, the sparse tundra gave way to lusher vegetation – grasslands and forests – which provided hunter-gatherers with much richer pickings. In some places, the environment was so productive that groups that knew how to exploit it could stay put rather than having to move on constantly. With greater quantities of food available, populations grew, and this in turn meant that people had to devise ways of surviving through leaner periods, by learning how to store food. One of the easiest foods to store, because they do not decay when kept dry, are cereals – the seeds of various grasses.

It was no doubt a gradual process by which certain groups learned to look after the wild

A hidden danger

Reliance on a diet of cereals contained a hidden danger. Many skeletons from the ancient world show evidence of appalling abscesses in the jaw, a result of teeth shattering when biting on fragments of rock from the stones used to grind the grain.

6500–6000 BC	6000 BC
Cattle herded in Middle East and North Africa	Farming begins in south-east Europe and Nile valley. Irrigation used in Mesopotamia. Small towns found in places such as Jericho and Çatal Höyük in Anatolia.

6And Abel was a keeper of sheep, but Cain was a tiller of the ground.9

Genesis, 4:2, on the sons of Adam and Eve

plants that they found most useful as food sources. Keeping off pests and clearing away weeds was a start, and at some point people made the connection between sowing seed and harvesting the resulting crop. In the Fertile Crescent, wheat and barley were the key cereals; in the Americas it was maize, in sub-Saharan Africa sorghum, in northern China millet, while in southern China and south-east Asia it was rice. Other crops were also important in various parts of the world, for example beans, yams, potatoes, gourds and peppers.

Domesticating wild animals The first animal to be domesticated was the dog, which is a direct descendant of the wolf. Dogs were used in hunting and as guards long before people became settled farmers – the feral dingo of Australia, for example, is a descendant of the dogs that the first humans brought to the continent some 50,000 years ago.

But it was not until after arable farming began in the Middle East that livestock farming – the rearing of animals for food and other products such as leather – began. The first animals to be tamed were cattle, sheep, pigs and horses, which in their domesticated form spread from the Middle East across Asia. Cattle and donkeys began to be used to pull ploughs, sleds and eventually wheeled wagons. In South America, the llama was bred as a pack animal, while guinea pigs were reared for food.

What agriculture has done for us Food production based on agriculture continues to provide the bedrock of modern civilization. But the coming of agriculture was not an unmixed blessing. Comparison of the skeletons of earlier hunter-gatherers with those of later farming peoples shows that on the whole the former were better built and healthier, reflecting their more varied diet. The first farmers – and this is still the case with hundreds of millions of subsistence farmers around the world – had a very plain diet, largely

timeline

5500 BC	4700 BC	4400 BC
Pigs reared in parts of Europe, the Middle East and China	Maize grown in Mesoamerica	Horses domesticated on Eurasian steppes

consisting of a staple carbohydrate crop. Protein, in the form of meat or dairy products, was very much a rarity.

Before the coming of farming there was some division of labour. In hunter-gatherer societies the women usually did most of the gathering and the men most of the hunting, while certain individuals, sometimes with some form of disability, became shamans. But generally speaking, the development of occupational specializations and social hierarchies, with kings and priests at the top and slaves at the bottom, came only after the establishment of sedentary farming communities. Settled communities, food surpluses and the manufacture of artefacts such as pottery or ceremonial stone axes also gave rise to trade over considerable distances – amber from the Baltic, for example, has been found in Neolithic sites across Europe.

By 6000 BC some of these communities – such as those at Jericho in the Jordan valley and at Çatal Höyük in Anatolia – had grown into small towns. The emergence of urban civilization in the form of the first city-states and empires was only a matter of time.

Milk drinkers and milk haters

Originally, no humans could digest milk once they had been weaned from their mother's breast. Then around 7,500 years ago a new gene arose amongst a tribe of cattle herders living between the Balkans and central Europe. This gene enabled them to continue digesting lactose – the sugar found in milk – through adulthood, so giving rise to the addition to the diet of such items as butter, cheese and yoghurt. However, this gene, which is commonest in people of northern European origin, is absent in half the world's population, who continue to be intolerant of lactose.

in a nutshell
Agriculture fundamentally changed the way we live

4300 BC	4000 BC	4000–3000 BC
Cotton grown in Indus valley and Mesoamerica	Agriculture spreads across Europe and sub-Saharan Africa	First cities in Mesopotamia

02 The first cities

Today, most people in the Western world live in cities – and this is increasingly also the case in rapidly developing countries such as India, China and Brazil. Mass urbanization is a relatively recent phenomenon, associated with industrialization and the mechanization of agriculture over the last two centuries.

Prior to this the vast majority of people lived in the countryside, working the land. But cities have existed since the very beginning of recorded human history, over five millennia ago, and were from the start important centres of power, as well as engines of cultural and technological change.

❛Nile Flood, be green and come! Give life to humankind and cattle with the harvest of the fields!❜

Hymn to the Nile,
ancient Egypt, *c.*1500 BC

Cities largely grew from towns, which in turn started as villages. The first permanent villages came with the beginnings of agriculture in the Middle East some 10,000 years ago, although some settlements may have begun not as farming communities, but as markets at the intersection of trade routes. Trade certainly played an important role in the development of larger towns and cities, but growing urban populations could have not have been sustained without an intensification of agriculture, which in many places was only made possible by large and complex irrigation schemes.

The importance of water Between 4000 and 2000 BC, the first urban civilizations arose independently in four different parts of the world: between the Tigris and Euphrates rivers in Mesopotamia (modern Iraq); in

timeline

4000–3000 BC	3300 BC	3000 BC
World's first cities built in Mesopotamia	Earliest written texts in Uruk in Mesopotamia	Memphis becomes capital of unified Upper and Lower Egypt

Egypt's Nile valley; in the Indus valley in what is now Pakistan; and along the Yellow River (Huang He) and the Yangtze (Chang Jiang) in China.

All of these great rivers are prone to seasonal variations in flow, with flood alternating with drought. To maximize agricultural production, it was necessary to build dams to store the flood waters in reservoirs, and then dig ditches to water the fields during the dry season. Once this technology was developed, farmers found that they could move into more arid areas, such as southern Mesopotamia – although here the deposition of salts caused by irrigation eventually left the land barren. Irrigation could mean that instead of just one crop a year, two or even three crops could be harvested.

Constructing such irrigation schemes required an accurate calendar to predict when the floods would come, and a high degree of social organization, necessary for establishing land ownership and recruiting a large labour force. Recording ownership of property spurred not only accurate measurement (hence the beginnings of mathematics) but also the first writing. In addition, the management of big construction projects required a tightly defined hierarchy that dictated who would do the digging and who would give the orders and reap most of the benefit.

Social and political organization The same degree of social stratification and mobilization of labour was required to construct the first cities, which were built on the back of the agricultural surpluses generated by irrigation schemes. These first cities were more than just collections of dwellings and workshops. They contained great monumental structures such as temples and palaces, ceremonial avenues, storehouses for tributes, taxes and traded goods, defensive walls, and, linked into the irrigation systems, canals and aqueducts to bring fresh water to the population. The great planned cities of the Indus valley, Mohenjo Daro and Harappa, built around 2600 BC, also had systems of covered drains to take away waste water and sewage.

2600 BC	**2550 BC**	**2350 BC**
Emergence of cities and writing in Indus valley	Great Pyramid built at Giza	First Mesopotamian empire established by Sargon of Akkad

Often different classes – labourers, artisans, merchants, priests and princes – lived in different quarters of the city, the size and quality of their dwellings reflecting their social status. Large numbers of labourers (whether free or slaves) were required to build the great religious and civic monuments – the ziggurats (temple towers) of Mesopotamia, the pyramids of Egypt, the temples and great ritual baths of the Indus. Artisans produced pottery, textiles, jewellery, stone carving, metalwork and other goods, both utilitarian and luxury, and these, together with agricultural produce, were widely traded by the merchant classes. Trade was not just local: in the later 3rd millennium BC, for example, the cities of the Indus were trading with those of Sumeria in what is now Iraq.

❛Create Babylon, whose construction you requested! Let its mud bricks be moulded, and build high the shrine!❜

The Epic of Creation, dating from the 1st millennium BC, which was recited every year before a statue of the Babylonian god Marduk

Over all ruled the kings, who often claimed descent from the gods, and who maintained their power via an assertion of divine authority – backed up by armed force where necessary. Armies were not just for keeping the king safe from his subjects. Human aggression and competition over resources in earlier periods had manifested itself in intermittent inter-tribal raiding. Now this escalated into a new phenomenon: war. In Mesopotamia, the Sumerian city-states of the 3rd millennium BC such as Eridu, Kish, Ur and Uruk were constantly fighting each other, and this in turn gave a boost to technological innovation in the form of city walls, war chariots, shields, spears and metal helmets. The period of warring city-states was succeeded by a period of empires – for example, those of the Akkadians, the Babylonians and the Assyrians. Political unity over a large area was also established in Egypt in around 3000 BC, and in China in the middle of the 2nd millennium BC under the first dynasty, the Shang.

In the 1st millennium BC, urban civilizations emerged in other parts of the world: in Persia, across India and south-east Asia, in Greece

timeline

2100 BC	2000 BC	1800 BC	1750 BC
Construction of Ziggurat of Ur	Palace-based Minoan civilization develops on Crete	Emergence of Shang dynasty in China	Law code issued by Hammurabi of Babylon

The beginnings of writing

The earliest forms of writing developed independently in the cities of Mesopotamia, China, the Indus valley and Mesoamerica. The first systems were generally pictographic – consisting of symbols representing things or ideas – but in Mesopotamia a more flexible syllabic script, known as cuneiform, had developed by 2800 BC. Writing helped the ruling elites to maintain control, being used to label and list property, and to name the succession of kings. Later, writing was also used for recording commercial agreements, for personal and government letters and, most importantly, for defining the laws – an important step in tempering the absolute power of the ruler. Literature, however, remained an oral phenomenon for much longer: one of the world's earliest known literary works, the Mesopotamian *Epic of Gilgamesh*, was only written down in the 7th century BC.

and the Roman empire. By the 1st millennium AD, great cities such as Teotihuacán – with a population of some 200,000 – were also flourishing in Mesoamerica, and also in the Andean region of South America. Although emerging in isolation from the rest of the world, these cities of the New World bore all the characteristics of the cities of the Old World – Teotihuacán, for example, is laid out on a grid, and is dominated by two great ceremonial monuments, the Pyramid of the Sun and the Pyramid of the Moon. And, like many other cities of the ancient world, all that is left are bare ruins, the reminder of a lost civilization.

in a nutshell
Cities provided an engine for political, social, cultural and technological development

800 BC	500 BC	400 BC	AD 100
City-states established in Greece	Civic-ceremonial centre established at Monte Albán, Mesoamerica	Beginnings of civilization based on city of Teotihuacán, Mesoamerica	Population of Rome may have exceeded 1 million

03 Egypt of the pharaohs

The kingdom of Egypt was one of the oldest and certainly the longest lived of the ancient civilizations, enduring for over three millennia. This long period was not without disruptions and upheavals, but Egyptian culture was so firmly rooted that even foreign conquerors were absorbed by it, and adopted the ways of Egypt's hereditary rulers, the pharaohs, who were regarded as sons of the supreme god Ra, the god of the sun.

Although evidence of the civilization of the ancient Egyptians was everywhere apparent, in the form of giant pyramids, vast statues and spectacular ruined temples, little was known of its detailed history, its society and its beliefs until its mysterious hieroglyphic (picture) writing was deciphered in the early 19th century, following the discovery of the Rosetta Stone.

Society and culture The lifeline of the ancient Egyptians was the River Nile, whose annual flood watered their fields and guaranteed bountiful harvests. Human settlement in ancient Egypt was confined to a strip either side of the river (Upper Egypt), and across its extensive delta (Lower Egypt). Apart from these areas, and the occasional oasis, the land was desert. The Nile valley was one of the first places in the world where agriculture developed, followed by some of the world's first towns and cities.

timeline

3100 BC	c.2630 BC	2600–2500 BC	2575–2134 BC
Menes unites Upper and Lower Egypt, and founds Memphis	Building of Step Pyramid of Saqqara	Construction of pyramids at Giza	Old Kingdom

> **"God is three of all gods
> Amun, Ra, Ptah, without any others . . .
> Their cities on earth endure to eternity –
> Thebes, Heliopolis, Memphis, forever."**
>
> **A hymn** from *c.*1220 BC, praising the three aspects of the state god of
> the New Kingdom. The Egyptians in fact worshipped many other gods,
> including Isis, Osiris, Anubis and Horus.

Around 3100 BC Upper Egypt and Lower Egypt were united by a king called
Menes, who became the first pharaoh. A new capital, Memphis, was built
at the junction of Upper and Lower Egypt, and this became the centre of
a highly centralized state, with the pharaoh
at the top of an efficient administrative
hierarchy. Such organization enabled great
building projects to be undertaken, and the
first pyramid – the Step Pyramid at Saqqara –
was built around 2630 BC as the burial place of
Pharaoh Djoser. By tradition it was designed
by the architect and physician Imhotep, and
provided the model for the famous pyramids
at Giza, built shortly afterwards. The Great
Pyramid at Giza, with a height of 138 m
(453 ft) was for four millennia the tallest
structure in the world.

The pyramids were tombs for the pharaohs,
and the bodies of the dead were surrounded
by all the objects that might be required in
the afterlife – which was imagined to be a
world very much like Egypt. In order that the
dead might enjoy the afterlife, it was crucial

The Rosetta Stone

The meaning of Egyptian hieroglyphic writing
was finally cracked following the discovery in
1799 of an inscribed stone at Rosetta (Arabic
Rashid), near Alexandria. Dating from 196 BC,
the stone carries a decree from Pharaoh
Ptolemy V in Egyptian in both hieroglyphic and
demotic (cursive) script, and also in ancient
Greek. This gave interpreters the key they
needed. The work of decipherment was begun
by the English polymath Thomas Young, and
was completed by the French scholar Jean-
François Champollion in 1822. The Rosetta
Stone is now in the British Museum in London,
although the Egyptian government has
requested its return.

2134–2040 BC	2040–1640 BC	1640–1552 BC	1552–1070 BC
First Intermediate Period: Egypt divided between various local rulers	Middle Kingdom: Egypt reunited, and conquers Nubia	Second Intermediate Period: rule by Hyksos, a foreign dynasty	New Kingdom: Egyptian empire at its greatest extent, with capital at Thebes

that their bodies were preserved, and to this end the Egyptians developed sophisticated techniques of mummification. Although initially such elaborate burials were confined to the upper echelons of society, over the centuries even the poor were provided with modest grave goods to provision their needs in the life to come.

Trade, empire and conquest Although Egypt was rich in agricultural and mineral resources, it lacked such things as timber, wine, oil, ivory and precious stones. In order to fulfil demand, great trading expeditions were mounted to Sinai and the Levant in the north-east, to Libya in the west, and to Nubia and Punt (the Horn of Africa) in the south. In the wake of these commercial contacts, the Egyptians sought to expand their power as well as their horizons, and between 1500 and 1000 BC they built an empire extending from Syria to the Sudan. Huge amounts of wealth poured into Egypt from the new provinces in the form of tribute, enabling the building of a great new religious centre at Thebes, and the huge temple at Karnak.

Akhenaten's religious revolution

In 1379 BC Pharaoh Amenophis IV came to the throne and instigated a religious revolution. He replaced the worship of the state god Amun-Ra and the pantheon of other gods with that of a single god, the Aten, the sun's disc. He himself took the name Akhenaten (meaning 'favourable to the sun disc'), built a new capital, Akhetaton (modern el Amarna), and initiated a naturalistic style of royal portraiture in place of the tradition of highly stylized depictions. Akhenaten neglected his empire in western Asia, and lost northern Syria to the Hittites. At home he met with considerable opposition from the powerful priests of Amun, and after his death in 1362 BC he was succeeded by the young Tutankhamun, and traditional religious practices were restored.

timeline

1379–1362 BC	1285 BC	1070–712 BC	712–332 BC	675 BC
Akhanaten's short-lived religious revolution	Egyptians and Hittites fight great battle at Kadesh	Third Intermediate Period: rule of Egypt divided between pharaohs and priests of Amun	Late Period	Assyrian invasion of Egypt

**❝I met a traveller from an antique land
Who said:– Two vast and trunkless legs of stone
Stand in the desert. Near them on the sand,
Half sunk, a shatter'd visage lies . . .❞**

Percy Bysshe Shelley, 'Ozymandias', 1819. The poem alludes
to the numerous giant statues of the Pharaoh Rameses II that lie
in ruins in the deserts of Egypt and the Near East.

This expansion brought the Egyptians into contact with powerful
neighbouring empires, and diplomatic relations were established with the
Hittites of Anatolia, the Babylonians and the Assyrians. Contact brought
competition and conflict: in 1285 BC the powerful Pharaoh Rameses
II fought a mighty battle against the Hittites at Kadesh in Syria, and
subsequently Egypt faced attacks from the mysterious 'Sea Peoples' of the
eastern Mediterranean.

Around 700 BC the Assyrians invaded Egypt and sacked Thebes. Another
invasion, this time by the Persians, came in 525 BC, and Egypt became a
Persian province until it surrendered without a fight to Alexander the Great
in 332 BC. Alexander made a journey across the desert to the Oracle of
Amun at the Siwa Oasis, and here he was endorsed by the priests as the new
pharaoh. After Alexander's death, one of his generals, Ptolemy, established
a dynasty of pharaohs who similarly gained the support of the people and
the priesthood by honouring the gods of Egypt. Even after Egypt became a
Roman province in 30 BC, its Graeco-Egyptian culture thrived until finally
extinguished by the Muslim Arab conquest of the 7th century AD.

in a nutshell
A magnificent civilization that endured for over 3,000 years

525 BC	332 BC	305 BC	30 BC	AD 640s
Persian conquest	Alexander the Great takes Egypt	Ptolemy, one of Alexander's generals, establishes dynasty of Graeco-Egyptian pharaohs	Egypt becomes a Roman province	Arab conquest of Egypt

04 Classical Greece

Much of our art and architecture, our literature and philosophy, our democratic politics and our science we owe to the ancient Greeks. That Greece should have had such a powerful cultural influence on the Western world is all the more surprising, given that there was never a unified Greek state. Instead, classical Greece consisted of a collection of rival city-states, with colonies scattered all around the Mediterranean and the Black Sea.

These city-states had begun to emerge in the 8th century BC, and each one had its own strongly maintained identity, centred around an acropolis – a citadel in which temples were dedicated to the city's favoured god or goddess. This robust sense of independence was partly engendered by the geography of the country, with each city and its surrounding agricultural land isolated from its neighbours by mountain ranges and the sea.

The advent of democracy At first, power in each city-state was in the hands of the leading noble families, although assemblies of adult male citizens might be consulted on certain issues (women and slaves were entirely excluded). But a number of developments ushered in a shift in power. First of all, the spread of literacy and the public display of the laws of the state in written form meant that the power of the nobles was circumscribed and opened to question. Secondly, the establishment of new colonies overseas gave citizens the opportunity to establish new patterns of land ownership and political organization. Thirdly, the development of new and highly effective military tactics, in which the traditional aristocrats in their war chariots were replaced by formations of heavily armed warrior-citizens called hoplites, gave every freeman a very real sense of power, which the state was obliged to respect.

timeline

*c.*1600 BC	*c.*1150 BC	*c.*800 BC	*c.*750 BC
Start of Bronze Age Mycenaean civilization in Greece	Beginning of Greek 'dark age'	Emergence of Greek city-states	Homeric epics written down

These developments helped to give birth to democracy in a number of Greek city-states, most notably in Athens, the most powerful of them all, where decisions were made by assemblies of all adult male citizens. Democracy was by no means universal, or permanent. There were periods of rule by 'tyrants', or by small groups of leading citizens known as 'oligarchs'.

The rise and fall of Athens Attempts by the mighty Persian empire to the east to conquer Greece in the early 5th century BC were defeated by a combination of the Athenian navy and the army of the other major Greek power, Sparta. In the wake of this victory, Athens began to impose itself on its less-powerful neighbours and allies, some of whom turned to Athens's rival, Sparta. Tensions culminated in the protracted and destructive Peloponnesian War (431–404 BC). With the defeat of Athens, Sparta became the dominant power – and as resented as Athens had been, leading to a further succession of internecine wars. Greece, thus weakened, became an easy prey to an ambitious warrior-king to the north: Philip II of Macedon, father of Alexander the Great. With Philip's victory at Chaeronea in 338 BC, Greece at last became united – but under a foreign ruler.

Greek philosophy and science All these wars had little negative impact on Greece's intellectual life. It is unclear why the spirit of inquiry should have been so keen in ancient Greece, but that it was is reflected in the fact that our word 'philosophy' comes from the Greek word *philosophos*, meaning 'lover of wisdom'. For the Greeks the remit of philosophy covered not only such fields as ethics, metaphysics and logic, but also the whole of what we now call science.

The early Greek philosophers, from the 6th century BC, rejected earlier mythological explanations of the physical world, and sought instead a single element that they believed underlay all things. The followers of Pythagoras

❝If the people of Greece could achieve political unity they could control the rest of the world.❞

Aristotle, *Politics,* 4th century BC

*c.*590 BC	507 BC	490 BC
Solon establishes legal code in Athens	Democratic reforms of Cleisthenes in Athens	Greeks defeat Persian army at Marathon

looked at how nature might be described in terms of number, while others examined via paradoxes the nature of infinity and such questions as whether change, as represented by motion, is a reality or an illusion.

In the 5th century BC the Athenian philosopher Socrates turned the focus onto ethical and political issues, devising a dialectical method of question and answer to examine the logical validity of propositions. Socrates' follower Plato asserted that the ultimate nature of reality cannot be grasped via the senses, holding that the physical world we experience is but a shadow of the ideal forms of things.

Plato's pupil Aristotle had a more analytical approach, attempting to define, catalogue and explain the world in which he lived. Thus as well

Some notable Greek scientists

- **Pythagoras** (6th century BC): realized the Earth is a sphere, and established the numerical basis of musical harmonics.

- **Empedocles** (c.490–430 BC): held that all matter consisted of four elements.

- **Democritus** (c.460–370 BC) and Leucippus (5th century BC): suggested that matter was made up of minute, identical, indivisible particles called atoms.

- **Hippocrates** (c.460–c.377 BC): became known as 'the father of medicine'.

- **Euclid** (fl.c.300 BC): set out the principles of geometry.

- **Aristarchos of Samos** (c.310–230 BC): realized that the Earth rotates about its own axis and orbits the Sun.

- **Archimedes** (c.287–c.212 BC): pioneered the field of mechanics and invented many ingenious devices.

- **Eratosthenes of Cyrene** (c.276–c.194 BC): calculated the circumference of the Earth with a creditable degree of accuracy.

timeline

480 BC	440 BC	431 BC
Greeks defeat Persian navy at Salamis	Athens reaches peak of its power under Pericles	Outbreak of Peloponnesian War between Athens and Sparta and their allies

as examining issues in ethics, aesthetics, metaphysics and politics, he also turned his attention to subjects such as biology, physics and cosmology. The teachings of Aristotle dominated both Islamic and Western thought until the Scientific Revolution of the 16th and 17th centuries.

Artistic influence The Greek approach to art and architecture reflects their philosophy. Their sculptures seek to embody a Platonic ideal of ultimate beauty, rather than depicting actual individuals with all their supposed flaws. Greek architecture based on geometric forms, embodies the Pythagorean belief in the overriding significance of number and ratio in nature and encapsulates all that is meant by 'classical art' – balance, proportion, calm, perfection. Greek aesthetic values were borrowed wholesale by the Romans, but largely forgotten after the collapse of the Roman empire. Their rediscovery in Europe in the 15th century led to some of the greatest artistic achievements of the Renaissance.

The Renaissance also saw a renewed popularity, as the subject matter for both art and literature, of the Greek myths and the tales of the Trojan War and its aftermath, as told by Homer and others, notably the Roman poet Ovid. Equally profound in their influence were the great Greek playwrights such as Aeschylus, Sophocles and Euripides, whose tragedies explore how humans behave in the most extreme circumstances, eliciting in the audience what Aristotle characterized as 'pity and terror'. Their plays have been enormously influential on Western drama, and indeed on the whole way we see ourselves as human beings.

in a nutshell
Greek culture lies at the root of Western identity

404 BC	**338 BC**
Defeat of Athens	Philip of Macedon defeats Greek city-states at Chaeronea

05 Alexander the Great

By the time of his death at the age of just thirty-two, Alexander the Great of Macedon had conquered much of the world then known to the ancient Greeks, from Anatolia, Syria and Egypt in the west through Mesopotamia, Persia and central Asia in the east, even as far as India.

Alexander's meteoric career, feats of arms, magnanimity to the defeated and restlessly inquiring mind turned him into the overarching hero of antiquity. In the Middle Ages he was held up as one of three great chivalrous 'worthies' of the pagan world – alongside Hector, the legendary hero of Troy, and Julius Caesar. Today, Alexander's innovative military tactics are still studied in military academies around the world.

Alexander's empire was short-lived, however, and after his death was carved up among his squabbling generals. Although political unity proved fleeting, the cultural impact of Alexander's empire-building turned out to be much more enduring, and a new Hellenistic era, combining both Greek and native elements, prevailed in the eastern Mediterranean and western Asia until the Arab conquests nearly a thousand years later.

The rise of Macedon The mountainous kingdom of Macedonia or Macedon lay to the north of the Greek heartlands of Thessaly, Aetolia, Boeotia, Attica and the Peloponnese. The Macedonians themselves, although they spoke a Greek dialect, were for long regarded as uncouth

timeline

359 BC	338 BC	336 BC	334 BC
Philip II succeeds to throne of Macedon	Philip defeats Greek city-states at Chaeronea	Alexander succeeds Philip on latter's assassination	Alexander defeats Persians at Granicus

and backward outsiders by the other Greeks, partly because they maintained a hereditary monarchy, in contrast to the political systems of the Greek city-states.

The constant warfare between and within the Greek city-states from the later 5th century BC created a weakness that Macedon was able to exploit. In 359 BC Alexander's father, Philip II, came to the throne, and determined to seize the opportunity offered by the power vacuum to the south. Philip undertook a reorganization of the Macedonian army, adding cavalry and mobile light infantry to the unwieldy hoplite (heavy infantry) formations known as phalanxes, which were used to break the enemy line. Having secured his northern borders, Philip turned his attentions southward, using diplomacy and arms to achieve dominance over the Greek city-states, culminating in his decisive victory at Chaeronea in 338.

Philip's son Alexander was only eighteen when he commanded the left wing of the Macedonian army at Chaeronea. His father had long seen his potential and his ambition, and had employed the great philosopher Aristotle to be tutor to the young prince and his companions. It was from Aristotle that Alexander acquired his interest in philosophy, medicine and literature, and one of his most treasured possessions was the annotated copy of Homer that Aristotle had given him.

A decade of conquest Philip was planning a campaign against Greece's traditional enemy, the Persian empire, when he was assassinated in 336 BC. Alexander lost no time in fulfilling his father's ambitions. In 334 he led his army of nearly 50,000 veterans across into Asia, and proceeded to win a series of victories against the Persians as he advanced through Anatolia, Syria, Egypt and Mesopotamia. In 331 he faced the Persian king, Darius III, on the vast plain of Gaugamela, north of the River

> **❝At my age Alexander was already king over so many peoples, while I have never yet achieved anything really remarkable . . . ❞**
>
> **Julius Caesar, quoted in Plutarch, *Life of Caesar*, 1st–2nd century AD**

333 BC	**331 BC**	**326 BC**	**324 BC**
Alexander defeats Persians at Issus	Final defeat of Persians at Gaugamela	Alexander wins Battle of the Hydaspes in the Punjab	Mutiny forces Alexander to return westward

Tigris. Although his army was at least twice the size of Alexander's, Darius could not match his enemy's military genius, and as his own formations were outmanoeuvred and broken he fled the field. Darius was later murdered by one of his disgruntled generals – much to Alexander's disgust.

Alexander declared himself Darius' successor as 'king of kings', and advanced through the Persian provinces of central Asia, such as Parthia and Bactria, increasingly relying on Persian soldiers and administrators, and marrying a Bactrian princess, Roxana. Being so far from home, Alexander recognized the necessity of cooperating with conquered peoples and adopting their customs – such as having himself declared a god – but the Greeks and Macedonians in his army were dismayed by such developments. Although he led them in a successful campaign over the mountains into the valley of the River Indus and the Punjab, in 324 BC his army mutinied and refused to march any further east. Returning westward, Alexander arrived in Babylon, where he began to plan new campaigns – against Arabia, and then perhaps into the western Mediterranean to take on the growing might of Carthage and of Rome. But these plans were never fulfilled, as in 323 Alexander died of a fever after a drinking bout.

Alexander's horse

When Alexander was a youth there was a horse so wild and high-spirited that no one could ride it. But Alexander managed to mount it and break it in, giving it the name Bucephalus. Thereafter Bucephalus became Alexander's favourite steed, sharing in all the privations of his campaigns, and letting no other rider mount him. At the age of twenty-four Bucephalus bore Alexander in the key cavalry charge at the Battle of Gaugamela, and then accompanied him all the way to India. Here, at the age of thirty, Bucephalus died, from exhaustion and age. So fond was Alexander of his horse that he named the city he founded to the east of the River Indus in his honour, calling it Bucephala.

The legacy of Alexander At the time of Alexander's death, his wife Roxana was pregnant, but there were no clear rules of succession. Legend has it that, when Alexander was asked on his deathbed to whom he bequeathed his empire, he responded,

timeline

323 BC	312 BC	306 BC	305 BC
Alexander dies in Babylon	Seleucus founds Hellenistic empire in western Asia	Antigonus establishes Antigonid dynasty in Macedon and Greece	Ptolemy becomes ruler of Egypt

'To the strongest.' The ensuing power struggle between Alexander's generals – during which both Roxana and her son were murdered – lasted a dozen years or more, after which three main power blocks emerged. Seleucus ruled a vast swathe of western Asia, roughly equivalent to the old Persian empire; Antigonus ruled Greece and Macedon; and Ptolemy ruled Egypt. The Seleucid empire gradually broke up into a number of kingdoms, and in the 2nd century BC Macedon and Greece fell to the Romans. In Egypt, the Ptolemies adapted themselves to local tradition, becoming pharaohs and holding sway until 31 BC, when the celebrated Queen Cleopatra VII was defeated – together with her lover, the Roman general Mark Antony – by Octavian, the future Emperor Augustus, and took her own life.

> **❛In body he was very handsome and a great lover of hardships . . . but as for pleasures of the mind, he was insatiable of glory alone.❜**
>
> **Arrian, *The Campaigns of Alexander*, 2nd century AD**

Alexander's legacy outlived even this defeat, however. Across his empire he had founded many cities, a number of them named Alexandria in his honour, and these cities were peopled with Greek merchants and artisans who spread the culture of their native land far and wide, and helped to bring East and West together into a single commercial sphere. The most famous of these Alexandrias, that in Egypt, became the intellectual centre of the Mediterranean world for many centuries, and its great library, under the patronage of the Ptolemies, became the repository of all the accumulated learning of the ancients.

in a nutshell
Alexander's conquests spread Greek culture and commerce across a huge area

247 BC	167 BC	146 BC	31 BC
Parthia breaks away from Seleucid empire	Romans conquer Macedon	Greece becomes a Roman province	Cleopatra defeated by the Romans at Actium

06 The spread of Roman power

Of all the great empires of the ancient world, that of the Romans was the greatest and the most enduring. The Greeks had spread their culture far and wide in the wake of the conquests of Alexander the Great, but had failed to establish a political unity.

In contrast the Romans, via force of arms, the imposition of their laws and the extension of citizenship to conquered peoples, created a homogenous imperium from the island of Britain to Egypt and the western fringes of Asia.

The origins of Rome are lost in the mists of time. According to Roman tradition, the city was founded in 753 BC by a shepherd called Romulus, after he had killed his brother Remus. Romulus was the first of seven kings of Rome, the last of whom, Tarquin the Proud, was banished by the citizens of the city in 509 BC.

Expansion under the Republic In place of the old monarchy, the Romans set up a republic. At first this was dominated by the patricians, a class consisting of a relatively small number of elite families. Every year the patricians elected two consuls to rule over them and command the army, and the consuls were in turn advised by an elected assembly, the Senate. In times of emergency, a single dictator was appointed, but for no more than six months at a time. Domination by the patricians led to unrest among the remainder of the citizens, the plebeians, who eventually gained some political rights, with their own assembly and elected representatives, known as tribunes.

timeline

753 BC	509 BC	390 BC	287 BC	284–241 BC	275 BC
Traditional date for the foundation of Rome	Rome expels last king and becomes a republic	City sacked by Celtic raiders	Plebeians gain right to make laws	First Punic War	Romans defeat King Pyrrhus, ending Greek ambitions in Italy

To begin with, Rome had been just one of a number of Latin-speaking city-states in central Italy. Gradually, combining diplomacy with military adventurism, Rome became the dominant power in the region, and the neighbouring peoples their allies in the conquest of the whole peninsula, which was completed by the early decades of the 3rd century BC. Rome then turned its attention overseas. The greatest power in the western Mediterranean at that time was Carthage, a city in North Africa that had been founded by Phoenician traders from the Levant. Rome fought three wars against Carthage, successfully resisting the invasion of Italy by the Carthaginian general Hannibal and taking over the extensive Carthaginian territories in Spain and elsewhere. In 146 BC, at the end of the third Punic War (*Punicus* is Latin for 'Carthaginian'), the Romans razed Carthage to the ground. In the same year, Greece became a Roman province, and the Mediterranean became the 'Roman lake'. The Romans went on to add the Near East, North Africa, Gaul (modern France) and Britain to their empire, with the Rhine and Danube rivers providing their frontiers in mainland Europe.

❝Dulce et decorum est pro patria mori. [It is sweet and honourable to die for one's country.]❞

Horace, *Odes*, book III, no. 2. This famous line sums up the value the Romans put upon martial virtue and manly sacrifice.

Civil wars Imperial expansion was accompanied by extensive social and economic changes. Originally the Roman army had been made up of small-scale farmers, who served when required then returned to their land. But as the army campaigned further and further afield, these peasant farmers were unable to take care of their holdings, and as a result many fell into debt and were forced to leave their land and seek a livelihood in the city – where many remained unemployed, reliant on government handouts. At the same time, the wealthy elite were able to buy up these small landholdings and form them into larger estates, worked by the numerous enslaved captives that were one of the bounties of imperial conquest.

272 BC	218–202 BC	216 BC	202 BC	149–146 BC	146 BC
Romans complete conquest of Italian peninsula	Second Punic War	Carthaginian general Hannibal wins overwhelming victory over Romans at Cannae	Roman general Scipio defeats Hannibal at Zama	Third Punic War, followed by Roman destruction of Carthage	Greece becomes Roman province

❝**Roman, remember to rule the peoples of the world through strength – for these are your skills: to bring peace and impose law, to spare the conquered, and to bring down the proud by war.**❞

Virgil, in *The Aeneid*, book VI, provides a mission statement for the first emperor, Augustus

As the rich grew richer and the poor grew poorer, a number of successful generals from the dominant elite vied for power, gathering around them followers drawn from the ranks of the dispossessed. This led in the 1st century BC to a series of civil wars and oligarchies, involving such figures as Pompey and Julius Caesar. Caesar was suspected of seeking supreme power, which led to his assassination by his Republican enemies in 44 BC. More civil wars followed, ending only when Mark Antony and his lover, Queen Cleopatra of Egypt, were defeated by Octavian in 31 BC.

Imperial Rome Octavian went on to become the first emperor, taking the name Augustus. He was succeeded by a long line of emperors, some of them effective rulers and generals, some of them incompetent nonentities, some of them crazed despots, such as Caligula and Commodus. The hereditary principle was never firmly established, and succession often depended on assassination or the support given to a popular general by his legions.

Although there was often political instability at the top, for some centuries the *Pax Romana* ('Roman peace') reigned through much of the empire, which had reached its greatest extent by AD 200. The provinces were largely self-governing, run by the local elites with little reference to the emperor in Rome – as long as they did not cause trouble. The benefits of Roman citizenship were extended to those conquered peoples who were content to comply with Roman ways; those who offered any resistance were either put to the sword or enslaved. The army recruited from many

timeline

133 BC	88 BC	58 BC	48 BC	44 BC	31 BC	27 BC
The tribune Tiberius Gracchus is assassinated after attempting to introduce land reforms	Beginning of fifty years of intermittent civil war	Julius Caesar begins conquest of Gaul (modern France)	Caesar defeats Pompey and becomes dictator for life	Caesar assassinated	Octavian defeats Mark Antony, ending civil wars	Octavian becomes Emperor Augustus

Roman engineering

Although the Romans never quite matched the Greeks in the intellectual sphere, they were supremely practical, and were responsible for some of the greatest engineering accomplishments of the ancient world. Water was brought long distances to the cities by aqueducts, and sewage taken away by covered drains, while the villas of the wealthy benefited from underfloor central heating, Magnificent public buildings adorned every city, none more so than Rome itself, where the Colosseum – the arena for the perennially popular gladiator fights – could seat 50,000 spectators. It was the Romans who were the first to use the arch in a wide range of structures, and it was the Romans who built the first true domes, in such buildings as the temple known as the Pantheon – which employed another Roman innovation, concrete. Military considerations led to other impressive achievements, notably the network of roads that linked all parts of the empire, and the defensive walls, such as Hadrian's Wall in the north of England, that secured the frontiers of Roman power.

subject peoples, and army veterans settled in colonies across the empire, often marrying local women. New cities built on the Roman model – with forums, temples and amphitheatres – grew up all over the provinces, trade flourished, and people could travel freely across the empire, able to communicate wherever they went in either Latin or Greek. However, this state of affairs was not to last. From the 3rd century AD the empire began to come under increasing pressure from outside – pressure that was eventually to bring about a catastrophic collapse.

in a nutshell
Rome held sway in the Mediterranean and beyond for over half a millennium

AD 9	AD 14	AD 43	AD 101–6	AD 126	c.AD 200
Three Roman legions annihilated by German tribes in the Teutoburger Forest, ending Roman ambitions across the Rhine	Death of Augustus	Start of Roman conquest of Britain	Conquest of Dacia (modern Romania)	Completion of Hadrian's Wall	Roman empire reaches its greatest extent

07 The fall of Rome and its aftermath

From the time of the Renaissance, if not earlier, scholars looked back at the fall of Rome as a great discontinuity in Western civilization, marking the triumph of barbarism and the beginning of what became known as the 'Dark Ages'. But the collapse of Roman power was neither so sudden nor so universal as this picture paints it.

The eastern Roman empire, based in Constantinople (modern Istanbul), continued for another thousand years in the form of the Byzantine empire. In the west a number of kingdoms inherited the mantle of Roman power, while the Church of Rome kept both faith and scholarship alive.

For centuries, writers would use the fall of Rome to point a moral or adorn a tale. In the eyes of some, the Romans and their increasingly tyrannical emperors became decadent and effete, indulging in luxury and neglecting the simple military virtues. For others – notably Edward Gibbon in *The Decline and Fall of the Roman Empire* (1776–88) – the rot set in when the Romans abandoned the secular, enlightened values they had inherited from the ancient Greeks and embraced the superstitious, intolerant, irrational cult of Christianity. But the consensus today is that the reasons

timeline

235	250s	260	270s	284
The beginning of half a century of political instability and turmoil, with barbarian incursions along the northern frontiers	Collapse of Roman monetary system	Sassanian Persians overrun Syria, and capture Emperor Valerian	City walls built round Rome	Diocletian becomes emperor and restores order

for Roman decline were not internal, but external: as one modern historian has put it, 'The Roman empire did not fall – it was pushed.'

The barbarians at the gates The empire had reached its greatest extent by AD 200. From the middle of the 3rd century, the frontiers along the Rhine and Danube came under increasing pressure by groups of Germanic tribes such as the Franks, the Alemanni and the Goths. These tribes were referred to by the Romans as 'barbarians', but were in fact at least partly Romanized, enjoying trading relationships with the empire and increasingly serving as mercenaries in the Roman army. Their territorial incursions into the Roman provinces were not so much a result of expansionist ambition as a response to pressure from warlike nomadic horsemen from the steppes to the east, such as the Huns.

> **Under the authority of God we conduct war victoriously, make peace with honour and uphold the condition of the state.**
>
> **The Emperor Justinian I,** *c.*530, claims divine sanction for his earthly powers

When the financial demands of defending the empire could not be met by the Roman taxpayer, the authorities responded by debasing the coinage, bringing the economy close to collapse. The disruption to trade and agriculture resulted in famine and lawlessness, while emperor succeeded emperor in a succession of revolts, civil wars and assassinations. Some degree of stability was restored from the late 3rd century under the Emperor Diocletian, and then in the early 4th century under Constantine. Constantine made Christianity the official religion of the empire, and moved his capital from Rome to the old Greek city of Byzantium, which he renamed Constantinople. Thereafter there were separate emperors in the east and west.

At the beginning of the 5th century the Germanic tribes poured over the frontiers and overran Gaul (modern France), Spain, North Africa and Italy, setting up kingdoms and obliging the western emperor to recognize them as

303	306	313	330	395
Beginning of Diocletianic persecution of Christians	Constantine becomes emperor	Edict of Milan proclaims religious toleration	Constantine moves Roman capital to Constantinople	Roman empire divided between east and west

allies. The emperor's new allies were restless, however: the city of Rome itself – untouched by foreign invasion for some eight centuries – was sacked by the Visigoths under Alaric in 410, and in 476 the last western Roman emperor was ousted by the Germanic general Odoacer, who made himself king of Italy.

Christianity: from Jewish cult to imperial religion

Christianity was just one of a number of messianic Jewish sects that arose during the Roman occupation of Israel, partly as a form of spiritual resistance to the foreign oppressor. At first, only Jews could become Christians, until St Paul began to proselytize to the Gentiles in Cyprus, Asia Minor, Greece and elsewhere. Paul not only turned the teachings of Jesus into a set of theological doctrines, he also began the work of establishing a universal church, with a strong, centralized organization.

Christianity, with its appeal for the poor and the oppressed, spread rapidly around the Roman empire, but also met with considerable antipathy among those who regarded the refusal of Christians to worship the 'official' Roman gods as a treason against the state. The Emperor Nero used the Christian community as a scapegoat for the fire of Rome in AD 64, putting many to death in a variety of unpleasant ways; but most of the early persecutions were unsanctioned outbreaks of mob violence. The pressures that began to build up on the fringes of the empire through the 3rd century, however, led to a series of severe official persecutions, most notably that under Diocletian at the beginning of the 4th century. By creating so many martyrs, these persecutions served only to recruit more converts.

It was the Emperor Constantine who recognized that Christianity, with its hierarchical organization and hold over people's loyalties, could provide a useful means of wielding power, and in 313 he issued an edict of religious toleration. From his time on Christianity became the official religion of the Roman empire, and the church an extension of the state.

timeline

410	451	476	527–65	7th C.
Rome sacked by Visigoths	Combined force of Visigoths and Romans defeat Huns at Châlons-sur-Marne	Last western emperor deposed	Reign of Emperor Justinian, who reconquers territory in the west	Byzantine empire loses much territory to Arabs

How dark were the Dark Ages? The 'barbarian' tribes who established kingdoms in what had been the western Roman empire – Visigoths in Spain, Vandals in North Africa, Ostrogoths in Italy and Franks in Gaul and western Germany – largely abandoned their old gods and adopted Christianity, in one form or another. However, as contact was lost with the great cultural centres of the eastern Mediterranean, such as Alexandria, literacy and learning declined, preserved only in the monasteries.

In the west the Franks, via force of arms, rose to be the dominant power, and under their most famous king, Charlemagne, they carved out an empire that covered not only France, but also Italy and much of Germany. On Christmas Day in the year 800 Charlemagne was crowned 'emperor of the west' by the pope in Rome. His capital at Aix-la-Chapelle (Aachen) became a great centre of learning, and he and his successors did much to preserve the legacy of the Greeks and Romans, in art, literature and scholarship.

In the east, the Byzantine empire experienced a great revival in the 6th century under the Emperor Justinian, who reconquered Italy and parts of Spain and North Africa. But this success was short-lived, and in the following centuries the Byzantine empire was gradually whittled away, first by the Arabs, and then by the Turks. And yet through all the long centuries of decline, the Byzantines, though speaking Greek, regarded themselves as the true inheritors of the mantle of Rome.

> **❝When I heard that the bright light of all the world was quenched . . . then indeed, "I became dumb and humbled myself and kept silence from good words."❞**
> **St Jerome, 'Preface to Ezekiel',** recalling his reaction on hearing of the sack of Rome in 410

the condensed idea
The legacy of Rome survived its fall

800	843	1054	1071	1453
Charlemagne, king of the Franks, is crowned 'emperor of the west'	Charlemagne's empire divided into three by his successors	Schism between churches of Rome and Constantinople	Turks begin assault on Byzantine empire with victory at Manzikert in eastern Anatolia	Constantinople falls to the Turks, marking end of Byzantine empire

08 The rise of Islam

At the beginning of the 6th century AD a new religion was born in the deserts of Arabia. This was Islam, a word meaning 'submission to God'. Its prophet, Mohammed, told his followers that the word of God had been directly revealed to him by the angel Gabriel.

Such was the appeal and charisma of Mohammed that he united the tribes of Arabia under the banner of Islam, and over the next 150 years the Arabs spread their power and their new religion from Spain in the west to the fringes of central Asia and India in the east.

Mohammed did not claim that Islam was a new religion. It was rather, he said, the perfection of the old monotheistic religions, Judaism and Christianity, which traced their roots back to Abraham. The revelations began in 610, and were eventually written down in the Qur'an. Mohammed's preaching against the idolatry of the polytheistic inhabitants of Mecca led to his expulsion to Medina in 622. He took his followers with him in a migration called the *Hijra*, which marks the first year of the Islamic calendar. Eight years later he returned to Mecca in force and conquered the city. By the time he died in 632, Mohammed was ruler of the whole of the Arabian peninsula.

Out of Arabia Before his death Mohammed had urged his followers to mount a *jihad* (holy war) against all non-believers. His successors as rulers of the Muslim community took the title of *caliph* (literally 'successor'), and over the next three decades they led the Arabs in a series of remarkable campaigns, seizing Egypt and Syria from the Byzantine empire and

timeline

c.570	610	622	630–50	632	661
Birth of Prophet Mohammed	Mohammed begins to receive revelations	Mohammed exiled from Mecca	Arabia, Egypt, Syria, Mesopotamia and Persia all come under Muslim rule	Death of Mohammed	Murder of Caliph Ali, Mohammed's son-in-law

Mesopotamia and Iran from the Sassanian Persians. The Arabs went on to lay siege to Constantinople, the Byzantine capital, not just once, but twice (674–8 and 717–18).

The policy of the conquerors to the conquered was to offer the rights and privileges of Muslims to all converts; those who did not wish to convert, whether Christian or Jew, were tolerated as long as they did not resist, although they were subjected to higher taxation. This pluralist approach was in contrast to the religious intolerance of the Greek Orthodox Byzantines and Zoroastrian Persians, and ensured that many welcomed the new conquerors.

The Muslim armies spread across North Africa, and in 711 an army of Moors (Muslim Berbers) crossed the Strait of Gibraltar and proceeded to conquer most of the Iberian Peninsula. Sardinia and Sicily also fell, and in 846 the Arabs sacked Rome itself. The same year that the Berbers crossed to Spain, an Arab army advanced from eastern Iran and conquered a large stretch of the Indus valley. Over the following centuries, Islam spread to the Turkish peoples of central Asia, and thence across much of India. Arab traders also brought Islam to sub-Saharan Africa, south-east Asia and Indonesia.

> **Persia was extinguished and Byzantium was crushed, as also were Indian cities; they were everywhere invincible.**
>
> **Tu Yu, 8th-century Chinese official,** describes the extent of the conquests of the Arabs, recording that they even sent an embassy to the Chinese imperial court to present tribute

It was not long before conflict arose within the Islamic world. Ali, the fourth caliph and Mohammed's son-in-law, was murdered in 661, and his followers, the Shi'at 'Ali ('party of Ali') formed the minority Shia sect, while the majority, the Sunnis, adhered to the *sunna* ('tradition'). The first dynasty of caliphs, the Umayyads, had their base in Damascus, but were replaced in 750 by the Abbasid dynasty, who moved the capital to Baghdad. The Abbasid court came to a peak of magnificence in the late 8th century under the fifth Abbasid caliph, Harun al-Rashid, who

661–750	674–8	711	717–18	750–1258	945
Umayyad dynasty of caliphs, based in Damascus	Arabs besiege Constantinople	Moorish invasion of Spain. Arab army conquers province of Sind in Indus valley.	Second Arab siege of Constantinople	Abbasid dynasty of caliphs, based in Baghdad	Buyids from northern Persia seize political power in Baghdad

exchanged gifts with Charlemagne and who features in the *Thousand and One Nights*. But thereafter the power of the Abbasids across the Arab empire declined. In 929 the emir of Córdoba in southern Spain proclaimed

Islamic science

For many centuries after the fall of Rome, while much of classical learning was lost to the Christian West, Islamic scholars and polymaths such as Ibn Sinna (Avicenna, 980–1037) and Ibn Rushd (Averroës, 1126–98) kept alive the intellectual flame of ancient Greece. This learning began to be recovered from the 12th century, when Gerard of Cremona translated many Arabic versions of Greek texts into Latin. It was via this process that the works of Aristotle and many others came to be known in Christendom, having an enormous impact on theology, natural philosophy and medicine.

But Arabs, Persians and others within the medieval Islamic world also came up with numerous original contributions. The Arabic system of numerals, including the key symbol for zero (derived from India), made possible far more complex mathematics than the Greeks or Romans had managed with their cumbersome number systems. The very word 'algebra' derives from the Arabic word *al-jabr*, first used

in a mathematical context in 820 by the Persian mathematician Al-Khwāzmī in his treatise on solving polynomial equations. Similarly, the word 'alcohol' derives from the Arabic *al-kuhl*, and it was Jabir ibn Hayyan (Geber, *c.*721–*c.*815) who first identified alcohol as the flammable vapour released by boiling wine. He also understood the workings of acids and alkalis (he named the latter), and is credited as the first to develop alchemy into an experimental science – chemistry.

There were great technological achievements too. In 850 the Banu Musa brothers of Baghdad published their *Book of Ingenious Devices*, which contains descriptions of numerous mechanical contrivances such as automatons and automatic musical instruments. A few years later, in the emirate of Córdoba in southern Spain, the Moorish inventor Abbas Ibn Firnas made himself a pair of wings and appears to have glided through the air for some distance before coming back to earth with a bump.

timeline

969–1171	1040s	1071	1099	1187	1206
Fatimid dynasty of caliphs, based in Cairo	Seljuk Turks sweep through Middle East	Seljuks defeat Byzantines at Manzikert	Crusaders seize Jerusalem and establish states in Syria and Palestine	Sultan Saladin retakes Jerusalem from Crusaders	Establishment of Islamic sultanate of Delhi in India

❝There was in the centre of the room a large basin filled with quicksilver; on each side of it eight doors fixed on arches of ivory and ebony, ornamented with gold and precious stones of various kinds, resting upon pillars of variegated marble and transparent crystal.❞

Al-Maqqari, the 11th-century writer,
describes a Moorish palace in the emirate of Córdoba in southern Spain

himself caliph, and for a century he and his successors presided over a golden age, marked by great prosperity and cultural flowering, with the erection of magnificent mosques, gardens and palaces and great advances in science, philosophy, history and geography. A further weakening of Abbasid power came in 969, when the Fatimids, a Shiite dynasty claiming descent from Ali and Fatima (Mohammed's daughter), declared themselves caliphs in Egypt and North Africa.

In addition to these internal divisions, there were also external pressures. In the 11th century the Seljuk Turks, Muslim converts from central Asia, swept down through the Middle East, while at the end of the century Christian armies from western Europe mounted the first of a succession of crusades to retake the Holy Land from the Muslims. At the same time, the Christian kingdoms in the north of the Iberian Peninsula began a long campaign of reconquest of Muslim Spain. In the 13th and 14th centuries the Mongols and the Ottoman Turks began their onslaughts – the latter creating an empire in the Middle East that was to last until the 20th century.

in a nutshell
A rapid expansion of a new religious and political phenomenon

1219	1250	1258	1260	c.1300
Genghis Khan begins Mongol attacks on Middle East	Mamelukes (Turkish warrior-slaves) seize power in Egypt	Mongols sack Baghdad, ending Abbasid caliphate	Mamelukes defeat Mongols at Ain Jalut	Foundation of first Ottoman Turkish state

09 The Vikings

Between the 8th and 11th centuries, waves of raiders and migrants swept out of Scandinavia and stamped their mark on a period that has come to be known as the 'Viking Age'. Long feared as brutal pillagers and deliverers of merciless slaughter, the Vikings were also expert seafarers, long-distance traders and fine craftsmen, and in many places settled down as peaceful farmers, generally integrating with the indigenous peoples and cultures. By the end of the 11th century nearly all had swapped their pagan beliefs for Christianity.

The term Viking is unknown in modern English before the early 19th century. It may owe its origins to Old English *wíc*, a temporary camp, or Old Norse *vík*, an inlet, suggesting the kinds of places these marauders may have been encountered. To their contemporaries, they were simply Norsemen – the men from the north.

The men from the north As far as England was concerned, the Viking Age commenced when the abbey on the island of Lindisfarne, off the Northumbrian coast, was destroyed by a fleet of Norse longships on 8 June 793. All the monks were killed. The event sent shockwaves through the Christian kingdoms of north-west Europe: 'Never before,' recorded the contemporary scholar Alcuin of York, 'has such an atrocity been seen.' Two years later, in search of further treasure, the Vikings attacked the abbey on the small Hebridean island of Iona, the cradle of Christianity in Scotland. Many more such raids were to follow, the Danes attacking the east coast of England and north-west France, while the Norwegians

timeline

793	834	853	856	860	865	866
Vikings begin raids on British Isles	Beginning of Viking raids on north-west France	Olaf, son of the king of Norway, establishes Viking kingdom in Ireland, with Dublin as his capital	Vikings sack Paris	Failed Viking attack on Constantinople	Major Danish invasion of East Anglia	Vikings capture York, and establish rule over Northumbria

concentrated on the Hebrides, the western seaboard of Scotland, the Isle of Man and the coasts of Ireland. They also occupied the Orkney, Shetland and Faroe Islands, and established colonies on Iceland and Greenland, and even a short-lived settlement in North America that they called 'Vinland', which may have been on Newfoundland, or even in Maine.

❝Then the wolves of the slaughter, careless of water, Came wading westward through shimmering rivers, Bearing shields landward . . . ❞

The Battle of Maldon, an anonymous Anglo-Saxon poem, *c.*1000, describing a Viking victory over the English in 991

Vikings from Sweden turned their attention eastward across the Baltic to Russia, sailing down the Volga to the Caspian Sea and the Dnieper to the Black Sea, and even mounting an attack on Constantinople, capital of the Byzantine empire. Although this failed, the Byzantine emperors were so impressed by the fighting skills of the Vikings that they later recruited large numbers to form their personal bodyguard, known as the Varangian Guard. In Russia, the Swedes were known as the Rus, and established the most important early Russian principality, based on Kiev.

Quite what prompted the Viking expansion is the subject of some debate, but it is likely that in their harsh northern homelands agricultural production lagged behind population growth, prompting many to eye up the richer, more temperate lands to the south. The raiders may also have been aware of weaknesses in their target territories: England at this period consisted of a number of competing Anglo-Saxon kingdoms, while across the Channel the Frankish empire created by Charlemagne was beginning to crumble following the death of Louis the Pious in 840.

The Vikings in the British Isles At first in north-west Europe the Vikings came as raiders, but before long they began to settle, and a number of Norse kingdoms, such as those centred on Dublin and York, began to emerge. By the later 9th century the Vikings had overwhelmed

871	**c.874**	**877**	**c.880**	**886**	**896**	**911**
Alfred the Great becomes king of Wessex and begins effective resistance against Vikings	Norwegians reach Iceland	Danes take over Mercia	Swedes establish state of Kievan Rus, the nucleus of modern Russia	Danelaw established by treaty in England	Alfred defeats new Danish invasion of England	Viking leader Rollo becomes first duke of Normandy

The Normans

In 896 a Viking 'great host' invaded north-west France. In 911, to buy peace, King Charles the Simple granted Rollo, one of the Viking leaders, extensive lands around the mouth of the River Seine, an area that became known as Normandy ('Norman' being a corruption of 'north-man'). In return, Rollo agreed to be baptized, and recognized Charles as his king. The dukes of Normandy went on to adopt the language and culture of France, although frequently asserting their political independence. The Normans carried on the military adventurism of their Norse ancestors, carving out territories for themselves in southern Italy and Sicily, while in 1066 Duke William defeated the English at Hastings and became William the Conqueror. French became the language of the English court for the next 300 years.

the Anglo-Saxon kingdoms of Northumbria, Mercia and East Anglia. Only Wessex, under King Alfred the Great, held out, and over the course of the following century his successors fought back and succeeded in unifying England. However, a large swathe of eastern England had been settled by the Danes, and until the late 11th century Danish laws and customs prevailed in this area, known as 'the Danelaw'. Viking influence can still be detected in many English place names: for example, the common suffix -by, Old Norse for 'farm' or 'village', is found in such names as Grimsby, Whitby and Derby.

The late 10th century witnessed a renewal of large-scale Viking attacks, and the English king, Ethelred the Unready, sought to buy the raiders off with large sums of money known as 'Danegeld'. Ethelred's sobriquet 'Unready' is from Old English *unraed*, meaning 'lacking good counsel', and he justified this description when in 1002 – perhaps in an attempt to restore national pride – he ordered the massacre of all the Danes in England. Among the slaughtered was the sister of the king of Denmark, Sweyn Forkbeard, who ordered an escalation in Danish attacks and who in 1013 arrived in England in person. Ethelred fled, and Sweyn was proclaimed king. Although Sweyn died the following year, his son Cnut was to rule England for two decades, a period of peace and relative

timeline

914	930	965	c.986	995	c.1000
King Edward the Elder begins English reconquest of Danelaw	Foundation of the Althing, the Icelandic assembly	Christianity adopted in Denmark	Eric the Red reaches Greenland from Iceland, giving it its name to attract settlers	Beginning of conversion of Sweden to Christianity	Leif Eriksson establishes Norwegian settlement in North America, 500 years before Columbus discovers the 'New World'

prosperity. Cnut himself, who was also the most powerful figure in Scandinavia at this time, was received in Rome by the pope and the Holy Roman emperor as a Christian prince among Christian princes.

Danish rule of England came to an end with the death of Cnut's son Harthacnut in 1042. But Norse ambition was still focused on England, and in 1066 the invasion of the Norwegian king Harold Hardrada was brought to an end when he was killed at Stamford Bridge near York. Shortly afterwards, Duke William of Normandy, the French-speaking descendant of Viking raiders, landed in Sussex. His victory at the Battle of Hastings was to change the course of English history.

> **❛Rollo, disdaining to kneel down, seized the king's foot and hoisted it to his mouth as he stood upright. The king fell flat on his back, and all the Norsemen broke out in laughter.❜**
>
> **William of Malmesbury,** *c.*1125, describes how the first Duke of Normandy kissed the foot of Charles the Simple of France in mocking homage

Elsewhere in the British Isles, Norse rule continued. In Ireland, Dublin, Wexford, Waterford and Limerick remained largely Viking towns until the Anglo-Norman invasion of the later 12th century. In Scotland, the Hebrides remained in Norwegian hands until the Scots defeated King Haakon IV of Norway at Largs in 1263. Orkney and Shetland were only transferred to the Scottish Crown in 1472, as part of the dowry for a dynastic marriage, and the people of those islands, with their Norse ancestry, still do not regard themselves as an integral part of Scotland.

in a nutshell
Raiders who terrorized northern Europe later became peaceful settlers

1013–42	1014	1066	1169	15th C.
England ruled by Sweyn Forkbeard of Denmark and his successors Cnut, Harold Harefoot and Harthacnut	Brian Boru, high king of Ireland, defeats Vikings at Clontarf	**SEPTEMBER** Harold Hardrada of Norway killed at Stamford Bridge. **OCTOBER** Duke William of Normandy defeats English under Harold II at Hastings.	Anglo-Norman invasion marks end of Gaelic-Norse kingdoms in Ireland	Norse colony on Greenland dies out, possibly owing to climate cooling

10 The Crusades

For two centuries, from 1096 to 1291, the rulers of western Europe mounted a series of military campaigns against the Muslims of the Near East in an attempt to recover the holy places – especially Jerusalem – for Christendom. The Crusades were preached by the Roman Catholic Church, which granted remission of sin to those who vowed to become Crusaders.

No doubt the motives of many of those who 'took the Cross' were idealistic – at least at first. But as is so often the case, religious zealotry brought with it an inhuman cruelty towards non-believers. And, as is also often the case, wars that were launched with the purest of motives soon degenerated into undignified scrambles for power and profit.

❝Let those who were brigands become soldiers of Christ . . .❞

Pope Urban II preaches the First Crusade at Clermont, 1095

Although the best-known Crusades were those dispatched to the Holy Land, there were also religiously motivated campaigns mounted against pagans such as the Slavs and Balts of north-east Europe, against heretics such as the Cathars of southern France, and against the Muslim rulers of Spain in a process called the Reconquista. These campaigns too were marked by fervour, intolerance and savagery.

The First Crusade The First Crusade originated in an appeal from Alexius I, the Greek Orthodox ruler of the Byzantine empire, who begged help from Pope Urban II in resisting the Muslim Seljuk Turks. Following the decisive Battle of Manzikert in 1071, the Seljuks had occupied most of Anatolia, and Alexius requested the assistance of western mercenaries in dealing with the threat to his empire.

timeline

638	1071	1095	1096	1098	1099
Muslim Arabs take Jerusalem	Seljuk Turks defeat Byzantines at Manzikert	Pope Urban II preaches First Crusade	First Crusade embarks for Holy Land	Crusaders take Antioch	Crusaders capture Jerusalem and set up states in Syria and Palestine

The Greek Orthodox Church in the east and the Roman Catholic Church in the west had become increasingly alienated from each other, and the pope saw in Byzantine misfortune an opportunity to assert the primacy of Rome over all Christendom, and to reverse the advance of Islam over lands that had previously been Christian. In 1095 he preached a sermon in Clermont in his native France, citing atrocities carried out by the Muslims against Christian pilgrims in the Holy Land – although generally speaking the Muslims had been tolerant towards Christian pilgrims, realizing that they were a significant source of income.

On the uses of propaganda

Baha ad-Din, the friend and biographer of Saladin, related how, in order to rouse the spirits of the warriors of Christendom for a Third Crusade, Conrad, Marquis of Montferrat, had a painting made showing a mounted Muslim knight trampling on the tomb of Christ in Jerusalem, while his horse urinated on the holy spot. This painting was widely circulated, and served as an effective means of recruiting a huge army.

The impact of Urban's sermon proved to be electrifying. Western Europe at that time was undergoing a period of population expansion, economic prosperity and spiritual self-confidence, and Urban's sermon helped to focus the ambitions of many restless warrior-barons – many of them Norman or French – who saw an opportunity of carving out a niche for themselves in the east while aiding fellow Christians and saving their own souls.

Within a year a number of armies had set out for the Holy Land. In 1098 they captured Antioch in Syria from the Seljuks after a long siege, and in 1099 took Jerusalem itself and proceeded to put its Muslim and Jewish inhabitants – men, women and children – to the sword. 'If you had been there,' wrote a contemporary Christian chronicler, 'your feet would have been stained up to the ankles with the blood of the slain.' The city's mosques were also destroyed. The Crusaders established a new kingdom of Jerusalem, under which were three vassal states: the counties of Tripoli and Edessa and the principality of Antioch.

1144	1146–9	1187	1189–92	1200–4	1209–29
Turks capture Crusader state of Edessa	Second Crusade fails to take Damascus	Saladin defeats Crusaders at Hattin and captures Jerusalem	Third Crusade captures Acre but fails to take Jerusalem	Fourth Crusade sacks Constantinople and establishes Latin empire	Albigensian Crusade against Cathar heretics of southern France

The later Crusades It has been said that the First Crusade was successful because no kings – and thus no national rivalries – were involved. The Second Crusade was a more royal affair, being led by King Louis VII of France and Conrad III, the German emperor. It was prompted by the recapture of Edessa by the Muslims in 1144, but had little success – the Crusader siege of Damascus was a failure, and was abandoned.

The Reconquista

The Christian campaign to reconquer the Iberian Peninsula from the Muslim Moors took some four centuries, and, unlike the Crusades in the Near East, its success was permanent. The northern Christian kingdoms of Castile and Aragon began to seize territory from the Moors in the mid-11th century, and after the decisive victory at Las Navas de Tolosa in 1212, the process became irreversible. Granada, the last Muslim possession in Spain, fell in 1492. But whereas the Muslims in Spain had presided over a generally tolerant and pluralistic culture, the country's new Christian rulers, King Ferdinand and Queen Isabella, forced the country's Jews and Muslims to convert, or face death or expulsion. Subsequently, even converts were subjected to the attentions of the Spanish Inquisition, and those suspected of secretly practising their original religion were burned at the stake.

In 1187 Saladin, sultan of Egypt and Syria, recaptured Jerusalem, prompting the Third Crusade, led by the German emperor, Frederick 'Barbarossa' (who died en route), King Philip II of France, and King Richard I ('Lionheart') of England. After the capture of Jerusalem, Saladin had spared the Christians and left their churches and shrines largely untouched; in contrast, when Richard I captured Acre, he slaughtered some 3,000 prisoners. The Crusaders failed to retake Jerusalem, but before he left the Holy Land Richard negotiated a treaty with Saladin, by which Christian pilgrims would be given safe passage by the Muslims.

The Fourth Crusade turned into an utterly cynical exercise. At the behest of the Venetians, the Crusaders diverted their attention from the Holy Land to the Byzantine empire, Venice's trade rival in the eastern Mediterranean. In

timeline

1212	1216–21	1228	1244	1248	1261	1268
Battle of Las Navas de Tolosa, decisive Christian victory over Moors in Spain	Fifth Crusade fails to take Cairo	Sixth Crusade secures recovery of Jerusalem by treaty	Jerusalem retaken by Muslims	Seventh Crusade: Louis IX of France (St Louis) captured while attempting to take Cairo	Restoration of Byzantine rule in Constantinople	Fall of Antioch to Mamelukes

1204 Constantinople itself was captured and its holy places desecrated, and a Latin state established there that lasted half a century. This marked the final breach between the eastern and western branches of Christianity.

Later Crusades to Egypt and the Holy Land achieved little, while the Muslims steadily recaptured the remaining Crusader strongholds along the coast of Syria and Palestine. Although Jerusalem was recovered by treaty in 1228, it was lost again in 1244, and in 1291 Acre, the last Crusader stronghold in the Holy Land, fell to the Mamelukes of Egypt.

> **❝Jerusalem is for us an object of worship that we could not give up even if there were only one of us left . . .**
> **Richard I to Saladin**

> **Jerusalem is ours as much as yours; indeed it is even more sacred to us than to you . . . ❞**
> **Saladin to Richard I**
> This correspondence was recorded by Saladin's biographer, Baha ad-Din, himself an eyewitness of the Third Crusade

The Crusades – which the German philosopher Friedrich Nietzsche characterized as 'nothing but superior piracy' – left a legacy of enduring bitterness against the West in the Muslim world. President George W. Bush's use of the word 'crusade' to describe his 'war on terror' after 9/11 caused widespread consternation outside the USA; and Islamist radicals deliberately characterize Western forces in Iraq and Afghanistan as 'Crusaders', knowing full well how that word conjures up the bloody atrocities committed in Jerusalem and Acre a millennium ago.

in a nutshell
European military adventurism in the Muslim world left a bitter legacy

1270	1271–2	1289	1291	1420–34	1492
Eighth Crusade is diverted to Tunis, where Louis IX dies	Ninth Crusade ends in failure	Fall of Tripoli to Mamelukes	Fall of Acre, last Crusader stronghold in Near East	Crusade against Hussites, proto-Protestants of Bohemia	Fall of Granada, last Muslim possession in Spain

11 The Black Death

In the middle of the 14th century, Europe was visited by a calamity the like of which it had never previously known, with a rate of mortality unsurpassed even by the two world wars of the last century. It is estimated that across the entire continent, around one-third of the population died within the space of three years.

The cause was a plague pandemic – known at the time as the Great Pestilence and subsequently as the Black Death. More than one contemporary chronicler noted that 'the living did not suffice to bury the dead'.

The consequences of the Black Death extended beyond the devastatingly high mortality. It was a grievous blow to the collective psyche of medieval Europe. Gone were the certainties and optimism of the High Middle Ages. It seemed that God was delivering an awful chastisement to his people, not seen since the times of the Old Testament. There was surely something rotten in the heart of humanity to warrant such devastation, and something particularly rotten in God's church, which could do nothing to stem the deadly tide of the disease. To many people, it seemed that the Last Days had come, that time of tribulation for humanity that was to precede the second coming of Christ.

The nature of the beast In the Middle Ages, people had no idea as to what caused disease, and thus found themselves helpless to prevent its spread or to effect a cure. It was not until the end of the 19th century that scientists identified the bacterium, *Yersinia pestis*, that causes

timeline

6th C. AD	1330s	1346	1347
First great plague pandemic spreads from Egypt to Constantinople and across Mediterranean	Second great plague pandemic erupts in the steppes of central Asia	Plague reaches Black Sea port of Kaffa	Plague reaches Sicily, Constantinople, Naples, Genoa and Marseille

plague, and realized that it was transmitted by the bites of fleas carried by black rats.

The commonest form of the disease suffered during the Black Death was probably bubonic plague – so called after the hard black buboes, the size of an egg or even an apple, that appeared in the groin and armpits. Those infected became fevered and delirious, suffered violent chest pains, and vomited blood. Few lived for more than three or four days, and many died in a matter of hours. In winter, the pneumonic strain of the disease, spread by coughing, was more common, while a third strain, septicaemic plague, infected the blood and killed its victims before any symptoms appeared. Some scientists today believe the pandemic may in fact have been viral in origin.

'Many died daily or nightly in the public streets . . . ; the whole place was a sepulchre.'

Giovanni Boccaccio, in *The Decameron*, 1350–3, describes the plague in Florence.

Out of Asia The Black Death probably originated in the steppes of central Asia, and spread via the trade routes to Europe. In one account, the Tartars besieging the Black Sea port of Kaffa (modern Theodosia) in the Crimea in 1346 were forced to abandon operations because of the disease, but before they left they catapulted the corpses of those who had died over the walls in the hope of infecting the inhabitants. The following year Genoese traders – or the rats aboard their ships – carried the disease from Kaffa to Messina in Sicily, and in 1348 it swept right across the Mediterranean lands and reached England.

By 1349–50 the plague had devastated France, all of Britain, Scandinavia, Germany and central Europe. 'It passed most rapidly from place to place,' recorded the English chronicler Robert of Avesbury, 'swiftly killing ere midday many who in the morning had been well . . . On the same day twenty, forty, sixty and very often more corpses were committed to the same grave.' In the English port of Bristol, the grass grew long in the silent streets. In some places, the mortality reached as high as 60 per cent, and across Europe, at the lowest estimate, some 25 million people perished.

1348	**1349**	**1349–50**	**1351**	**1358**
Plague spreads across the Mediterranean and western Europe, reaching as far as southern England. Pope Clement VI issues a Bull declaring the Jews innocent of causing the disease.	Pope issues a Bull condemning flagellants	Plague affects all of northern and central Europe	Statute of Labourers in England	Jacquerie uprising in France (named after French nickname for a peasant). Revolt in Bruges.

The challenge to the old order Humanity had fallen out of God's favour, and across Europe a new mood of pessimism prevailed. The literature and art of the period are filled with images of death and damnation – visions of Hell and the Devil, the Dance of Death, the Grim Reaper, the Four Horsemen of the Apocalypse. The realization of the deadly consequences of sin led to a growth in piety, and with it criticisms of the laxity and worldliness of the clergy. Various protest movements

Fear and loathing

In the face of the almost unimaginable horror of the Black Death, people resorted to all sorts of desperate remedies. The disease was most commonly attributed to bad air, so doors and windows were kept shut, aromatic substances burned, and those who ventured out carried sponges soaked in vinegar. Some blamed the water supply, which, they said, must have been polluted with spiders, frogs and lizards – embodiments of earth, dirt and the Devil – or even with the flesh of the basilisk, a mythical serpent who could kill a man with a single glance. Scapegoats were sought everywhere – the lepers, the rich, the poor, the clergy and, most popularly, the Jews, who were subjected to widespread pogroms.

The avoidance of unclean living and the purgation of hidden sin became something

of an obsession, and mass outbreaks of self-flagellation swept across Germany, the Low Countries and France. The flagellants, who spurned the company of women, adopted such names as the Cross-bearers, the Flagellant Brethren and the Brethren of the Cross, and in their ritualized and bloody sessions they sought to purge not only their own sins, but to take on the sins of the world and so avert the plague and the complete annihilation of humankind. The flagellants thus attracted great popular approbation, and at first they were tolerated and even encouraged by the ecclesiastical and secular authorities. However, once the flagellants appeared to threaten the established order, they were roundly condemned, and in October 1349 Pope Clement VI issued a Bull for their suppression.

timeline

1370s	1381	1382–4	1414	1420–34
Popular unrest in several Italian cities	Peasants' Revolt in England	A number of Flemish towns rebel	Suppression of Lollard rebellion in England	Hussite Wars in Bohemia

emerged, such as the Lollards in England and the Hussites in Bohemia, and their rejection of papal authority foreshadowed the Protestant Reformation of the 16th century.

It was not just the established authority of the church that was challenged. Once the pestilence passed, those agricultural workers who survived found their services much sought after, leading to demands for better pay. Such demands were resisted by the landowning classes; in England, for example, the Statute of Labourers of 1351 attempted to freeze wages at pre-plague levels. The resulting discontent among both peasants and townspeople, exacerbated by heavy taxes, led to popular rebellions – the Jacquerie of 1358 in France, for example, and the Peasants' Revolt in England in 1381. There was also unrest in the cities of Flanders and Italy. Although such rebellions were suppressed, by the end of the century the shortage of labour had led to the abandonment of serfdom in many parts of Europe, and real wages for the mass of the population had risen to hitherto unknown levels. For many, the Black Death ushered in a golden age of relative plenty.

> **And no bells tolled and nobody wept no matter what his loss because almost everyone expected death . . . and people said and believed, "This is the end of the world."**
>
> **Agnolo di Tura,** called the Fat, a tax collector in Siena, in 1348. He had buried his five children with his own hands.

in a nutshell
The plague pandemic brought about a new questioning of authority

1664–6	1666–70	1679–84	1720	late 19th C.
Last great outbreak of plague in London kills 70,000 people	Plague in western Germany and Netherlands	Plague in central Europe	Last major European outbreak, in Marseille	Third great plague pandemic across China and India

12 Precolonial India

The cultures that now flourish in Egypt and the Middle East bear little resemblance to those that flourished there in ancient times. Conquests by Greeks, Romans and Arabs created dislocations with the far distant past. In contrast, the Hindu culture that still flourishes in India today represents the continuation of a civilization that can trace its history back over three and a half millennia.

The history of India is, of course, even older. By 5000 BC farming was established in the Indus valley, where around 2600 BC one of the world's first urban civilizations emerged, centred around the highly planned cities of Harappa and Mohenjo Daro.

The emergence of Hindu culture After 1700 BC, the cities of the Indus valley went into a decline, possibly owing to an influx from the west of a nomadic people, the Aryans, who spoke an early Indo-European language (known as Sanskrit in its later written form). Their earliest writings, a collection of Sanskrit hymns, invocations, charms and rituals known as the *Vedas*, date from around 1500 BC, and mark the emergence of Hinduism. This polytheistic religion evolved a complex and highly colourful hierarchy of gods and goddesses, many of whom are still worshipped across India to this day.

timeline

5000–2000 BC	2600–c.1700 BC	800 BC	c.500 BC	326 BC
Farming spreads across India	Indus valley civilization	A number of Hindu states have been established in Ganges basin	Beginning of Buddhism	Alexander the Great reaches Indus

The early Hindu kingdoms established by the Aryans in the Ganges basin were themselves rigidly hierarchical, with the king assuming divine status upon death. Beneath him were layer upon layer of tightly defined groups – priests (Brahmins), soldiers and nobles, farmers and artisans, and, at the bottom, bonded labourers. Over the millennia this religiously sanctioned structure became more and more rigid, and forms the basis of the hereditary caste system that still plays an important part in modern Indian society, despite the efforts of reformers to abolish it.

> **His mouth became the Brahmin; his arms were made into the Warrior, his thighs the People, and from his feet the Servants were born.**
>
> 'Hymn of Man' from the *Rig Veda*, (*c.*1500 BC), an early outline of the caste system

Around 500 BC a number of new religious sects arose, notably Jainism and Buddhism. These dispensed with the colourful panoply of Hindu gods, but shared many of the core concepts of Hinduism, such as the cycle of death and rebirth (*samsara*), the idea that individuals suffer the consequences of their actions (*karma*), and the concept of *dharma*, variously interpreted as 'law', 'way', 'duty' or 'nature'.

The ebb and flow of power By and large, ancient India comprised a mosaic of small kingdoms, but there were times when one ruler or dynasty came to have power over many others. One such ruler was Chandragupta Maurya (reigned 321–297 BC), who founded the Mauryan dynasty, based in the kingdom of Magadha in western Bengal. Chandragupta conquered much of the north of the subcontinent, from Afghanistan in the west to Assam in the east, and as far south as the Deccan plateau. Chandragupta's grandson Ashoka (reigned 272–232 BC) turned his grandfather's conquests into a centrally controlled empire, administered according to Buddhist precepts: Ashoka was particularly aware of the obligation placed upon the ruler to do the right thing.

After Ashoka, Mauryan power was gradually whittled away. It was not until the 4th century AD that another dynasty, the Guptas, built an empire

321–297 BC	272–232 BC	2nd C. BC	1st C. AD	c.320–540	606–47
Much of northern India united under Chandragupta Maurya	Reign of Ashoka, greatest ruler of the Mauryan empire	Graeco-Indian civilization in Indus valley	Kushans from central Asia begin to settle in Indus valley	Gupta empire in northern India	Harsha rules Buddhist empire in northern India

to match that of Ashoka. The Guptas ushered in a golden age in the arts and sciences, but the Gupta empire fell apart in the middle of the 6th century. Parts of their empire were briefly reunited in the early 7th century by a Buddhist ruler called Harsha. After his time the influence of Buddhism in India waned, although it took more permanent root in south-east Asia, Tibet, China and Japan.

Muslim India India first came into contact with Islam in 711, when an Arab army invaded from Iran and occupied Sind, the region around the mouth of the Indus. Future Muslim invasions came from a different direction, from Afghanistan in the north-west, and were led by a variety of rulers of Turkish origin. Raiding began in the early 11th century, but it was

The golden age of the Guptas

The period of the Gupta empire, from the 4th to the 6th centuries AD, is regarded in India as a golden age. In literature, the ancient Sanskrit Hindu epic the *Mahabharata* reached its final form, while the great poet Kalidasa – who has been described as the Sanskrit Shakespeare – created new epics, together with lyrical poetry and dramas. In architecture, one of the greatest Gupta monuments is the ornate Mahabodhi Temple in Bodh Gaya, the place where the Buddha attained enlightenment, while the mysterious 7m (22 ft) Iron Pillar in Delhi – which to this day shows no sign of rust

– is a remarkable metallurgical achievement. In science, the astronomer Aryabhatta proved – among other things – that the Earth revolves around the Sun and rotates on its own axis, while the astronomical and mathematical treatise known as the *Surya Siddhanta* contains a definition of the sine function used in trigonometry. Of greatest significance, however, was the development of the decimal number system and the use of zero, innovations that were later picked up by Muslim mathematicians, and eventually transmitted to Europe.

timeline

711	early 11th C.	late 12th C.	1206	1336–1565	1398
Arab army conquers Sind	Mahmud of Ghazni, Turko-Afghan ruler, raids north-west India	Muhammad of Ghur, another Turko-Afghan ruler, conquers much of north-central India	Foundation of Muslim sultanate of Delhi	Hindu empire of Vijayanagar in southern India	Delhi sacked by Timur (Tamerlane), who claimed descent from Genghis Khan

not until 1206 that the Islamic sultanate of Delhi was established. This was the first and most powerful of a number of Muslim states established across northern India in the following centuries, during which period a significant minority of Indians converted to Islam. Hinduism remained in power in the south, however, where the Vijayanagar empire held sway for some 200 years until its eventual collapse in 1565.

The Turko-Afghan invader who had the most enduring impact was Babur of Kabul, who in 1526 overthrew the Delhi sultanate and established a dynasty that went on to conquer all of the subcontinent, bar the southern tip. These were the Moguls – so-called because they claimed descent from the Turkic Mongols of central Asia. The Moguls presided over a magnificent court culture, notable for its Persian-influenced poetry and delicate miniature paintings. They were also responsible for some of India's finest buildings, from Delhi's Red Fort to the Taj Mahal in Agra. Under Babur's grandson Akbar the Great (reigned 1556–1605), India achieved a hitherto unsurpassed degree of unity, partly owing to his policy of encouraging capable men from the Hindu majority to participate in the administration of his empire.

Under the Emperor Aurangzeb (reigned 1658–1707), however, religious toleration was abandoned, to the detriment of political unity and administrative efficiency. Power across the subcontinent became increasingly localized, and internal struggles and weaknesses made India a relatively easy prey for the Europeans, who, having found a sea route to Asia, sought to exploit the continent's vast wealth for their own advantage.

in a nutshell
One of the world's oldest civilizations

1497–9	1526	1556–1605	1658–1707	1757
Vasco da Gama establishes sea route from Europe to India	Babur of Kabul overthrows Delhi sultanate and establishes Mogul empire	Reign of Akbar the Great	Mogul empire begins to decline under Aurangzeb	British win Battle of Plassey and secure control over much of India

13 Imperial China

China's earliest historical rulers, the Shang, emerged some 3,500 years ago – the first of a number of imperial dynasties that ruled China right up to the 20th century. It was under the Shang that there evolved the elements of a recognizably Chinese culture, both in the form of an ideographic script of a type still in use today, and in the style of its artefacts – bronze, pottery, silk and jade.

China is so vast, its population so huge and its resources so rich that for millennia the Chinese saw no need to look beyond the distant frontiers of their own land, which they called the Middle Kingdom. Beyond lay nothing but benighted barbarians, while China itself flourished – economically, artistically and technologically. Until the beginnings of the Scientific Revolution in the West in the 16th century, China had been far in advance of Europe in terms of science and technology, and it is to China that we owe four key inventions: the compass, gunpowder, papermaking and printing.

The early dynasties China is dominated by two great rivers, the Yellow River (Huang He) in the north and the Yangtze (Chang Jiang) in the south. It was on the fertile flood plain of the Yellow River that agriculture first appeared in China, around 4000 BC, spreading from there to the Yangtze basin. As Chinese society became more complex, various important ceremonial centres emerged, and by the time of the Shang dynasty, these had evolved into planned cities, laid out on a grid oriented to the points of the compass. The Shang, who claimed they had a 'mandate from heaven', ruled over much of northern China from their

timeline

4000 BC	c.1500 BC	c.1000 BC	500–300 BC	481–221 BC	221 BC
Farming begins in valley of Yellow River	Foundation of first historical dynasty, the Shang	Zhou dynasty replaces Shang	Emergence of Daoism and Confucianism, two of China's main religions	Period of the Warring States	Shi Huangdi becomes first emperor, establishing short-lived Qin dynasty and building Great Wall

power base in the valley of the Yellow River. As in ancient Egypt, the royal tombs of the Shang were furnished with rich goods to sustain the dead in the afterlife. The Shang went further, though, sacrificing men, women and children to bury in the tomb, so that the departed would not lack for servants.

The Shang were overthrown around 1000 BC by the Zhou state to the west. The Zhou claimed they had inherited the 'mandate of heaven' and established their own dynasty, which endured until early in the 5th century BC, when China entered the period of the 'Warring States'.

The first emperor The period of the Warring States came to an end in 221 BC when Zheng, king of the small western state of Qin, emerged victorious over his rivals. He adopted the name Shi Huangdi, declared himself emperor of all China, and extended its frontiers to central Asia and the South China Sea.

Confucianism and the state

Around 500 BC a scholar-official called Kongfuzi – known in the West as Confucius – taught that, in order to conform to the 'will of heaven', people should show the same respect to the emperor as they do to the head of their family. This emphasis on hierarchy within both family and state – accompanied by the Confucian values of self-improvement, wisdom, sincerity, loyalty, piety and compassion – has had an enduring influence on Chinese society to this day.

Shi Huangdi centralized the administration, standardized weights and measures and built many roads and canals. But he earned the hatred of his people by his ruthless crushing of all opposition and his forced conscription of hundreds of thousands of young men to work on the Great Wall in the far north. Earlier rulers had built various defensive walls against the northern nomads, but Shi Huangdi determined to connect and reinforce the existing fortifications. Tens of thousands of labourers died as a consequence.

210 BC	**202 BC**	**C.AD 100**	**AD 265–316**	**386–533**	**589–618**
Death of Shi Huangdi	Han dynasty starts to expand empire and introduce administrative reforms	Buddhism spreads to China	Jin dynasty, eventually destroyed by nomad invasion	Nomadic Wei dynasty in northern China	Sui dynasty reunites northern and southern China

The rise and fall of dynasties After Shi Huangdi died in 210 BC he was buried along with a remarkable 'terracotta army' consisting of thousands of life-sized statues of soldiers. Shortly afterwards a new dynasty, the Han, took over. The Han, who ruled China for 400 years, improved administration by instituting entrance exams for the civil service and by posting administrators far from their homes in order to prevent corruption. The Han oversaw improvements in agriculture and a further expansion of the empire, and controlled the Silk Road as far as central Asia. It was via the Silk Road – the system of overland routes named after China's most valued export – that trading links were established with peoples far to the west, including the Roman empire, whose frontiers lay at the other end of Asia.

> **'The state established by the emperor is the greatest ever seen.'**
> Inscription made on the order of Shi Huangdi on becoming emperor in 221 BC

The Han were followed by a succession of dynasties, whose rigidly planned imperial capitals, with populations approaching a million, were the greatest cities in the world between the fall of Rome and the meteoric growth of London in the 18th century. New dynasties tended to start strongly, with an effective and even-handed central administration, but over time they were weakened by rival power bases in the provinces, by peasant revolts against excessive taxes, and by invasions of nomadic horsemen from the north. Two such invasions led to the foundation of new dynasties: in the 1270s the Mongols under Kublai Khan completed their conquest of China, establishing the Yuan dynasty, and in 1644 a clan from Manchuria overran the country and established the Manchu or Qing dynasty, the last dynasty of imperial China.

Looking inward and outward The Chinese had developed considerable skills in shipbuilding, seafaring and navigation – it was they who had invented the compass – and in the early 15th century the imperial government sent a great fleet under Admiral Zheng He to conduct a series of trading voyages to the East Indies, India, Arabia and East Africa. But this policy of broadening China's horizons, and possibly establishing an overseas

timeline

618–907	960–1279	1127	1215	1271–1368	1270s	1368–1644
Tang dynasty: Chinese culture experiences its classical age	Song dynasty: great commercial expansion	Invasion by Jin nomads, restricting Song rule to southern China	Mongols under Genghis Khan overwhelm Jin in northern China	Yuan (Mongol) dynasty, first established by Kublai Khan	Kublai Khan destroys southern Song	Ming dynasty: Chinese withdraw from overseas trading expeditions and build Forbidden City in Beijing

> **'The serfs had risen in swarms . . . They sharpened their hoes into swords, and took to themselves the title of "Levelling Kings", declaring they were levelling the distinction between rich and poor.'**
>
> **A contemporary scholar** describes an outbreak of popular unrest in 1645, just one of many peasant revolts that punctuated the history of imperial China

trading empire, was suddenly abandoned in the early 1430s. The emperor was apparently persuaded that China possessed all the resources it needed, and that it would do better to concentrate on defending its northern frontiers.

China withdrew into itself just as Europeans were beginning to look beyond their own shores – and on the verge of overtaking China in terms of technological advance. In the middle of the 16th century the Portuguese established a trading post on the southern coast of China, and by the early 19th century Western powers such as Britain were pressing the reluctant Chinese to trade with them, in particular to agree to the import of opium from British India. The resulting 'Opium Wars' ended with the Western powers gaining control of a number of ports in China. Weakened by internal revolts and continued external pressure, the reactionary imperial court turned its back on all thoughts of modernization and reform, while European troops occupied Beijing itself. The Chinese people had had enough, and in 1911 the last emperor was overthrown in a nationalist revolution. Thus ended three and a half millennia of imperial rule.

in a nutshell
Imperial China's inwardness became its undoing

1644–1911	1839–42	1851–64	1856–60	1894–5	1900–1	1911
Qing (Manchu) dynasty: China at its greatest power and prosperity, until decline sets in	Britain defeats China in First Opium War and gains Hong Kong as a colony, plus access to five 'Treaty Ports'	Millions die in Taiping Rebellion	Second Opium War: British and French troops occupy Forbidden City	Japan at war with China, taking Korea and Taiwan	Boxer Rebellion: attacks on foreigners encouraged by imperial court; suppressed by Western powers	Nationalist revolution overthrows last emperor

14 The Mongols

In the 13th century an obscure nomadic people from the steppes of north-eastern Asia created the largest contiguous land empire the world has ever seen, stretching from Hungary in the west to Korea in the east, and taking in virtually all of Asia apart from India and the south-east of the continent.

These people were the Mongols, and under the leadership of Genghis Khan and his sons and grandsons they burst out of their homelands in Mongolia and wreaked havoc across much of the known world. In the process, they were responsible for slaughter on a scale undreamed of until the era of Hitler and Stalin.

The pagan Mongols were feared and detested by Christians and Muslims alike – and yet they showed respect and toleration for the religions of others, as long as they submitted to Mongol power. And while in the West the name Genghis Khan is synonymous with merciless brutality, in his native Mongolia, and among other Turkic peoples, he is hailed as a great hero – to this day, many male children in Turkey are given the name Genghis. Modern historians take the long view of Genghis, pointing out that, in creating his vast Eurasian empire, he enabled contacts between Europe and the much more technologically advanced civilization of China, to the immense enrichment of the former.

The horsemen from the steppes For millennia, the sedentary farming peoples of Europe, the Middle East and China had been subjected to waves of invasion by nomadic peoples from the remote grasslands at the heart of Asia. In the ancient world, the Greeks wrote of the Scythians

timeline

4th C. AD	451	6th C.	796	1071	1162
Huns from Asian steppes migrate into Europe	Huns under Attila defeated at Châlons-sur-Marne	Avars, another steppe people, establish themselves in eastern Europe	Avars defeated by Charlemagne and integrated into Frankish empire	Seljuk Turks defeat Byzantines at Manzikert and occupy much of Anatolia	Birth of Genghis Khan

and Sarmatians who lived to the north of the Black Sea, while in the 4th and 5th centuries AD the Huns swept through Europe, pushing the Germanic tribes across the frontiers of the Roman empire. At the same time, a related people, whom the Chinese called the Northern Wei, seized control of the fertile basin of the Yellow River (Huang He). Another group of nomads, the Magyars – the ancestors of modern Hungarians – were only stopped from sweeping across Europe by the German emperor, Otto I's decisive victory over them at Lechfeld in 950.

These peoples, and the Mongols who followed them, were all magnificent riders. Their military tactics were highly mobile: they avoided traditional pitched battles, instead harrying the enemy with surprise attacks. They would then disappear into the immensities of the steppes, luring their opponents into following after them, usually with fatal consequences. Their traditional weapon was the bow, later joined by the lance, which became doubly effective with the appearance of the stirrup in the 5th century AD.

> **❝They are to bring the whole world into subjection to them.❞**
>
> **John of Plano Carpini,** the pope's envoy to the Mongols in the 1240s

The descendants of Genghis Khan

In 2003 a group of geneticists published the results of a 10-year study of populations living in what had been the Mongol empire, stretching from the Pacific Ocean to the Caspian Sea. They found that 8 per cent of men living in this region – some 16 million individuals, amounting to 0.5 per cent of the entire male population of the world – shared nearly identical Y-chromosomes. This indicated that they were all descendants of just one man who lived around 1,000 years ago – and that this single man was an ancestor of Genghis Khan and his close male relatives. During the course of the Mongol conquests, the leaders would have had first choice of the most beautiful women, either as wives or concubines. It was recorded at the time that Genghis's eldest son, Tushi, fathered forty sons, while his grandson Kublai Khan, who conquered China, had twenty-two legitimate sons, and added thirty new virgins to his harem each year.

1206	1215	1219	1227	1238
Genghis Khan unites Mongolian tribes	Mongols complete conquest of northern China	Beginning of Mongol campaigns of conquest in Middle East	Genghis Khan dies and is succeeded by his son Ogodei	Mongols cross Volga and begin conquest of European Russia

> **The greatest joy is to conquer one's enemies, to pursue them, to deprive them of their possessions, to reduce their families to tears, to ride on their horses, and to make love to their wives and daughters.**
>
> **Genghis Khan,** attributed remark

Contemporary descriptions of Mongol armies on the move relate how both men and women were able to endure long stretches of riding in either great cold or extreme heat. They carried their yurts (round felt tents) on wagons, and survived almost exclusively on meat and milk. According to the 13th-century papal envoy, John of Plano Carpini, 'They show considerable respect to each other and are very friendly together, and they willingly share their food, although there is little enough of it. They are also long-suffering . . .'

Genghis Khan and his successors In the first decade of the 13th century, a Mongolian chieftain called Temujin (meaning 'ironworker') united all the tribes of Mongolia under his rule. At a great gathering in 1206 he adopted a new name, Genghis Khan, meaning 'Lord of the Earth'. He then set about giving substance to this title, and by 1215 had conquered most of northern China. Four years later he turned westward and swept through Afghanistan and Iran. 'As there is one sky,' he proclaimed, 'so there should be one empire on earth.'

Genghis died in 1227, but his sons and grandsons carried on his work, crossing the Volga in 1238 and pushing into European Russia, subduing the Turks of Anatolia, and in 1258 destroying the Abbasid caliphate based in Baghdad. The Christians had hoped that the invaders from the east would become their allies in their campaign against the Muslims, but when in the 1240s the pope sent an envoy to the Mongols, he returned with a demand that all the princes of Europe submit to the Great Khan.

timeline

1258	1260	1271	mid-14th C.
Genghis's grandson Hulagu destroys Abbasid caliphate based in Baghdad	Mongols defeated at Ain Jalut in Palestine by Mamelukes	Hulagu's brother Kublai Khan proclaims himself first emperor of the Yuan dynasty in China	Collapse of Ilkhanate in Middle East

Mongol expansion in the Near East came to an abrupt halt in 1260, when they were decisively defeated at Ain Jalut by the Mamelukes of Egypt. The victors cut off the head of the Mongol commander and used it in a game of polo. But expansion continued in the east, where in the 1270s Genghis's grandson Kublai Khan overthrew the Song rulers of southern China and established his own imperial dynasty, the Yuan.

By 1300 the Mongol empire had split into a number of khanates, which gradually disintegrated over the following centuries. There was something of a revival in the later 14th century under a chieftain called Timur or Tamerlane, who claimed descent from Genghis Khan.

The sack of Baghdad

In 1258 Genghis Khan's grandson Hulagu captured Baghdad, capital of the Abbasid caliphs, and put thousands of the inhabitants to the sword. The caliph himself was rolled up in a carpet and trampled to death by horses, the Mongols believing that it would offend the earth to shed royal blood. The Grand Library was ransacked and its books hurled into the Tigris in such numbers that it was said that a man could ride on horseback across the river – which, in the words of one Arab historian, 'ran black with the ink of scholars and red with the blood of martyrs'.

He conducted a long campaign of destruction across the Middle East, central Asia and into India, but never consolidated his conquests into an empire. In 1526 a descendant of Timur, Babur of Kabul, invaded India and established an Islamic dynasty that was to rule the subcontinent for centuries, creating a magnificent culture marked by such monuments as the Taj Mahal. They called themselves 'Moguls', in recognition of their descent from the Mongols (see p. 51).

in a nutshell
The Mongols briefly created an empire extending from eastern Europe to the Pacific

1368	1369–1405	late 15th C.	1526	1678
Mongol Yuan dynasty in China overthrown by first Ming emperor	Reign of Timur (Tamerlane)	Collapse of khanate of the Golden Horde on Russian steppes	Babur of Kabul establishes Mogul dynasty in India	Jagatai khanate in Turkestan finally extinguished

15 Japan, the island empire

It has been said that all countries are different from each other, but that Japan is 'differently different'. Perhaps because of its geographical isolation, on an archipelago of islands off the east coast of Asia, Japan for much of its history kept itself from the rest of the world.

Even its remarkably rapid modernization and industrialization in the later 19th century only touched the surface of Japanese life, and did not alter the country's strong adherence to its traditional customs, values and outlook on the world.

The islands of Japan were first settled by humans some 40,000 years ago during the last Ice Age, when lowered sea levels created a land bridge from the Asian mainland. These Stone Age Japanese were hunter-gatherers, and from about 10,000 BC began to make pottery – one of the first cultures in the world to do so. However, it was not until around 400 BC that another wave of immigrants – possibly from China or Korea – brought agriculture and metalworking skills. There were certainly contacts with the well-developed Chinese civilization to the west, which by the 1st century AD was exacting tribute from the numerous clans of Japan. It was from China that Japan went on to acquire its written script and Confucian and Buddhist beliefs, which became melded with the native Shinto religion, with its emphasis on ancestor worship and respect for tradition and native land. Despite these

timeline

10,000 BC	400 BC	1st C. BC	c.AD 400	6th C.	604
Jomon culture begins to make pottery	Beginnings of agriculture and metalworking	Tribute sent to China	Japan united under Yamoto dynasty	Arrival of Buddhism	'Seventeen-article Constitution' outlines duties and virtues required of officials under an omnipotent emperor

connections, the Japanese language is not related to Chinese, and possibly not to any other language.

Emperors and shoguns From the 3rd century AD Japan was a mosaic of military states, but around AD 400 one of these, Yamoto, began to dominate the others, and all Japanese emperors subsequently claimed descent from the Yamoto dynasty. By 607 the 'Emperor of the Land of the Rising Sun' (i.e. Japan) was writing to the 'Emperor of the Land of the Setting Sun' (i.e. China) as an equal in power and magnificence. In the 8th century the Japanese established an imperial capital along Chinese lines at Nara, and began to adopt the Chinese model of strong, centralized government. A new origin myth evolved, by which the emperors were said to descend from the legendary first emperor, Jimmu, who had, according to the myth, founded Japan in 660 BC and who was himself a descendant of the Shinto sun goddess, Amaterasu. The claim of the Japanese emperors to divine status was only abandoned after the Second World War.

In 794 the capital moved to Kyoto. Thereafter, contacts with China diminished, and the power of the emperors was eclipsed by the growing power of the noble Fujiwara family, who acted as regents. In the 12th century the Fujiwara were themselves challenged by a number of other aristocratic families. As a result, Japan collapsed into civil war, and a decentralized feudal society emerged, with power divided among a number of regional barons (daimyos), who maintained bands of samurai warriors, an elite military caste regarded as superior in rank to merchants, artisans and peasants. In 1159 a warlord called Yoritomo, of the Minamoto family, seized overall power, and from 1185 ruled from Kamakura (near Tokyo) as shogun (military dictator), while the emperor, secluded in Kyoto, was reduced to a figurehead.

Shoguns from various families remained the absolute rulers of Japan for many centuries, interrupted in the 16th century by a series of civil wars.

❝Harmony is to be valued, and an avoidance of wanton opposition to be honoured . . . ❞

Prince Shotoku, who became regent in AD 593, lays down the imperial law in the Seventeen-article Constitution of 604

710–84	794	10th C.	early 12th C.	1159	1185	1274,1281
Imperial capital at Nara	Capital moves to Kyoto	Power shifts from emperor to Fujiwara family	Civil wars	Minamoto Yoritomo takes power and becomes first shogun	Shogunate moves to Kamakura, near Tokyo	Unsuccessful invasion attempts by Mongols

Kamikaze

Such was their isolation during the Middle Ages that the Japanese were unused to facing threats from across the sea. So it came as a terrible shock when in 1274 and again in 1281 the Mongols – who under Kublai Khan had conquered all of China – attempted massive sea-borne invasions of Japan. On both occasions, the Mongol fleet was devastated by a typhoon – known thereafter by the Japanese as *kamikaze*, meaning 'divine wind'. The legend resurfaced towards the end of the Second World War, when, in a hopeless bid to stop the Allied advance on the home islands, Japanese pilots adopted the name *kamikaze* as they deliberately crashed their bomb-laden planes onto enemy ships.

By 1600 Japan was reunited, and a noble from the Tokugawa family called Ieyasu established a new shogunate, based in Edo (Tokyo), while the emperor remained powerless in Kyoto.

The Tokugawa shoguns exercised tight control over the daimyos, forcing them to spend much time in Edo, and away from their regional power bases (just as Louis XIV successfully emasculated the turbulent nobility of France in the later 17th century by requiring them to live in his great palace at Versailles). The Tokugawa shoguns also turned their backs on European contact. Traders and Christian missionaries had begun to arrive in the 16th century, and many peasants were converted. The shoguns feared this heralded a European takeover, and from 1635 imposed a policy of isolation, banning all contact between Japanese and foreigners. The only exception was the small Dutch trading concession on an island in Nagasaki harbour.

Out of isolation This isolation was forcibly ended when on 8 July 1853 four US warships under the command of Commodore Matthew Perry sailed into the bay at Edo. Having demonstrated his ships' firepower, Perry requested that the Japanese open their doors to foreign trade. Japan was subsequently pressed to sign a number of treaties with Western powers, granting the latter trading rights that effectively compromised Japan's sovereignty.

timeline

1333	15th–16th C.	1549	1585	1600	1635
Kamakura period ends with advent of Ashikaga shogunate	Civil wars and feudal anarchy	Arrival of the first Christian missionary, the Jesuit Francis Xavier	Having reunited Japan, Toyotomi Hideyoshi becomes regent	Tokugawa Ieyasu establishes Tokugawa shogunate in Edo (Tokyo)	Edict banning all contact with foreigners

These forced changes marked the end of Japan's long Middle Ages. After a coup by modernizers in 1868 the shogun resigned, and in 1869 the emperor was installed with restored powers in Edo, which was renamed Tokyo. He himself took the throne name Meiji, meaning 'enlightened government'. There followed a remarkable period in which Japan underwent in three decades a process of industrialization that had taken nearly two centuries in Europe. It was not only manufacturing that was transformed: education, the armed forces, the economy and the political system were all modernized along Western lines.

As Japan's power grew, the 'unequal' treaties were put aside. Aiming to become the dominant regional power, Japan fought a war with China in 1894–5 and gained Korea and Taiwan. Then in 1904–5 it took on Russia over which of them should control Manchuria. Japan scored a decisive naval victory over the Russians at Tsushima – the first victory in modern times of an Asian nation over a European power. By the outbreak of the First World War, Japan was being treated as an equal, having become an ally of Great Britain. During the war it attacked German bases in China and seized some of Germany's island possessions in the Pacific. After the war Japanese delegates attended the Paris Peace Conference, and Japan was awarded a League of Nations mandate over all former German colonies in the Pacific north of the equator. Japan had flexed its muscles; more was to come (see p. 168).

> **❝If any Japanese attempts to go abroad secretly, he must be executed . . . If any Japanese returns from overseas after residing there, he must be put to death.❞**
>
> **The shogun Tokugawa Iemitsu**
> issued an edict in 1635 shutting Japan off from foreign contact

in a nutshell
A remarkable transformation from medieval to modern

1853	1868–9	1894–5	1902	1904–5	1914	1919
US fleet ends Japanese isolation	Overthrow of last shogun; power restored to Meiji emperor	First Sino–Japanese War	Japan forms alliance with Great Britain	Russo–Japanese War	Japan declares war on Germany	Japan acquires mandates over former German Pacific colonies in the Mariana, Caroline and Marshall Islands

16 Incas and Aztecs

The people of medieval Europe had some idea that there were other magnificent cultures and powerful rulers apart from their own – the sultans and caliphs of the Muslim world, the Great Khan of the steppes, the emperor of far Cathay. But they had no idea that west across the Atlantic, beyond the setting sun, there lay a vast continent where there flourished civilizations of unimagined wealth and brilliance.

The irony is that, when they did come across these civilizations – those of the Incas and the Aztecs – a handful of European adventurers succeeded, in just a few short years, in bringing about their utter destruction.

The first humans reached the North American continent from eastern Asia some time during the last Ice Age, when the two continents were linked by a land bridge. This migration may have been made as early as 25,000 years ago, and certainly no later than 8000 BC, when rising sea levels drowned the land bridge across the Bering Strait. Thereafter, human settlement spread rapidly right down the Americas. The beginning of agriculture can be traced back to the 7th millennium BC in the Andean region of South America, spreading from there to other parts of the continents.

Early civilizations As agricultural surplus enabled societies to become more complex, the first great ceremonial centres appeared in both Mesoamerica and the Andes. Some of the most striking monuments – including plazas, pyramids and colossal stone heads – were those built from

timeline

8000 BC	6500 BC	4700 BC	1500 BC	1200 BC
Rising sea levels drown land bridge between Asia and North America	Beans, squash and peppers grown in Peruvian Andes	Maize grown in Mesoamerica	Large ceremonial centres begin to appear in Mesoamerica and the Andes	Emergence of Olmec civilization in Mesoamerica and Chavin civilization in Andes

around 1200 BC on the Caribbean coast of Mesoamerica by the Olmec people. Ceremonial centres grew into temple-cities laid out geometrically on astronomical principles, such as Tiahuanaco in the Andes and Teotihuacán in the Mexico valley. By the 1st millennium AD Teotihuacán had a population of some 200,000, far larger than any European city of the time, apart from Rome before its fall. But by the end of the millennium Teotihuacán, along with the great city-states of the Maya people in the Yucatán peninsula, had been abandoned – for reasons that are not entirely clear.

Many of the enduring characteristics of Mesoamerican cultures had their origins in these early societies. At the heart of their cities and ceremonial centres stood lofty stepped temple-pyramids. There was also a great interest in astronomy and the calendar, and the Maya in particular developed sophisticated mathematical systems, such as place-value notation for numbers, as well as a form of writing that was still in use in Mesoamerica at the time of the Spanish conquest. Finally, there was the practice of sacrificing humans in order to propitiate the blood-hungry gods and to ensure the cycle of the seasons. 'When they sacrifice a wretched Indian,' wrote a European eyewitness in the 16th century, 'they saw open the chest with stone knives and hasten

The Nazca lines

The Nazca Desert of Peru is littered with hundreds of giant linear figures. Some are simple geometrical shapes while others depict animals such as monkeys, killer whales, lizards and hummingbirds. These mysterious figures were created over a period of nearly 1,000 years, from around 200 BC to AD 700, and were made by removing dark stones from the surface of the desert to reveal the paler ground beneath. They are so vast that their outlines can only be made out from the air, so those who made them could never have seen them in their entirety. However, the method of making such giant figures is not complex, and it is likely that they were used for various shamanistic rituals, during which worshippers would process along the lines before making offerings to the gods.

400 BC	200 BC	AD 100	AD 300	early 7th C.
Beginning of Zapotec civilization centred round city of Monte Albán in Mesoamerica	Foundation of city of Teotihuacán in Mexico valley	Beginning of Moche civilization in northern Peru	Beginning of Mayan civilization and writing system in Yucatán	Terraces, aqueducts and drainage channels built by Nazca, Huari and Tiwanaku cultures in Andean region

to tear out the palpitating heart and blood . . .' Human sacrifice was also a characteristic of some of the Andean cultures.

The last empires When the first Europeans arrived on the American mainland in the early 16th century, two great empires held sway over large areas of territory. Much of Mesoamerica was under the control of the Aztecs, while the Andean region, from Ecuador to northern Chile, was ruled by the Incas of Peru. The Aztecs were the last of a number of warlike states to dominate Mesoamerica in the Pre-Columbian era, and from their magnificent capital Tenochtitlán (on the site of present-day Mexico City) they extorted tribute and human sacrificial victims on a massive scale from neighbouring peoples.

> ❝**Many lords walked before the great Moctezuma, sweeping the ground where he would tread and spreading cloths on it, so that he should not tread on the earth.**❞
>
> **Bernal Díaz del Castillo,** *The Conquest of New Spain,* **1560s, describing the progress of the Aztec emperor**

The Inca state appears to have been less bloodthirsty (although human sacrifice was not unknown) and more unified. The task of central government was made easier by a network of well-built roads, which extended for thousands of miles across the length and breadth of the empire. However, nowhere in the Americas was the wheel in use; transport depended on foot or – in the Andes – on the principal beast of burden, the llama. As an aid to communication the Incas had a system of knotted strings called *quipu*, used for accounts and censuses, although, unlike the Maya script, it does not appear to have developed into a more flexible writing system.

The Spanish conquest When the Spanish conquistadores first encountered these civilizations, they were astonished by their magnificence, but also prepared to exploit their own technological superiority. Not only did the indigenous people lack the wheel, their tools and weapons were still made of stone. So when confronted with Spanish

timeline

mid-7th C.	by 900	12th C.	*c.*1200	1345
Decline of Teotihuacán	Collapse of Mayan city-states; rise of Toltec civilization, based at Tula in Mexico valley	Collapse of Toltec empire	Foundation of Inca dynasty	Aztecs found Tenochtitlán

soldiers with steel helmets and breastplates, steel swords, firearms and horses, they were quite overwhelmed.

In Mexico, the conquistador Hernán Cortés found that the neighbours of the Aztecs were only too happy to join the Spaniards in attacking their rulers, whose insatiable demands for human sacrifices they had long resented. In just over a year, in 1519–20, Cortés and a few hundred Spanish troops had defeated the might of the Aztecs, whose emperor Moctezuma believed Cortés to be a manifestation of the god Quetzalcoatl ('the Feathered Serpent'), and so offered little resistance.

It was a similar story in Peru, where Francisco Pizarro, another ruthless Spanish adventurer in search of gold and power, led fewer than 200 men against the Incas. In 1532 he lured the Inca emperor, Atahualpa, into a trap, massacred his escort of thousands of men, and took the emperor captive. Atahualpa offered Pizarro a roomful of gold in return for his release, but when he got the gold Pizarro went back on his word and ordered that Atahualpa be burned at the stake. When, faced with death, the emperor converted to Christianity, Pizarro relented and had him garroted instead. The conquest of Peru was completed in 1535 with the capture of Cuzco, the Inca capital. Both here and in Mexico, the new colonial power set about enslaving and forcibly converting its subjects, and destroying all residues of their cultures.

❛Some of our soldiers even asked whether the things we saw were not a dream.❜

Bernal Díaz del Castillo,
a conquistador who accompanied Cortés, describes the Spaniards' reaction to the wonders of the Aztec capital, Tenochtitlán

in a nutshell
Millennia-old civilizations were wiped out in just a few years

14th–15th C.	15th C.	1519–21	1532–5
Chimú empire in Peru	Inca empire expands to greatest extent	Spanish conquest of Aztec empire	Spanish conquest of Inca empire

17 Empires and kingdoms of Africa

When European explorers first studied the ruins of Great Zimbabwe in the later 19th century, they were convinced that this extensive royal palace-complex, with its high stone walls and towers, could not have been built by the local African people. The ruins must, they asserted, have been the work of Phoenicians or Arabs, and stories arose linking the site with King Solomon's fabled mines and the Queen of Sheba.

It simply did not fit in with the European colonial project to consider black Africans capable of developing a society with the wealth and complexity necessary to produce such magnificence.

There was a similar sense of disbelief when Europeans first encountered the stunning brass heads from Ife in what is now south-western Nigeria. Both aesthetically and technically these statues, dating from the 12th to the 16th centuries, exceeded or were on a par with anything being produced in Europe at the same time. But as the archaeological evidence accumulated, both in Ife and Great Zimbabwe, it became clear that in both these places prosperous and powerful indigenous kingdoms had flourished during the time of the European Middle Ages. And these were just two of a number of wealthy kingdoms and empires that thrived in sub-Saharan Africa in the precolonial era.

timeline

4000 BC	8th–7th C. BC	500 BC	AD 1–500	AD 100	4th C.
Farming established in the Sahel	Nubian dynasty rules Egypt	Iron smelting developed by Nok culture of West Africa	Bantu migration	Foundation of kingdom of Axum	Abyssinia adopts Christianity

The cradle of humanity It was in Africa that our earliest human-like ancestors first evolved, around 4 million years ago. Some 2 million years later, *Homo erectus*, an early human species, began to spread out of Africa, reaching as far as Europe and eastern Asia. Modern humans, *Homo sapiens sapiens*, also first evolved in Africa, around 200,000 years ago. From 100,000 years ago some of these modern humans began to migrate to Europe and Asia, and from there reached Australia, Oceania and the Americas.

Africa itself was affected by climatic change after 5000 BC, resulting in the formation of the Sahara Desert. This created a physical barrier between the peoples on either side of it, and those who lived to the north of the desert fell within the ambit of the Mediterranean and Near Eastern worlds. Their history is mingled with that of ancient Egypt, of Carthage, of the empires of Alexander the Great, Rome, the Arabs and the Ottoman Turks.

On the other side of the great divide, developments occurred largely independently. By 4000 BC farming communities had been established in the grasslands of the Sahel, the area just south of the Sahara, iron smelting emerged in West Africa in the 1st millennium BC, and some substantial settlements arose, thriving on the trade with the desert nomads to the north and the forest peoples to the south.

Between 2,000 and 1,500 years ago Iron Age farming communities began to spread south-eastward from West Africa, in what is known as the Bantu migration. The indigenous hunter-gatherers to the south were marginalized: the pygmies of central Africa took refuge in the dense tropical rainforest, while the San (Bushmen) of southern Africa were confined to the Kalahari Desert.

Cultural contacts In places, contacts did occur between sub-Saharan Africa and the peoples to the north. The Nile provided a link between

> **❝Among the gold mines of the inland plains ... there is a fortress built of stones of marvellous size ...❞**
>
> **Vicente Pegado,** captain of the Portuguese garrison of Sofala on the coast of Mozambique, gives the first European description of Great Zimbabwe, 1531

7th C.	8th–11th C.	11th C.	12th–16th C.	13th–15th C.	14th–15th C.
Islam spreads across North Africa	Empire of Ghana	Islam established in the Sahel	Kingdom of Ife	Empire of Mali	Construction of Great Zimbabwe

the Egypt of the pharaohs and the darker-skinned peoples to the south, in Nubia (northern Sudan). Nubia was conquered by the Egyptians early in the 2nd millennium BC, and some of the later pharaohs were actually of Nubian origin. It was the Nubians who, around AD 100, established the kingdom of Axum along the Red Sea coast. Initially Axum also ruled part of Arabia, but later the rulers moved further inland to form the kingdom of Abyssinia in what is now Ethiopia. Abyssinia adopted Christianity in the 4th century AD, and succeeded in maintaining its identity and independence against Muslim-Arab influence and European invasion until the Italian occupation of 1935–41.

> **‘Here are great store of doctors, judges, priests and other learned men, that are bountifully maintained at the king's cost and charges.’**
>
> **Leo Africanus, *History and Description of Africa*, 1550 describes Timbuktu, capital of the empire of Mali**

Elsewhere in Africa, Islam began to dominate. Having spread rapidly across the north of the continent in the 7th century AD, it then began to percolate southward via the trans-Saharan trade routes, and was established in the Sahel by the 11th century. Arab seafarers also spread their religion and culture down the east coast of Africa, where they established a number of trading posts such as Mombasa.

Gold, ivory and slaves It was the trade in gold with the Arabs on the coast of East Africa that supplied the wealth necessary to build Great Zimbabwe in the 14th and 15th centuries. The export of gold, ivory and slaves via the trans-Saharan caravan routes also underpinned the wealth and power of a number of empires and kingdoms that successively dominated parts of West Africa and the Sahel. From the 8th to the 11th centuries, the empire of Ghana extended over parts of modern Mauritania and Mali, and it was said its rulers could muster an army of 200,000 men. In the 13th–15th centuries, the empire of Mali ruled over the upper reaches of the River Niger, and westward to the Atlantic coast. Other empires followed: Songhai in the 15th and 16th centuries, which was

timeline

15th C.	15th–16th C.	16th–19th C.	1652	17th C.	17th–18th C.
Portuguese establish trading posts down the west coast of Africa	Songhai empire	Atlantic slave trade	Dutch establish colony at Cape Town	Bornu empire and kingdom of Benin at their peaks	Oyo empire flourishes

larger even than Mali; and Bornu, centred around Lake Chad, which reached its peak in the 17th century.

The commerce in slaves increased dramatically when from the 15th century the Portuguese established trading posts along the Atlantic coast of Africa. The Portuguese were followed by the Dutch, the French and the English, and a number of inland African kingdoms – Benin, Oyo and Ashanti – flourished partly by satisfying the insatiable demand for slaves. The slave trade – by which millions of black Africans were shipped across the Atlantic to work the plantations of the New World – had an appallingly destructive effect on traditional African society. This 'African Holocaust', as it has been described, left the continent ripe for the European colonial takeover of the later 19th century. Only a few African kingdoms – such as Ashanti in West Africa and the Zulus in southern Africa – were able to mount an effective resistance, and in the end even they were crushed.

The munificence of Mansa Musa

Such was the wealth of the Mali empire that when its devout ruler, Mansa Musa, made a pilgrimage to Mecca in 1324 he took with him tens of thousands of followers – soldiers, slaves, wives and court officials – together with 100 camels, each carrying 100 pounds (45 kg) of gold. When he reached Cairo, he spent so much gold, 'flooding the city with his kindness', that the cost of goods and services soared, and the local currency took some years to recover its value.

in a nutshell
Wealthy and powerful empires once flourished in what Europeans called 'the dark continent'

1820s	1824–1901	1875–1900	1879	1896
Shaka forms powerful Zulu empire in southern Africa	Ashanti kingdom resists British	'Scramble for Africa': continent divided between European colonial powers	Zulus defeat British at Isandlwana	Ethiopians defeat Italian invasion

18 The Renaissance

It was not until the 19th century that cultural historians began to apply the term *Renaissance* – the French word for 'rebirth' – to the revival of classical models in art and literature that took place in Europe from the 14th to the end of the 16th centuries. Alongside this revival they discerned a movement away from a God-centred view of the world towards a world in which humans took centre stage.

In the Victorian era, historians often saw history as a story of progress, in which humanity steadily improved itself through the ages, moving from barbarism and superstition towards rationality, enlightenment and sober good manners. According to this narrative, Western civilization had suffered a setback with the fall of Rome, and had declined into the long 'Dark Ages' of the medieval period, only to move towards the light again after the rediscovery of classical values – those of ancient Greece and Rome.

The visual arts The notion that humans had achieved something new and remarkable in the period we now call the Renaissance goes back further than the 19th century, and owes much to the Italian artist and biographer Giorgio Vasari (1511–74). In his *Lives of the Painters* (1550), Vasari describes how from the later 13th century Tuscan painters such as Giotto had reacted against the Gothic art of the Middle Ages and begun to 'purge themselves of this crude style'. 'Those who came after,' Vasari continues, 'were able to distinguish the good from the bad, and abandoning the old style then began to copy the ancients with all ardour and industry.' Vasari's version of the history of art culminates in the

timeline

11th C.	12th C.	13th C.	c.1305	c.1321	1341
Foundation of first European university, in Bologna	Foundation of universities of Paris and Oxford	St Thomas Aquinas attempts to combine philosophy of Aristotle with Christian theology	Giotto's frescoes in the Arena Chapel, Padua, the first great paintings of the Renaissance	Dante completes *The Divine Comedy*	Petrarch, 'father of humanism', crowned poet laureate in Rome

perfection achieved, or so he avers, by his friend, the painter and sculptor Michelangelo (1475–1564). 'He surpasses not only those who have, as it were, surpassed Nature,' Vasari gushes, 'but the most famous ancients also, who undoubtedly surpassed her. He has proceeded from conquest to conquest, never finding a difficulty which he cannot overcome by the force of his divine genius . . .' It was a brilliant piece of public relations, one that was to set the agenda not only of art history, but of cultural history more generally, for several centuries. The focus moved from the collective, often anonymous, efforts of medieval artists, such as the builders of the great cathedrals, to the individual genius, the human being in whose blood a divine flame burned.

> ❛The Renaissance . . . stands for youth, and youth alone – for intellectual curiosity and energy grasping at the whole of life . . . ❜
>
> **Bernhard Berenson,**
> *The Venetian Painters,* 1894

It is certainly true that in the visual arts there were a number of notable innovations and developments during the Renaissance, spreading from Italy to other parts of Europe. In architecture, the Gothic style was abandoned in favour of the revival and adaptation of Greek and Roman models. (The term 'Gothic' was coined during the later Renaissance, suggesting the style of the High Middle Ages was as barbarous as the Goths who sacked Rome.) In painting, a new discovery was made – perspective, which gives the illusion of three-dimensional space. In both painting and sculpture there was an increasing secularism. The subject matter of medieval art had been predominantly religious, and was largely commissioned by or for the church. Although religious subject matter continued to be important during the Renaissance, secular patrons wanted to show off their wealth by adorning their palace walls with stories drawn from Greek myth – not least because such stories provided plenty of opportunities for depicting beautiful bodies without any clothes on. Where the church taught the doctrine of original sin and the shamefulness of nakedness, the artists of the Renaissance peddled the attractive notion of the perfectibility of the human being – especially as far as physical appearance was concerned.

1408	**c.1410–15**	**1420–36**	**c.1426**	**c.1450**	**1471**
Donatello's statue of *David*	Italian architect Filippo Brunelleschi rediscovers mathematical laws of perspective known to ancients	Construction of Brunelleschi's dome for Florence Cathedral	Masaccio begins to apply principles of perspective to painting	Gutenberg begins printing with movable type	Birth of Albrecht Dürer, one of the greatest artists of the Northern Renaissance

Renaissance humanism The idea of the perfectibility of man was important in the movement known as 'Renaissance humanism'. This originated in Italy in the 14th century when the poet Petrarch (1304–74) – who was the first to coin the term 'Dark Ages' – encouraged a new interest in the works of ancient Greek and Roman authors. Many of these works had been rediscovered over the previous two centuries – notably, numerous Greek texts had been preserved by Arab scholars, and had subsequently been translated by Europeans into Latin (which was much more widely understood than Greek). The word 'humanism' actually derives from the Latin term *studia humanitatis*, the name given to the new educational syllabus proposed by the followers of Petrarch. This syllabus, based on classical literature, covered five core subjects: rhetoric, poetry, grammar, history and moral philosophy.

The Italian *umanisti*, as the classical scholars became known, sought not only to imitate the style of the ancient authors, but also to adopt their mode of intellectual inquiry, unshackled by the constraints imposed by Christian doctrine (although they did not go so far as to reject the teachings of the church). The study of what constitutes virtue was of particular importance – how should the virtuous man act in the political sphere, on the battlefield, and so on. Style was important though: by adopting the rhetoric of

'Renaissance Man'

The idea of human perfectibility was embodied in the concept of the all-round 'Renaissance man', eloquently articulated by Baldassare Castiglione in his book *The Courtier* (1528). 'This courtier of ours should be nobly born,' he wrote, 'endowed not only with talent and beauty of person and feature, but with a certain grace.' He should be an expert soldier, a fine horseman, be able to 'speak and write well', and demonstrate proficiency in music, drawing and painting. The book was immensely popular, but this was perhaps because it was re-articulating the ideal of the 'parfit, gentil knight' that had been central to the medieval concept of chivalry for several centuries.

timeline

1474	1486	*c.*1503	1508–12	1509	1509–11
William Caxton prints first book in English	Botticelli, *The Birth of Venus*	Leonardo da Vinci, *Mona Lisa*	Michelangelo paints ceiling of Sistine Chapel	Erasmus, *The Praise of Folly*, a satirical attack on abuses within the Roman Catholic Church	Raphael, *The School of Athens*

such figures as the Roman orator Cicero, the humanists believed they could instil virtue in others and in the state as a whole.

The spirit of open inquiry espoused by the humanists spread in due course to northern Europe, where the Dutch scholar Desiderius Erasmus (1466–1536) became highly critical of the Roman Catholic Church. But he never endorsed the break with Rome initiated by Martin Luther, and the degree to which the spirit of the Renaissance influenced the Protestant reformers is debatable. Similarly debatable is the extent to which this spirit initiated the Scientific Revolution of the 16th and 17th centuries, given that the great astronomers and anatomists of that period rejected the teachings of classical writers – and of the church – where they conflicted with the observed facts. And it was the Scientific Revolution, rather than Renaissance humanism, that ushered in the far-reaching intellectual, ethical and philosophical revolution of the 18th-century Enlightenment, in which so many of our modern Western values are rooted.

Printing

Printing with movable type had been in use in China since the 11th century, but was unknown in Europe until the technique was invented independently by the German printer Johannes Gutenberg around 1450. Prior to this, texts had been laboriously copied by hand, severely limiting the number of books – and thus the amount of knowledge and opinion – in circulation. Printing with movable type allowed for the mass production not only of books, but also of broadsheets, ballads and pamphlets. This allowed for the transmission to a wider international audience of the work not only of the Renaissance humanists but also of the religious reformers, contributing significantly to the spread of the Protestant Reformation.

in a nutshell
A move away from the god-centred discourse of the Middle Ages, but not a revolution

1513	1516	1516	1528	1550
Niccolò Machiavelli, *The Prince*, a treatise asserting that to maintain political power and stability, the ends justify the means	Erasmus publishes his edited version of the Greek New Testament, with a Latin translation	The English humanist Sir Thomas More publishes *Utopia*, outlining an ideal society	Castiglione describes the all-round 'Renaissance man' in *The Courtier*	Vasari glorifies Renaissance art in *Lives of the Painters*

19 The Ottoman empire

To an Englishman writing in 1603, the Ottoman Turks were 'the greatest terror of the world'. It was a view universally shared among the Christians of Europe.

Over the previous two centuries the Ottomans had snuffed out the last vestiges of the Roman empire in the east, conquered the entire Balkan peninsula, and appeared in force at the gates of Vienna itself, threatening to bring all of central Europe under the Islamic caliphate. Their power stretched from the Red Sea and the Persian Gulf to Hungary and the Barbary Coast of North Africa, and they had come close to dominating the entire Mediterranean.

The Ottoman empire takes its name from its founder, Osman or Othman I, a nomad leader who at the end of the 13th century declared his small state in Anatolia independent of the Seljuk Turks, then the dominant power in the region. It was said that Osman, while staying at the house of a holy man, dreamed that a moon rose out of the holy man's chest and settled in his own. 'As soon as it did so,' the story continues, 'a tree sprouted from his navel and its shade covered the whole world.' The holy man told Osman that this dream foretold the sovereignty of him and his descendants.

'Covering the whole world' Osman and his successors set about turning this dream into a reality, extinguishing the Byzantine presence in Asia Minor and expanding into the Balkans, where the Christian

timeline

1299	1389	1396	1453	1460	1514	1514–16	1517
Osman I, founder of the Ottoman dynasty, declares independence from Seljuk Turks	Serbia conquered after Ottoman victory at Kosovo	Conquest of Bulgaria	Constantinople falls to Ottoman siege	Ottomans take southern Greece	Sultan Selim I defeats Persians at Chaldiran	Selim conquers Armenia	Selim takes Egypt, Syria and western Arabia

peasantry found they were treated better under the Ottomans than they had been under their earlier Christian masters. The Byzantines – inheritors of the eastern Roman empire – were confined to their capital, Constantinople, until this too fell in the great siege of 1453, marking the end of two millennia of Roman history and sending shockwaves across Europe. The Ottomans made Constantinople their capital, renaming it Istanbul – 'the city'.

The sultan who had captured Constantinople, Mehmet II, also completed the conquest of Greece and established a foothold across the Black Sea in the Crimea. His successors, Bajezid II and Selim I, conquered Syria, the Levant, Egypt and part of Arabia, including the Muslim holy cities of Medina and Mecca.

Ottoman power reached its zenith under Selim's son, Suleiman I (ruled 1520–66), known as 'the Magnificent'. Suleiman seized Mesopotamia from the Persians, conquered Hungary and Transylvania, and in 1529 laid siege to Vienna, only withdrawing with the onset of winter. Suleiman also created an effective navy, which he used to take the island of Rhodes from the Knights of St John, while Ottoman power was extended into the western Mediterranean via the corsairs of the Barbary Coast, who became vassals of the sultan.

To western Christendom, 'the Turk' presented a threat to its very existence, and numerous stories of Ottoman atrocities were in circulation.

Sultans and caliphs

In the Muslim world, the title 'caliph' – meaning 'successor' – was given to those who followed Mohammed as leaders of the entire Islamic community, and in the centuries after Mohammed the title was held by a number of Arab dynasties. The title 'sultan' was given to those who held power behind the throne of the caliph, and was adopted by the Ottomans in the 14th century. Leadership of the caliphate itself was assumed by the Ottoman sultans in the 16th century following their conquest of Egypt and the death of the last Abbasid caliph. The Ottoman caliphate was finally abolished in 1924 by the new secular Turkish republic.

1522	1526	1529	1565	1571	1669	1768–92
Ottomans take Rhodes	Suleiman the Magnificent conquers Hungary after victory at Mohács	Unsuccessful Ottoman siege of Vienna	Knights of St John resist Ottoman siege of Malta	Ottomans capture Cyprus, but are defeated at Lepanto	Crete taken from Venice	Wars with Russia lead to loss of territory around Black Sea

On the whole, however, the Ottoman sultans showed tolerance towards the religious practices of their Christian and other non-Muslim subjects – in stark contrast to the religious persecutions conducted by Europe's Christian princes before, during and after the Reformation.

'The sick man of Europe' Ottoman ambitions in the western Mediterranean were finally crushed in 1571, when the Turkish fleet was defeated by a joint Spanish and Venetian force at Lepanto, off the coast of Greece. Thereafter, the Ottoman story is one of slow decline. Looking back from the perspective of the late 19th century, a Turkish historian pictured the fortunes of the Ottoman state after the time of Suleiman the Magnificent as an oscillation between 'autumnal decay and distress' and 'spring restoration and rejuvenation'. But the general drift was one way: towards decay. Turkey, once the scourge of Christendom, became known as 'the sick man of Europe'.

> **❝I who am the sultan of sultans, the sovereign of sovereigns, the shadow of God on earth . . . ❞**
>
> **Suleiman the Magnificent**
> writes to Charles V, the Holy
> Roman emperor, June 1547

Various reasons for this decline can be identified. The sultans themselves were partly to blame, sinking into isolated self-indulgence in their luxurious palaces, surrounded by their harems and their sycophantic courtiers. At the same time, the centralized administration established by Suleiman disintegrated as local administrators – the pashas – assumed greater power. The effectiveness of central government was also weakened by the increasing tendency to award administrative jobs on the basis of heredity rather than merit. Another factor was a growing conservatism within the Muslim world, once a hotbed of intellectual and technological innovation. Thus the Ottoman empire was largely untouched by two crucial developments that transformed Europe and America in the 18th and 19th centuries: the Enlightenment and the Industrial Revolution.

As the vigour of the Ottomans diminished, the neighbouring powers began to nibble away at the edges of their empire. After another

timeline

1804–13	1829	1853	1853–6	1876	1878
Successful Serb revolt against Turkish rule	Greece, supported by Britain, France and Russia, achieves independence from Turkey	Russian occupation of Ottoman provinces of Moldavia and Walachia (later united as Romania)	Turkey, Britain, France and Piedmont fight Russia in inconclusive Crimean War	Savage Turkish repression of Bulgarian revolt	Congress of Berlin: Romania, Serbia and Montenegro granted independence from Turkey; Bulgaria gains autonomy

unsuccessful Ottoman siege of Vienna in 1683, the Austrians went on the offensive and conquered Hungary, while in the later 18th century the Russians seized much of the northern coast of the Black Sea. In the 19th century, nationalist unrest increased among the Ottomans' Christian subjects in south-eastern Europe, and the Ottomans responded with increasing savagery – to the horror of popular opinion in the West. However, the Western powers were alarmed by Russian ambitions as Ottoman power declined in the Balkans and eastern Mediterranean, fearing an upset to the balance of power. Britain in particular believed that Russia threatened its route to India, its most important imperial possession. A series of wars and diplomatic crises followed, as Austria and Russia vied for dominance in the disintegrating Balkans. This rivalry was to culminate in the outbreak of the First World War, in which Turkey allied itself with Austria and Germany against Russia, Britain and France. Turkey's ultimate defeat in that war led to the final dismantling of the Ottoman empire.

The Barbary Corsairs

From the 16th century, corsairs from the Barbary Coast – modern Tunisia, Algeria and Morocco – raided all round the western Mediterranean and as far as southern England and Ireland, capturing hundreds of thousands of Christians and selling them as slaves. It was only in the early 19th century that the piracy of the corsairs was suppressed by the Western powers, including the USA. European colonization of their homelands followed.

in a nutshell
The disintegration of the Ottoman empire affected the balance of power in Europe

1891	1912–13	1918	1920	1921–2	1923
Young Turk movement formed to encourage reform	Turkey involved in First and Second Balkan Wars	Turkey defeated in First World War	Former Ottoman territory in Middle East divided between Britain and France	Turks successfully resist Greek invasion	Kemal Atatürk declares Republic of Turkey and begins process of Westernization

20 The voyages of discovery

'Discovery' is a highly relative, Eurocentric term in the context of the history of exploration. The lands that the likes of Vasco da Gama, Columbus and Cabot 'discovered' were already inhabited by other peoples – it was just that Europeans had not been there before. Nevertheless, these 'discoveries' were to have profound consequences for both the discoverers and the discovered, and for the world as a whole.

The great exploratory voyages embarked upon by European navigators from the mid-15th century were by no means unprecedented. For thousands of years those extraordinary seafarers the Polynesians had been sailing across thousands of miles of the Pacific Ocean in their outrigger canoes, navigating by the stars to colonize far-flung islands. Around the end of the 9th century AD, the Vikings had established a colony in Greenland, and in 1000 Leif Eriksson established a short-lived settlement called Vinland somewhere in north-east North America – possibly on Newfoundland, or in Maine. Around the same time, Arab merchants had established trading settlements down the east coast of Africa, and at the beginning of the 15th century the Chinese admiral Zheng He had also reached East Africa, and also Arabia, India and the East Indies. But none of these voyages of discovery had quite the enduring impact of the European 'discovery' of the Americas and the opening up of new sea routes to Asia and beyond.

timeline

1402	1420	1430	1434	1444
Spanish begin conquest of the Canary Islands	Portuguese sailors sponsored by Prince Henry the Navigator discover Madeira	Portuguese settlement of the Azores	Portuguese sail round Cape Bojador on the north-western coast of Africa	Portuguese reach Senegal River, establishing a sea route for slaves and other goods and so bypassing the Muslim-controlled trans-Saharan routes

Round the Cape It was not in furtherance of scientific knowledge that the early European voyages of discovery were undertaken. The principal motive was commercial – in particular, a desire to get a share in the extremely valuable spice trade. Spices originated in the Indies (as southern and south-eastern Asia was known), and came to Europe via long and difficult land routes across central Asia and the Middle East. The break-up of the Mongol empire and the expansion of the Ottomans in the 14th century made these routes more problematic. The small but powerful maritime republic of Venice controlled the trade from the Near East across the Mediterranean to Europe, and this motivated its trading rivals to seek alternative routes.

The kingdom of Portugal, situated on the Atlantic, took the lead, largely owing to the encouragement of Henry the Navigator (1394–1460), younger son of King John I. Prince Henry established a school of navigation, encouraged the colonization of Madeira and the Azores, and sponsored a series of exploratory voyages down the west coast of Africa, where a number of trading posts were established. All this was made possible by the development of sailing vessels more suited to the open ocean than the oar-powered Mediterranean galley, and by new navigational aids, such as the magnetic compass (first used by the Chinese, and then by the Arabs), the quadrant and the astrolabe.

❝The gums of . . . some of our men swelled, so that they could not eat under any circumstances and therefore died.❞

Antonio Pigafetta, who accompanied Ferdinand Magellan on his first circumnavigation of the world, describes the effects of scurvy

Prince Henry's patronage of explorers was continued after his death by King John II of Portugal. Under the latter's auspices, in 1488 Bartolomeu Dias rounded the Cape of Good Hope at the southern tip of Africa, demonstrating that a new way to the East lay open. In 1498 another Portuguese navigator, Vasco da Gama, sailed round the Cape, then continued up the east coast of Africa and across the open ocean to Calicut, in south-west India. He returned with a small quantity of spices.

*c.*1460	1488	1492	1493–6	1494
Italian and Portuguese navigators discover Cape Verde Islands	Bartolomeu Dias rounds the Cape of Storms, later renamed the Cape of Good Hope	Christopher Columbus reaches San Salvador Island in the Bahamas, and visits Hispaniola	Columbus's second voyage: visits Guadeloupe, Puerto Rico and Jamaica, and establishes settlement on Hispaniola	Treaty of Tordesillas divides New World between Spain and Portugal

> ❝Your highness . . . will soon convert to our holy faith a multitude of people, acquiring large dominions and great riches for Spain. Because without doubt there is in these lands a very great quantity of gold.❞

Christopher Columbus, letter to his patron,
King Ferdinand of Spain, October 1492

Others followed in his footsteps, reaching as far as the fabled Spice Islands (the Moluccas) in the East Indies. The charts they made of their complex routes through the dangerous waters of the Malay archipelago became worth more than their weight in gold.

To the New World Christopher Columbus had no idea of the existence of the Americas when he sailed west in 1492. It had long been known that the world was round, but Columbus, thinking the Earth was smaller than it actually is, believed that by sailing west he would reach the Indies much more quickly than by sailing round Africa. In the event, it took his three ships thirty-three days to make landfall on the Bahamas, and such was his conviction that he had reached the Indies that he referred to the inhabitants as *Indios*.

Columbus was an Italian, but his patrons were Ferdinand and Isabella, king and queen of a newly united Spain. Ferdinand and Isabella were ardent Catholics, and Columbus reported that this 'New World' was full of heathens ready for conversion to the true faith – and also full of gold. The Spanish Crown's claim to the new lands to the west was challenged by Portugal, and by the Treaty of Tordesillas of 1494, brokered by the pope, the Americas were divided between the two countries, with Portugal gaining Brazil and Spain the rest. The English also took an interest in the New World, and in 1496 King Henry VII sponsored an Italian navigator, John Cabot, who the following year reached north-east North America.

timeline

1497–9	1498–1500	1500	1502–4	1510	1519–21
Vasco da Gama sails to India and back via the Cape	Columbus's third voyage: reaches Trinidad and South American mainland	Pedro Álvares Cabral lands in Brazil and claims it for Portugal	Columbus's fourth voyage: explores Caribbean coast of Central America	Portuguese establish permanent settlement at Goa, on west coast of India	Spanish conquest of Aztec empire in Mexico

Colonization and domination It was to be another ninety years before the English attempted to establish settlements in North America, but further south the Spanish and Portuguese were quick to take advantage of their technological superiority over the natives. The mighty empires of the Aztecs and the Incas were soon overthrown, their gold and silver looted, and the indigenous people enslaved and forcibly converted. 'For these people,' wrote a Jesuit missionary in 1563, 'there is no better preaching than by the sword and iron rod.' Millions died from European diseases to which they had no immunity.

The European domination of the world had begun. But there were consequences. As the European powers facing the Atlantic – Spain and Portugal, and then the Netherlands, Britain and France – thrived on the wealth from the new-found lands, the Mediterranean turned into something of a backwater, and the great Italian trading cities of Venice and Genoa went into decline. Not all of the imports from the New World were beneficial, however. The huge amounts of silver brought back to Spain contributed to widespread economic inflation across Europe in the 16th century. Other imports, such as tobacco and syphilis, had a more insidious effect on European well-being, causing the deaths of countless millions over the centuries that followed.

Naming America

By a stroke of fortune, America was not named after Christopher Columbus, but rather after a Florentine merchant adventurer, Amerigo Vespucci, who in 1499 sailed along the north-east coast of South America and discovered the mouth of the Amazon. Columbus has had to content himself with giving his name to a South American republic, a North American river, a number of US cities, a federal district and a Canadian province.

in a nutshell
The voyages of discovery set the scene for European colonization and world domination

1519–22	1532–5	1597	1611
Ferdinand Magellan, a Portuguese navigator in the service of Spain, leads first circumnavigation of the world, establishing a new route to Asia round the tip of South America and across the Pacific. Magellan is killed in 1521, and only one of his five ships returns to Spain.	Spanish conquest of Inca empire in Peru	William Barents, a Dutch navigator, dies on the return from his third attempt to find a North-east Passage to the Indies along the north coast of Russia	Henry Hudson, an English navigator, is cast adrift by his mutinous crew after making the first of many failed attempts to find a North-west Passage to Asia via the Canadian Arctic

21 The Reformation

Until the later Middle Ages, the Roman Catholic Church had enjoyed unchallenged spiritual supremacy across western Europe. True, there had been outbreaks of heresy – such as Catharism in southern France in the early 13th century – but these had been efficiently and violently extinguished. There had also been fallings-out with secular rulers, where the interests of church and state had come into conflict – such as over who had the right to appoint bishops, or whether a king had the right to tax the clergy.

The church had experienced periods of laxity and abuse within its ranks, but had generally managed to reform itself, for example by the creation of new and stricter monastic orders, as the older ones grew rich and self-indulgent.

But the growing wealth and worldliness of the church led in the 14th century to a new mood of anticlericalism, and the church's claim that only its priests could mediate between God and lay men and women was increasingly challenged. One such challenge was offered by the English theologian John Wycliffe (?1330–84), who criticized the doctrine of transubstantiation (the belief that the bread and wine served at the Eucharist literally become the body and blood of Christ) and emphasized the role of individual action as opposed to priestly mediation. Wycliffe also oversaw the first translation of the Bible into English. Hitherto, the Bible had only been available in Latin, and thus its teachings were hidden to most people, who were obliged to rely on what the priests taught them. Wycliffe's ideas influenced the Bohemian (Czech) reformer Jan Hus, who

timeline

1377	1380s	1414	1415	1517	1520
John Wycliffe's criticism of Catholic doctrine condemned by the pope	Completion of Wycliffe's translation of the Bible into English	Suppression of the Lollards, Wycliffe's English followers	Jan Hus burned at the stake for his criticisms of the church	Luther launches Reformation with his ninety-five theses against indulgences	Ulrich Zwingli begins Reformation in Switzerland

was burned at the stake in 1415 for refusing to recant his views. However, his followers in Bohemia considered him a national hero and successfully fought off a crusade sent to crush them.

Calls for reform By the end of the 15th century the popes in Rome were behaving with all the ostentation, ruthlessness and materialism of Renaissance princes, lavishing money on great artistic projects, taking mistresses and appointing their illegitimate children to positions of power within the church. To fund this extravagance they offered high church offices up for sale and encouraged the practice of selling indulgences, by which those who confessed their sins would be granted remission, on condition that they paid for the privilege. This practice was particularly resented in Germany, where one of the most notorious practitioners was Johann Tetzel, who, according to one contemporary, said that a man would be forgiven even if he had slept with his own mother.

Such abuses were criticized by humanist scholars such as Erasmus (see p. 75). In 1516 Erasmus translated the New Testament from the original Greek into Latin, and in so doing showed up the flaws in the Vulgate, the Latin version endorsed by the church. This return to the original text of the Bible also showed up the disparity between the austerity of the early church and the flamboyance and corruption of the institution in Erasmus's own day. Erasmus, against church practice, also wanted the Bible translated into everyday language, so that everybody could understand the word of God.

Why 'Protestantism'?

The word 'Protestantism' derives from the 'protest' issued by a minority of delegates at the Diet of Speyer, an assembly called by the Emperor Charles V – the papacy's staunchest supporter – in April 1529. The 'protest' was against a resolution calling for an end to 'innovation in religion' – in other words, the teachings of reformers such as Luther. The 'Protestants' declared that individual conscience was paramount in such matters.

1521	1524–5	1527	1530	1533	1536
Luther is excommunicated then outlawed at the Diet of Worms	Peasants' War in Germany	Lutheranism adopted in Sweden	Augsburg Confession establishes separate Lutheran church	Henry VIII breaks with Rome and becomes supreme head of the church in England, which nevertheless remains Catholic in its doctrine	Jean Calvin outlines his reformed theology in his work *The Institutes*

Lutheranism Erasmus sought to reform the church from within, but others came to the conclusion that this would not be possible. In Germany, an Augustinian monk and priest called Martin Luther (1483–1546) also called for the text of the Bible to be made available to everyone, not just those who could read Latin – and to this end he translated the New Testament into German. Luther believed that religious truth was to be found in Scripture alone, and that salvation could only be attained by faith. This led him to excoriate the selling of indulgences, and confront Johann Tetzel with his famous ninety-five theses against the practice, which he nailed to the door of the castle church in Wittenberg on 31 October 1517. Luther also denied the special role of the priesthood, asserting that every man and woman stood alone and equal before God.

> **❝My conscience is captive to the word of God . . . Here I stand. I can do no other. God help me. Amen.❞**
>
> **Martin Luther** defies papal authority at the Diet of Worms, 18 April 1521

Luther's attacks on both priests and pope led to his excommunication in 1521, followed by a summons to appear at the imperial diet (assembly) in the city of Worms. Luther was a subject of Charles V, who as Holy Roman emperor was a staunch supporter of the papacy, but at the diet Luther refused to recant, and as a consequence was declared an outlaw by the emperor.

The new medium of print helped to disseminate Luther's ideas rapidly to a wide audience, and they found much support in Germany, both among the princes (Germany then comprised numerous small states, notionally under the emperor) and among the common people. The latter took Luther's rejection of both papal and imperial authority as a cue to free themselves from oppression, leading to the Peasants' War of 1524–5. But Luther was appalled by this revolt against temporal authority, and realized he needed the support of the princes against the attempts by Charles V to crush the Reformation he had initiated. He therefore urged 'everyone who can to avoid the peasants as he would the Devil himself', and supported the brutal suppression of the revolt.

timeline

1536–40	1541	1541	1546	1547	1553–8	1555
Dissolution of the monasteries in England	Calvin establishes a Protestant theocracy in Geneva	Counter-Reformation launched at Council of Trent	Lutheranism adopted in Denmark	Edward VI succeeds to throne of England and introduces Protestantism	Mary I restores Catholicism in England	Peace of Augsburg ends religious wars in Germany

The spread of Protestantism With the Augsburg Confession of 1530, which summarized the basic tenets of Lutheranism, the break with Rome became final. A series of religious wars followed in Germany, coming to an end with the Peace of Augsburg in 1555, by which it was agreed that each prince should have the right to determine the faith of his subjects. By this time Sweden and Denmark had also adopted Lutheranism, and the breakaway Church of England, of which the monarch was the head, also contained Lutheran elements. In England as elsewhere, the state profited by the confiscation of church property, and was strengthened by its power over ecclesiastical appointments.

> **❛A man with God is always in the majority.❜**
>
> **John Knox,** *c.*1505–72, Scottish reformer, inscription on the Reformation Monument in Geneva

Lutheranism was not the only strand of reformed religion. The most significant alternative, Calvinism, derived from the teachings of the French theologian Jean Calvin (1509–56). Calvin taught that salvation was predestined: no matter what one did in one's life, only those chosen by God would be saved. At the same time, Calvin urged the authorities to closely supervise the moral lives of church members, giving an austere and theocratic bent to his teachings. Calvinist churches were set up in Geneva, France, the Low Countries and Scotland, and were later established in New England. As in Germany, the reformers often met with violent opposition, particularly once the Roman Catholic Church began the process known as the Counter-Reformation (see p. 88).

in a nutshell
The spiritual monopoly of the Roman Catholic Church was broken for ever

1559	**1560**	**1562–98**	**1588**	**1598**
Elizabeth I reintroduces Protestantism in England	Scottish Parliament adopts John Knox's Calvinist *Confession of Faith,* thereby severing the church in Scotland from Rome	Wars of Religion in France between Huguenots (Calvinists) and Catholics	Failure of Spanish Armada against England	Edict of Nantes grants religious toleration to Huguenots (French Protestants)

22 The Counter-Reformation

The Reformation delivered a profound shock to the Roman Catholic Church, one that induced it to reform and reinvigorate itself. Now the Church Militant went on the offensive, purging itself of abuses, laxity and ill-educated clergy, and sending forth its soldiers, both spiritual and temporal, to strike down the heretical schismatics who had raised their banner against the authority of the pope in Rome.

It was to be a bloody business, marked by merciless zealotry on all sides, while increasingly complicated by secular politics and international realpolitik. The conflict between Protestants and Catholics culminated in the horrendous blood-letting that was the Thirty Years' War, which devastated much of central Europe. By the end of that war, the struggle was not so much between Protestants and Catholics, but between the rising (Catholic) power of France, and the fading (Catholic) power of the Habsburgs, rulers of Spain, Austria and the Holy Roman empire, which then comprised most of Germany.

Catholic renewal The rapid spread of the reformist teachings of Luther and Calvin across Europe threatened the very existence of the Roman Catholic Church. While on the pope's behalf the Holy Roman emperor Charles V fought the German Protestant princes, the church, realizing how far it had fallen from its own high standards, sought to renew itself. The main agent of reform within the Catholic Church was the

timeline

1521	1534	1541	1542	1553–8	1555
Excommunication of Martin Luther	Foundation of Society of Jesus (the Jesuits)	Counter-Reformation launched at Council of Trent	Pope Paul III sets up Holy Office with inquisitorial powers over all Catholics	Catholicism restored in England under Mary I	Peace of Augsburg ends first wave of religious wars in Germany

> **In the invocation of the saints, the veneration of relics and the sacred use of images, all superstition shall be removed, all filthy quest for gain eliminated, and all lasciviousness avoided . . .**

Decree of the twenty-fifth session of the Council of Trent, 3–4 December 1563

Council of Trent, a body that met in three sessions between 1541 and 1563 in the northern Italian town of Trento, conveniently close to the linguistic border between Italian- and German-speaking Europe. The Council issued numerous decrees regarding both doctrine and practice, and put in place measures to ensure that all priests were properly educated – not to mention celibate. A tighter rein was applied to the existing religious orders, whose moral slackness had given the reformers considerable ammunition. A number of new orders, both lay and monastic, were also established.

Most notable of the new orders was the Society of Jesus, whose members, the Jesuits, swore vows of poverty, chastity and obedience. This highly disciplined and effective body was founded in 1534 by a former Spanish soldier, Ignatius Loyola. Their task, in Loyola's words, was to 'fight for God under the banner of the cross' and to 'advance souls in Christian life and doctrine and to propagate the faith by the ministry of the word, by spiritual exercises, by works of charity and expressly by the instruction of children and unlettered persons in Christian principles'. The Society became one of the most powerful institutions in Catholic Europe, and was the leading Catholic missionary body elsewhere in the world.

In 1542 the Holy See established the Holy Office – the Supreme Sacred Congregation of the Roman and Universal Inquisition. This had responsibility for enforcing Catholic doctrine, and was possessed of inquisitorial powers over all Catholics. In a number of countries Inquisitions already existed, and in others one was introduced. The Spanish Inquisition had been active against

1559	1562	1564	1566	1567	1572
Pope Pius IV introduces Index of books that Catholics are forbidden to read	Beginning of Wars of Religion in France between Huguenots (Calvinists) and Catholics	Philip II orders that all the decrees of the Council of Trent be enforced in all Spanish territories	The Dutch resist the imposition of the Spanish Inquisition, and demand freedom of religion	Outbreak of the Dutch Revolt (the Eighty-Year War)	St Bartholomew's Day Massacre of Huguenots in France

The Index

In 1559, aware of the effect that print had had in spreading the teachings of the Protestant reformers, the pope introduced an 'Index' of books that Catholics were forbidden to read, prompting many to scour their shelves anxiously for anything not authorized. One scholar in Rome described it as 'a holocaust of literature'. It was also damaging to scientific advance: for example, Copernicus's *On the Revolutions of the Celestial Spheres*, in which he concluded that the Earth orbits the Sun and not vice versa, remained on the Index until 1835.

Jewish converts suspected of backsliding since 1478, and with the Reformation worked to snuff out Protestantism throughout the Spanish empire (which then included the Netherlands). These bodies tried suspected heretics in ecclesiastical courts, then handed them over to the secular authorities for punishment, 'not . . . for the correction and good of the person punished,' according to a 1578 manual for inquisitors, 'but for the public good in order that others may become terrified and weaned away from the evils they would commit'. Those found guilty of heresy were burned alive, usually in a great public spectacle called an *auto-da-fé* – meaning 'act of faith'. Between 1575 and 1610, in just one Spanish city, Toledo, 366 people suffered this fate. Thousands more shared their fate elsewhere.

Europe polarized As at other times, when opposing religious certainties clash, violence ensues. The son of Emperor Charles V, Philip II of Spain, although anxious to limit the power of the church in his own realms, emerged as the most zealous champion of Catholic Europe. His attempt to extirpate Protestant heresy in the Spanish Netherlands contributed to the outbreak of the Dutch Revolt in 1567. English support for the Dutch rebels prompted Philip to send the Spanish Armada against England in 1588, but this ended in ignominious failure. Philip also intervened in the French Wars of Religion (1562–98), in which the French Huguenots (Calvinists) fought for freedom of worship while Catholic and Protestant nobles vied for control of the crown. The worst excess occurred in 1572, when some 13,000 Protestants were killed in the St Bartholomew's Day Massacre. The war ended in 1598 with the Edict of Nantes, by which the Huguenots were granted religious freedom.

timeline

1588	1598	1609	1618	1620	1621
Spanish Armada scattered by an English fleet and by storms	Edict of Nantes grants religious toleration to Huguenots, ending French Wars of Religion	Truce declared in war between Spanish and Dutch	Revolt in Bohemia marks outbreak of Thirty Years' War	Bohemian revolt crushed at Battle of White Mountain. Spanish troops occupy Rhenish Palatinate in western Germany.	Hostilities resume between Spanish and Dutch

The Thirty Years' War Although France had for the time being resolved its internal religious differences, Europe soon became embroiled in a wider religious conflict, the Thirty Years' War. This was in fact a complex mix of conflicts, starting with a revolt within the Holy Roman empire by Protestant Bohemians against the imperial rule of the Austrian Habsburgs. Although the revolt was crushed, in 1620 the Spanish Habsburgs intervened against the Protestant princes in Germany, and were joined in this anti-Protestant crusade by the Emperor Ferdinand II. Alarmed at this development, Gustavus Adolphus, the powerful king of Protestant Sweden, intervened in 1630 and scored a number of victories until he was killed at the Battle of Lützen in 1632. Three years later, France joined in on the side of the German Protestants. The war from now on was more political than religious: France itself was a Catholic power, but it had been an enemy of the Habsburgs since the early 16th century, and now saw that its own place in Europe depended on containing the power of Spain and the empire. The war dragged on until 1648, when the Peace of Westphalia gave recognition to Dutch independence, and fixed the religious map of Europe in more or less its present form.

It was at a terrible cost: in Germany alone, through war and its constant companions, pestilence and famine, some 7 million men, women and children – some two-thirds of the population – had lost their lives. It was a reverse from which Germany took many generations to recover.

> **❛It was for me the best and most cheerful news which could come to me.❜**
> **Philip II of Spain,** August 1572, on hearing of the St Bartholomew's Day Massacre of French Protestants

in a nutshell
The religious map of Europe was only fixed after a century of violent conflict

1629	1630	1632	1635	1643	1648
Emperor Ferdinand II attempts to impose terms of 1555 Peace of Augsburg in Germany	Gustavus Adolphus of Sweden intervenes on Protestant side in Germany	Gustavus killed in battle	Catholic France intervenes on side of German Protestants against Habsburgs in Thirty Years' War	French score decisive victory over Spain at Rocroi	Peace of Westphalia ends Thirty Years' War; Dutch independence recognized by Spain

23 The English Revolution

In the 17th century England experienced a succession of sometimes violent constitutional upheavals by which it sought to shed the shackles of royal autocracy. The constitutional monarchy that emerged was to become a model that progressives in many other countries sought to imitate in the centuries that followed.

The power of the Crown in England had in theory been diluted since the Middle Ages by the institution of Parliament – although at this stage Parliament did not represent more than a tiny handful of nobles and other landowners, clergy and wealthy townsmen. Monarchs still behaved in autocratic ways, but they increasingly did so within the confines of laws passed by Parliament – albeit at the monarch's bidding. More crucially, the Crown relied on Parliament to raise taxes in order to carry out the business of government – from making war to building palaces. But Parliament only met irregularly, when summoned by the monarch.

Crown and Parliament Tensions between Crown and Parliament began to emerge towards the end of the reign of Elizabeth I. However, being a pragmatic politician, Elizabeth never pushed the constitutional issues to the test. Her successor, James I, was consumed by a belief in the 'divine right of kings' to do as they pleased, as their rule was sanctioned by God. This took him into a head-on conflict with Parliament, which fiercely defended its 'liberties and privileges'. In response, James attempted to rule

timeline

1598	1603	1621	1625	1629
James VI of Scotland outlines the doctrine of the divine right of kings in *The True Law of Free Monarchies*	On the death of Elizabeth I, James VI succeeds to the English throne as James I	James arrests two of his leading critics in the House of Commons	Charles I succeeds to the throne	Charles dissolves Parliament, which does not meet for another eleven years

without summoning Parliament, and raised money by various unpopular means, such as selling monopolies and titles.

James's son, Charles I, was brought up as a fervent believer in the divine right of kings, and was even less of a pragmatist than his father. A proud, pious, prickly man, Charles took any disinterested advice as personal criticism. When he succeeded to the throne in 1625, Parliament was dominated by Puritans, who disapproved of the lavish (albeit notionally Protestant) religious ceremonial favoured by Charles, and of his choice of wife, a French Catholic princess. Like his father, Charles preferred to rule alone, but when he could not raise sufficient money by his own devices he was forced to summon Parliament, which in 1628 issued the Petition of Right, declaring the illegality of raising taxes without parliamentary approval and condemning other abuses of monarchical power. Another parliamentary hiatus – the 'Eleven Years' Tyranny' – ended in 1640, when Charles's attempt to impose bishops on the Presbyterian Scots met with armed resistance. Needing money for war, Charles was once more obliged to summon Parliament.

The Long Parliament that began to sit in November 1640 gained Charles's reluctant approval to a number of demands, including an insistence that Parliaments be summoned at least once every three years, and that they could not be dissolved without their own consent. But in January 1642, after Parliament had demanded control of the army, Charles marched into the House of Commons at the head of 400 soldiers and attempted to arrest his five leading opponents. They had escaped, but within a matter of months both sides – Royalists and Parliamentarians – were openly at war.

Commonwealth and Protectorate The English Civil War, which continued in fits and starts until 1651, divided the country, and also drew in the Scots and the Irish. Charles was captured in 1646, and

> **❛Kings are justly called gods, for that they exercise a manner or resemblance of divine power upon earth.❜**
>
> **King James I,** speech to the English Parliament, 21 March 1610

1640

APRIL–MAY Charles summons Short Parliament to raise money for war with Scots, but dismisses it after it refuses to do his bidding. **NOVEMBER** Charles summons Long Parliament, which declares the king's revenue-raising methods illegal.

1641

Parliament issues the Grand Remonstrance, detailing Charles's abuses of power since his accession

1642

JANUARY Charles tries to arrest five of his leading opponents in the House of Commons. **AUGUST** Charles declares war on Parliament.

1644

Parliament achieves a decisive victory at Marston Moor

> **❝You have sat here too long for any good you have been doing. Depart, I say, and let us have done with you. In the name of God, go.❞**
>
> **Oliver Cromwell,** having won the Civil War for Parliament, dismisses that body in 1653

in January 1649 was put on trial for treason, found guilty and beheaded. Kings had been overthrown and killed before, usually by dynastic rivals, but never tried and convicted of treason. It amounted to a declaration that the people – as represented by Parliament – were sovereign, and not the monarch. Indeed, Parliament proceeded to abolish the monarchy and declared England a Commonwealth.

But Parliament was not the only power in the land. The army – which under its most successful general, Oliver Cromwell, had delivered victory in the Civil War – found the new Parliament too conservative for its taste. In 1653 Cromwell led a troop of soldiers into the House of Commons and expelled the members, and later that year he became 'lord protector'. On his death in 1658 Cromwell was succeeded, in monarchical fashion, by his son Richard. However, the new lord protector did not enjoy the support that his father had, and the resultant

The social contract

The philosopher John Locke published his *Two Treatises of Government* in 1690, implicitly justifying the recent overthrow of James II in the 'Glorious Revolution'. Locke stated that men are born with certain 'natural rights' – freedom, equality and independence – and only give up these rights 'by agreeing with other men to join and unite into a community, for their comfortable, safe, and peaceable living one amongst another'. Thus kings rule not by 'divine right' but through a 'social contract', by which subjects give up their 'natural rights' for 'civil rights'. If a ruler tries to deny these rights, the people are justified in seeking his overthrow. Locke's arguments were influential on both the American and the French revolutionaries of the later 18th century.

timeline

1646	1647	1648	1649	1651	1653	1657
Charles surrenders to Scots, and is handed over to Parliament	Charles refuses to agree to army proposals for constitutional reform	Hostilities resume; Charles's supporters defeated at Preston	Charles convicted of treason and beheaded. Parliament abolishes monarchy and House of Lords.	Charles II and his Scots allies defeated at Worcester	Oliver Cromwell becomes lord protector	Cromwell refuses Parliament's offer of the crown

power vacuum was filled when Charles I's son returned to England in 1660 to take the throne as Charles II.

The 'Glorious Revolution' So in the end the Civil War had failed to resolve the constitutional issues that had provoked it. The Restoration of 1660 did not bring a resolution either, as Charles II was too much of a skilled political operator to address the issues head-on. But on his death in 1685 Charles was succeeded by his Catholic brother, James II, who had none of Charles's cunning and all the doctrinaire obstinacy of his father. James's Protestant subjects increasingly feared that the king planned to reintroduce Catholicism and to reign in the absolutist fashion of Louis XIV of France. In 1688 a group of nobles invited James's Protestant son-in-law, William of Orange, to England. William arrived with 12,000 men and a proclamation that he would maintain 'the liberties of England and the Protestant religion'. James fled to France, and in 1689 the crown was offered to William and his wife, Mary (James's Protestant daughter), on condition that they accept the Bill of Rights, which limited the power of the Crown, and detailed the rights and liberties of the subject.

Thus the so-called 'Glorious Revolution' established England as a constitutional monarchy with a minimum of bloodshed. However, power was by no means devolved to the people as a whole, but was rather held in the hands of a small, largely aristocratic, landowning oligarchy. It was to take another two and a half centuries of agitation and struggle before a truly representative democracy was established in Great Britain, with every man and woman having a say in who was to govern the country.

in a nutshell
The beginning of the end of absolute monarchies in Europe

1658	1660	1679–81	1685	1688	1689
Death of Cromwell	Restoration of Charles II to the throne	Charles dismisses a number of Parliaments after they try to exclude his Catholic brother James (the future James II) from the succession	James II succeeds to the throne and suppresses a Protestant rebellion	William of Orange lands in England; James flees	William and his wife Mary jointly accept crown, accepting terms of Bill of Rights

24 The Scientific Revolution

Science is the method by which we understand and predict the workings of the physical world. Its rules are rigorous, its theories testable by experiment, and its laws once established immutable – unless new evidence proves them false.

Although today science and religion are regarded by non-fundamentalists as distinct activities involved in separate spheres of human experience, in the past the two came into conflict when science's accounts of the physical world contradicted Scripture or other accepted religious authority.

In Christian Europe in the Middle Ages, the scientific achievements of the ancient Greeks were largely unknown, and little of what we would call science was undertaken. Only in the Islamic world were the writings of the Greeks preserved and built upon, and it was only from the 12th century that Latin translations of Aristotle and others began to appear in Europe. St Thomas Aquinas worked the philosophy of Aristotle into Christian theology, while the teachings of the ancients regarding the nature of the physical universe – from the celestial sphere to the human body – came to be regarded as unchallengeable.

Copernican cosmology Although in the 3rd century BC the ancient Greek philosopher Aristarchos had concluded that the Earth rotates about its own axis and orbits the Sun, this account of a heliocentric (Sun-centred) universe had been overshadowed in the 2nd century AD

timeline

1543	1551–6	1556	1561	1572
Publication of Copernicus's *On the Revolutions of the Celestial Spheres,* and of Vesalius's *On the Workings of the Human Body*	Conrad Gesner, a Swiss physician, publishes *Histories of the Animals,* the basis of modern zoology	Posthumous publication of *On the Nature of Metals,* by Georgius Agricola, German founder of mineralogy	Publication of *Anatomical Observations* by the Italian anatomist Gabriel Fallopius, who discovered the tubes named after him	The Danish astronomer Tycho Brahe observes a supernova (explosive death of a star), indicating that celestial objects are not immutable

by Ptolemy of Alexandria, who held that it was the Earth, not the Sun, that was at the centre of the universe. The Ptolemaic system later became incorporated into Christian doctrine, in which the Earth and human life on it were the culmination of God's creation.

The Earth-centred version was universally accepted in Europe until the Polish astronomer and mathematician Nicolaus Copernicus (1473–1543) tried to calculate the future positions of the planets, and found the mathematics much easier if he assumed that they all (Earth included) orbited the Sun. He then realized that this would account for the observed fact that the planets at certain times appeared to reverse direction and go backwards relative to the Earth.

> **❝To affirm that the Sun is in very truth at the centre of the universe . . . is a very dangerous attitude . . . ❞**
>
> **Cardinal Roberto Bellarmino**
> of the Roman Inquisition, 12 April 1615

Aware that he risked criticism or worse from the church, Copernicus waited until 1543, the year of his death, before publishing *On the Revolutions of the Celestial Spheres*. This met with disapproval from both Catholics and Protestants. But after his death Copernicus's theory was backed up by detailed astronomical observations. These led Johannes Kepler (1571–1630) to work out that the planets traced ellipses around the Sun, rather than circles – which received wisdom held to be the more mathematically perfect figure. Further evidence in support of the Copernican system was produced by Galileo Galilei (1564–1642), who used the telescope he made to observe sunspots (rendering the Sun less of a perfect body than hitherto supposed) and the moons of Jupiter. Copernicanism was formally condemned by the Roman Catholic Church in 1616, and in 1633 Galileo, faced with a charge of heresy for which the punishment was burning at the stake, was forced to retract his support for the heliocentric theory. He remained under house arrest for the rest of his life.

The scientific method Copernicus had been anxious to find evidence that ancient authors had proposed a heliocentric universe,

1584	1600	1609–19	1610	1616	1620
The Italian monk Giordano Bruno goes beyond Copernicus in suggesting that the Sun is just one of many such bodies in the universe	Bruno burned at the stake for heresy. The English physician William Gilbert publishes his experiments on magnetism.	Kepler publishes his laws of planetary motion	Galileo publishes astronomical observations made with his telescope	The Roman Catholic Church condemns Copernicanism as heretical, and bans Galileo from further scientific work	Francis Bacon outlines the scientific method in *Novum Organum*

and was relieved to find references to such theories in his readings of Cicero and Plutarch. But the authority of the ancients did not remain unchallenged. The European voyages of discovery of the 15th and 16th centuries did much to alter perspectives: as the Irish scientist Robert Boyle pointed out in 1690, even an ordinary seaman travelling with Columbus to the New World 'was able at his return to inform men of an hundred things that they should never have learn'd by Aristotle's philosophy or Ptolemy's Geography'. Earlier in the same century, the English philosopher and statesman Francis Bacon had in the light of new discoveries rejected the old dogma that 'the bounds of the intellectual globe should be restricted to what was known to the ancients'. Bacon went on to assert that the recent invention of gunpowder, printing and the magnetic compass demonstrated that the moderns had already superseded the ancients.

Discovering the interior world

In the Middle Ages, the ultimate authority on medicine and human anatomy was the ancient Greek physician Galen. In Galen's day, human dissection was forbidden, and he had come to his conclusions about human anatomy by dissecting animals. When the Flemish anatomist Andreas Vesalius (1514–64) began to dissect the corpses of recently executed criminals, he found that Galen was often mistaken. The response of the traditionalists was that human anatomy must have changed since Galen's day.

Galen had had a notion of blood circulation, suggesting that blood seeped through tiny pores in the wall separating the two ventricles of the heart. Thus when the English physician and anatomist William Harvey (1578–1657) contradicted Galen when he published his account of the circulation of the blood in 1628, it caused considerable controversy. But by the time of Harvey's death his detailed description, based on his dissections and experiments on animals, was widely accepted.

timeline

1621	1628	1632	1655	1660
The Dutch physicist Willebrod Snell discovers his law of refraction	Publication of Harvey's *On the Motion of the Heart and Blood in Animals*	Galileo publishes *Dialogue on Two World Systems,* leading to his appearance before the Inquisition	The Dutch physicist and astronomer Christiaan Huygens begins work on optics, leading to his wave theory of light	Foundation of the Royal Society, Britain's leading scientific institution. Robert Hooke publishes his law on stress and strain in an elastic body.

Bacon was the pioneer of the process of induction – the derivation of general theories from observations of what actually occurs in the physical world. This contrasts with deduction, in which particular conclusions are argued from general principles – without reference to observation or experiment. Deduction is only valid in science if it is based on mathematics. Galileo himself had realized this, and was the first to insist on the use of mathematical analysis in physics.

The new scientific method, based on observation and experiment, and anchored in the remorseless logic of mathematics, was triumphantly vindicated in the work of Sir Isaac Newton (1642–1727). Newton's discovery of the three laws of motion and the law of gravitation provided a complete mechanical explanation of the universe, whose operations were shown to be as predictable as clockwork. Newtonian mechanics underscored the great technological advances that were to follow – from steam engines to space rockets – and, despite the conclusions of relativity and quantum physics, his laws still remain valid at most scales and for most practical purposes. It was Newton's intellectual breakthrough more than any other that laid the ground for the Enlightenment of the 18th century.

in a nutshell
Our understanding of the physical world became freed from ancient authority and religious dogma

1661	1663	1684	1686–7	1992
Robert Boyle publishes *The Skeptical Chymist*, showing that there are many more elements than the four espoused by the ancient Greeks, and distinguishing between elements, compounds and mixtures	Boyle publishes his law on the relationship between the pressure and volume of a gas	Gottfried Leibniz publishes his paper on calculus, starting a feud with Newton, who claimed he had invented it in 1666	Newton outlines his laws of motion and gravitation (discovered in the mid-1660s) in his *Principia Mathematica*	Galileo cleared of heresy by a Vatican commission

25 The age of empire

The voyages of discovery of the 15th and 16th centuries unveiled whole new worlds to the European eye, worlds full of new animals, new plants, new peoples. 'It ought not to go for nothing,' wrote Francis Bacon in 1607, 'that through the long voyages and travels which are the mark of our age, many things in nature have been revealed which might throw light on natural philosophy.'

But for many, the discovery of new worlds was not so much an intellectual opportunity as a commercial one. These new lands were rich in raw materials, which could be traded for European manufactured goods. They also offered possibilities of settlement, and a number of European countries began to plant their flags and their people in distant parts of the globe, often fighting each other for the right to do so.

War and trade Colonial rivalries were apparent from the very beginning. As Spain looted its newly conquered possessions in Mexico and Peru of gold and silver, English privateers such as Francis Drake preyed on the fleets of galleons taking plunder back across the Atlantic. The Americas and the Indies (south and south-eastern Asia) held other riches that made them worth fighting for: furs, timber, tobacco and fish from North America; coffee, sugar and tobacco from Central and South America and the West Indies; spices, silk, cotton, tea and coffee from the Indies. The 17th and 18th centuries were punctuated by frequent wars

timeline

1492	1494	1497–9	1500	1510	1519–21
Columbus reaches the Americas	Treaty of Tordesillas divides New World between Spain and Portugal	Vasco da Gama establishes sea route to India	Portuguese lay claim to Brazil	Portuguese settlement established at Goa, on west coast of India	Spanish conquest of Aztec empire in Mexico

❝To the natives . . . all the commercial benefits which can have resulted from those events have been sunk and lost in the dreadful misfortunes which they have occasioned.❞

Adam Smith, *The Wealth of Nations,* 1776, referring to 'the discovery of America, and that of a passage to the East Indies by the Cape of Good Hope'

between the British, French, Spanish, Dutch and Portuguese over trading rights and colonial possessions. The Dutch largely ousted the Portuguese from their scattered empire in the East Indies in the 17th century, and by the end of the Seven Years' War in 1763, Britain emerged as the dominant power in North America and India. The Portuguese held on to Brazil and the Spanish retained their colonies in Mexico and Central and South America, while the West Indies ended up as a mosaic of colonial settlement.

The cultivation of sugar, tobacco and other crops on the plantations of the Americas depended on slave labour. At first the Spanish tried to enslave the indigenous inhabitants of the West Indies, but within a matter of decades these peoples were wiped out by a combination of brutal treatment and European diseases to which they had no resistance. Thus began the great demand for African slaves, kick-starting the so-called triangular or Atlantic trade, by which slaves were taken from West Africa to the plantations of the Americas, American raw materials were transported to Europe, and European manufactured goods were sent both to the American colonies and to West Africa to purchase more slaves.

In the 17th and 18th centuries, most of the colonizing was carried out by government-chartered trading companies such as the British East India Company, founded in 1600, and its Dutch and French equivalents. A patent 'for the inhabiting and planting of our people in America' was granted by Queen Elizabeth I of England to Sir Walter Raleigh in 1584, and various

1532–5	1600	1602	1607	1652	1652–74
Spanish conquest of Inca empire in Peru	Foundation of British East India Company	Foundation of Dutch East India Company	Virginia Company founds colony at Jamestown, first permanent English settlement in America	Dutch establish colony at Cape Town	Anglo–Dutch wars over trade: England ousts Dutch from North America and West Africa

A new use for the colonies

The first European settlers of Australia – claimed for Great Britain by Captain James Cook in 1770 – were convicted criminals. Since the early 18th century, in the absence of a prison system, Britain had sent the convicts it did not hang to its American colonies to work on the plantations. But with American independence, Britain had to look elsewhere, and in 1788 the 'First Fleet', carrying hundreds of felons, arrived in New South Wales to establish a penal colony. Transportation continued for several more decades, and freed convicts were to play an important role in building the foundations of Australia's economy.

attempts were made to colonize the eastern seaboard until the first permanent settlement was established by the Virginia Company in 1607.

European governments at this period saw the creation of such settlements as a means of benefiting the mother country. This theory, known as 'mercantilism', was outlined by the great French *Encyclopédie* of 1751–68, which stated that colonies were established 'solely for the use of the metropolis [i.e. the mother country]', that they therefore 'should be immediately dependent upon it and consequently protected by it', and that the colonies 'should trade exclusively with the founders'. What the mercantilists did not recognize was the cost of defending by armed force the mother country's monopoly on trade to and from its colonies. It took Adam Smith, in his groundbreaking economic work *The Wealth of Nations* (1776), to recognize the truth: 'Under the present system of management . . . Great Britain derives nothing but loss from the dominion which she assumes over her colonies.'

The imperial mission In the 19th century, a new attitude began to emerge. Colonization was not to be undertaken merely for commercial reasons, but for the high moral purpose of spreading the benefits of Western civilization to peoples regarded as godless savages or as children in need of discipline and guidance. In Britain, the new attitude emerged out of the evangelical revival of the later 18th century, and in the 19th century became intertwined with pseudo-scientific racial theories as to

timeline

1664	1740s	1754	1763	1776	1788
Foundation of French East India Company	Britain and France begin to fight each other in India	Beginning of French and Indian War in North America	Britain emerges victorious in Seven Years' War, gaining Canada and India	Declaration of Independence by Britain's colonies in North America	British establish penal settlement in New South Wales

the superiority of the white races over those of different colours. In the 18th century the 'nabobs' of the British East India Company, in it only for the money and a life of luxury and ease, had been content to adopt native ways and marry native wives – and even, in some cases, convert to native faiths. In contrast, the colonial administrators and missionaries of the Victorian era observed a strict apartheid between rulers and ruled, while at the same time making strenuous efforts to build churches, schools, courthouses, railways and other pillars of Western civilization. For the colonized, it was something of a mixed blessing, and beneath the veneer of pious intent, the colonizers were still in it for power and profit, and any dissent was dealt with by armed force.

Armed force was still the means by which empires were extended. In the scramble to carve up Africa in the later 19th century, the Europeans used their massive technological advantage to crush all resistance from the indigenous peoples, as did the white Americans as they spread westward across the North American continent. A new fervour of competition arose among the Western powers: more colonies meant more raw materials, and more markets for manufactured goods. Many talked in quasi-Darwinian terms of 'the survival of the fittest'. This drive for imperial domination was to contribute to the mutual mistrust and hostility that culminated in the outbreak of the First World War.

> ❛It is a noble work to plant the foot of England and extend her sceptre by the banks of streams unnamed, and over regions yet unknown . . . ❜
>
> *The Edinburgh Review,* vol. 41, 1850

in a nutshell
From the 16th century the European powers began to take over the rest of the world

1853	1857	1875–1900	1898	1899–1902	1918
US fleet forces Japan to open up to trade	Indian Mutiny against British rule	'Scramble for Africa': continent divided between European colonial powers	USA takes Philippines, Guam and Puerto Rico from Spain. US annexation of Hawaii.	British defeat Boers (Dutch settlers) in South Africa, and take over Boer republics	Defeat of Turkey and Germany in First World War; their empires are divided among the victors

26 The Enlightenment

The Enlightenment is the name given to the era of intellectual and critical ferment that began in Europe and America in the late 17th century and continued through the century that followed. During this period a diverse range of thinkers – known as the *philosophes* in France – sought to replace the blindly accepted beliefs of the past with rational thought and rational practice – in everything from political economy to the treatment of criminals.

The thinkers of the Enlightenment shared no coherent programme, and indeed many were in disagreement with each other, but all sought to challenge the hitherto unquestioned assumptions of tradition and prejudice, and aspired to lead humanity out of the dark of superstition and into the light of reason. Their outlook was broadly liberal and humanitarian, and in general they were critical of the repressiveness and dogmatism of the Roman Catholic Church, and condemned those rulers who displayed a disregard for the welfare of their subjects.

The primacy of reason The thinkers of the Enlightenment looked back to the Scientific Revolution of the 16th and 17th centuries as their inspiration. Copernicus, Kepler, Galileo and others had demonstrated the falsity of the church's teaching that the Earth was at the centre of the universe, and Newton had, by inference from observations, come up with a complete explanation of motion, from that of a cannon ball through the

timeline

1637	1686–7	1688–9	1690	1734	1740
Descartes outlines his system of methodical doubt in *Discourse on Method*	Newton states his laws of motion and gravitation in *Principia Mathematica*	Constitutional monarchy established in England	Locke states empiricist case in his *Essay Concerning Human Understanding*, and in *Two Treatises of Government* defends the right of a people to overthrow any ruler who fails to protect their rights	Voltaire champions English values and ideas in *Philosophical Letters*	Hume develops empiricist philosophy in his *Treatise of Human Nature*

air to a planet orbiting the Sun. This and other advances in experimental science in the later 17th century – which had both explanatory and predictive power – led to the triumph of empiricism over Cartesianism, the system of the French philosopher René Descartes (1596–1650). Descartes held that all knowledge gained via the senses is unreliable, and all that we can know for certain must be deduced from the basic irrefutable premise, 'I think therefore I am.' The principles of empiricism, which contradicted those of Cartesianism, were enunciated by the English philosopher John Locke in his *Essay Concerning Human Understanding* (1690). In this, Locke argued that humans have no innate ideas, but derive all knowledge from experience, via 'sensation' and 'reflection'. This was what constitutes reason, he argued, 'as contra-distinguished to Faith'.

Few of the thinkers of the Enlightenment were out-and-out atheists, but many were adherents of deism. Deists rejected the divine revelations and miracles of Christianity, proposing a God whose existence could be established by reason, rather than surmised by faith. Thus God was necessary as the 'first cause' that brought the universe into being, and it was God who had designed the stars and the planets to run like clockwork in the way described by Newton. This God had endowed humans with reason and free will, but otherwise stood back from his creation.

> **Écrasez l'infâme – [stamp out abuses]**
>
> **Voltaire,** letter to M. d'Alembert, 28 November 1762

The influence of the Enlightenment The ideas of the Enlightenment were spread amongst the intellectual elites of Europe and America by works such as Voltaire's *Philosophical Letters on the English* (1734), which discussed the ideas of Newton and Locke and expressed admiration for British liberties – in contrast to the autocracy of the *ancien régime* in his native France. The most important repository of Enlightenment thought, however, was the 28-volume French *Encyclopédie*, compiled under the direction of Denis Diderot between 1751 and 1772, which contained all the latest scientific and philosophical developments.

1740–86	1748	1751–72	1759	1762
Reign of Frederick the Great of Prussia	Montesquieu publishes *Spirit of the Laws*	Publication of the *Encyclopédie* in 28 volumes	Voltaire publishes *Candide*, a satirical fable	In his *Social Contract*, Rousseau states that sovereignty resides in the people as a whole, while in *Émile*, his novel about education, he expounds his idea that it is only society that corrupts innate human goodness

Some leading figures of the Enlightenment

- **John Locke** (1632–1704), English philosopher: popularized the idea of the 'social contract' between government and governed, and championed empiricism – the belief that knowledge is ultimately derived via the senses.

- **Voltaire** (François-Marie Arouet, 1694–1778), French writer and philosopher: popularized ideas of Locke and Newton; champion of liberty and toleration; known especially for his satirical novella *Candide*.

- **Denis Diderot** (1713–84), French philosopher: editor of and principal contributor to the *Encyclopédie* (1751–72); opponent of Christianity and proponent of materialism.

- **Montesquieu** (Charles Louis de Secondat, Baron de Montesquieu, 1689–1755), French philosopher and writer: his *Esprit des lois* (*Spirit of the Laws*, 1748) showed how systems of law and government varied from society to society, giving rise to the concept of cultural relativism.

- **Cesare Beccaria** (1738–94), Italian legal theorist: his *Crimes and Punishments* (1764) expounded the principles behind criminal law, called for the abolition of torture and capital punishment, and inspired many countries to reform their penal codes.

- **David Hume** (1711–76), Scottish philosopher and historian: continuing in the empiricist tradition, he rejected the existence of innate ideas, examined the psychological basis of human nature, and applied an extreme scepticism to everything from supposed miracles to the concept of cause and effect, which he regarded as a 'constant conjunction' rather than a logical inevitability.

- **Adam Smith** (1723–90), Scottish philosopher and economist: in *The Wealth of Nations* (1776) he espoused free trade as against monopoly and regulation, upheld the role of self-interest in the creation of a wealthier society, and demonstrated the economic advantages of the division of labour.

- **Jean-Jacques Rousseau** (1712–78), French philosopher and writer: he held that human nature is innately good, but spoiled by corrupt society. He increasingly opposed rationalism, championing the primacy of individual feeling.

timeline

1762–96	1764	1769	1773	1775–83	1776
Reign of Catherine the Great of Russia	Publication of Voltaire's *Philosophical Dictionary* and Beccaria's *Crimes and Punishments*	Dissolution of hundreds of monasteries in Austria	Suppression of the Jesuits	American Revolutionary War	American Declaration of Independence. Adam Smith states the case for free markets in his *Wealth of Nations*.

Among those taken with the fashionable ideas of the *philosophes* were a number of Europe's autocratic monarchs, including Catherine the Great of Russia, Frederick the Great of Prussia and Joseph II of Austria. All of these 'enlightened despots' sought to impose 'rational' reforms in their countries. There were limits to their enlightenment, however. Frederick may have liberalized the Prussian legal code and introduced social and economic reforms, but he also waged ruthless wars of conquest. Catherine too waged wars of territorial expansion, and abandoned her proposal to emancipate the serfs of Russia in the face of opposition by the serf-owners. Joseph did succeed in emancipating the serfs within the Holy Roman empire, but then proceeded to impose taxes on them. He also introduced religious toleration and reforms in education, the legal system and administration – some of which he had to withdraw in the face of opposition by certain groups whose privileges he threatened.

Of more enduring political consequence was the impact the language and ideas of Enlightenment thinkers had on some of the key documents of both the American and the French Revolutions, the American Declaration of Independence and the Bill of Rights. These documents include ideas that continue to dominate political discourse in Western liberal democracies: equality, individual rights, the idea that government only rules with the consent of the governed, religious toleration and due process of law.

in a nutshell
The Enlightenment helped to establish the values of modern liberal democracies

1780–90	1788	1789	1791
Reign of Joseph II of Austria	Ratification of US Constitution	Beginning of French Revolution and drafting of Declaration of the Rights of Man and of the Citizen	Ratification of US Bill of Rights (first ten amendments to the Constitution)

27 The American Revolution

The American Revolution was more than just the war of independence that the American colonists fought against British rule between 1775 and 1783. It began with the resentments expressed by the colonists against the taxes and restrictions placed upon them by the British, and continued through the conflict itself to the postwar debates by which the independent United States decided what kind of country it was going to be.

The mutual antipathy that arose between the colonists and their rulers back in London had its origins in two very different views of what the colonies were for. To the British government, colonies existed entirely for the benefit of the mother country, and should make a financial contribution to their own defence. To the colonists, who had no voice in the Westminster Parliament, this was a negation of natural justice. The unwillingness of King George III and his ministers back in London to compromise made conflict inevitable.

Rumblings of discontent During the French and Indian War (the North American component of the Seven Years' War; see p. 101), the vast majority of the American colonists regarded themselves as loyal subjects of the Crown, and many – including George Washington – fought for the British against the French. Although the war had ended in 1763 with British victory, it had proved enormously costly, and Parliament determined that the colonists should henceforth pay for their own

timeline

1754–63	1763	1764	1765	1766
French and Indian War	British prohibit settlement beyond the Appalachians	British prohibit colonies from issuing their own paper money	Quartering Act requires some of the colonies to provision British garrisons. Stamp Act introduces stamp duty on all legal documents.	Parliament repeals Stamp Act, but passes Declaratory Act, proclaiming its right to levy taxes on the colonies

defence via taxation. It introduced a number of measures to this effect, and also prohibited settlement west of the Appalachians, to prevent further expensive conflict with Native American peoples. This prohibition and the Stamp Act of 1765 – introducing a stamp duty on legal documents and other transactions – provoked particular anger amongst the colonists, who had been used to a fair measure of self-government via their colonial assemblies. They argued that, given they were not represented in the British Parliament, only their own assemblies should have tax-raising powers – hence their slogan, 'No taxation without representation.' In the face of extensive agitation, Parliament repealed the Stamp Act, but still proclaimed its right to tax the American subjects of the Crown, and proceeded to levy duties on a variety of goods imported into the colonies.

> **❝The Revolution was in the minds of the people . . . before a drop of blood was shed at Lexington.❞**
>
> **Former President John Adams,** letter to Thomas Jefferson, **24 August 1815**

As the political temperature rose, many Americans began to adopt a radical new ideology in which they declared that their liberties as 'free-born Englishmen' were being threatened by a corrupt tyranny. In 1770 Parliament withdrew all the import duties except that on tea, and then in 1773, in order to help the struggling East India Company, dumped a large quantity of tea – still with its controversial duty – on the American market. This provoked the famous Boston Tea Party, in which a group of 'patriots', as they now called themselves, dressed themselves up as Native Americans, boarded the ship carrying the tea and threw its cargo into Boston harbour.

The Revolutionary War When Britain imposed repressive measures against Massachusetts (the colony where the Tea Party had taken place), delegates from the colonies came together in the First Continental Congress and voted to ban all imports from Britain. Confrontation turned to military conflict on 19 April 1775 when British troops in search of a cache of weapons were confronted at Lexington, near Boston, by armed farmers, and shots were exchanged.

1767	**1770**	**1773**	**1774**	**1775**
Townshend Revenue Act imposes duties on various imports into the colonies	Parliament repeals all Townshend duties except that on tea. Boston Massacre: a number of citizens are shot while demonstrating outside the headquarters of the customs service.	Dumping of Indian tea on American market provokes Boston Tea Party	Intolerable Acts introduce repressive measures against Massachusetts. First Continental Congress begins to meet.	Fighting breaks out at Lexington and Concord. George Washington becomes commander of the Continental Army. Americans claim victory at Bunker Hill. Second Continental Congress begins to meet.

As far as King George and his government were concerned, the colonists were now traitors, and a large force of British troops and German mercenaries was dispatched across the Atlantic to deal with the rebellion. As open warfare began, a Second Continental Congress assembled in September 1775. By the following summer it had reached a momentous decision, and on 4 July 1776 it endorsed the Declaration of Independence.

Declaring independence was not the same as achieving it. The British had at their command a disciplined, well-armed force, and a large number of Americans remained loyal to the Crown. However, the rag-tag of patriot militias had the advantage of knowing the terrain, and were forged into an effective fighting force by their commander-in-chief, George Washington. They could also be resupplied locally, whereas the British depended on much longer supply lines. The decisive American victory at Saratoga in 1777 encouraged the French to join in against their old enemy, the British, and in 1781 a large British force besieged by Washington's army and a French fleet in Yorktown was forced to surrender. Two years later, Britain recognized US independence at the Treaty of Paris, formally ending the war.

> **The tree of liberty must be refreshed from time to time with the blood of patriots and tyrants. It is its natural manure.**
>
> **Thomas Jefferson,** letter to W. S. Smith, 13 November 1787

Creating a new country Having achieved the independence of the United States, as the thirteen former British colonies now became, the question now arose as to what kind of country it was going to be. At first there was no strong central government, the states being reluctant to exchange one tyranny for another. The Second Continental Congress had drafted Articles of Confederation providing for a union between the states, but this was not adopted until 1781, when the Confederation Congress came into being. The states remained reluctant to surrender any powers to central government, and the Confederation Congress had no tax-raising powers. Two opposing factions arose: federalists, who saw the need for a strong central

timeline

1776	1777	1780	1781	1783	1786
Thomas Paine's radically anti-monarchical pamphlet *Common Sense* becomes a best-seller. Congress adopts Declaration of Independence.	Americans achieve decisive victory at Saratoga	Pennsylvania abolishes slavery, followed by several other northern states	British surrender at Yorktown. Articles of Confederation establish weak central government run by Confederation Congress.	Treaty of Paris ends war; Britain recognizes US independence	Shays's Rebellion in Massachusetts against high taxes and foreclosures

government to deal with external threats and internal disorder, and anti-federalists, who saw central government as threatening the rights of the states and the liberties of individual citizens. To resolve these difficulties, a Constitutional Convention was assembled in Philadelphia in 1787 to thrash out a new federal constitution.

What eventually emerged provided for a stronger central government, but with its powers separated between the executive (the president), the legislature (Congress) and the judiciary, and balanced and checked by the powers of the states and the people. The US Constitution was ratified in 1788, and to mollify the anti-federalists the Bill of Rights, comprising the first ten amendments to the Constitution, was adopted. Among other things this guaranteed freedom of religion, speech and the press, upheld due process of law, and reserved to the states all powers not specifically assigned to the federal government. However, neither the Constitution nor the Bill of Rights resolved the issue that was to tear the country apart over the following decades – the issue as to whether slavery was to be allowed to continue in any part of the Union.

The Declaration of Independence

The job of drafting the Declaration of Independence was given by Congress to a young Virginian planter called Thomas Jefferson, who was later to become the third president of the USA. Its sentiments, justifying rebellion against tyranny, still ring down the centuries: 'We hold these truths to be self-evident, that all men are created equal; that they are endowed by their Creator with inherent and inalienable rights; that among these, are life, liberty, and the pursuit of happiness . . .'

in a nutshell
A novel experiment in nation-building

1787	1787–8	1788	1789	1791
Constitutional Convention begins to meet	James Madison, Alexander Hamilton and John Jay put federalist case in *Federalist Papers*	US Constitution ratified	George Washington becomes first president of the USA	Bill of Rights ratified

28 The French Revolution

The shots fired at Lexington and Concord that sparked off the American Revolutionary War in 1775 may – in the words of Ralph Waldo Emerson – have been 'heard round the world', but it was the fall of the Bastille in Paris in 1789, and the upheavals that followed, that was to set all Europe ablaze. The French Revolution not only toppled France's own monarchy, it threatened all the other monarchies of the *ancien régime* in Europe and led to decades of warfare as the forces of reaction attempted to slay what they regarded as the monster in their midst.

The roots of the French Revolution go back to the time of Louis XIV, whose long reign lasted from 1643 to 1715. During Louis's minority, France had been racked by civil wars between various aristocratic factions, and once Louis began to rule in his own right in 1661 he determined to end the power of the nobility and centralize all power in himself, famously declaring '*L'État c'est moi*' – 'I am the state.' The aristocracy were obliged to spend most of their time at court, living in Louis's magnificent new palace at Versailles, outside Paris. Here, far from their provincial power bases, they were not in a position to raise rebellions against the king. However, cocooned in isolated luxury, both the nobility and the royal family were distanced from the common people and their growing grievances.

timeline

1776	1777	1781	1788	1789
Anne-Robert-Jacques Turgot, Louis XVI's finance minister, is dismissed after attempting to introduce reforms	France joins American colonists in war against Britain	Jacques Necker, Turgot's successor as finance minister, resigns after his proposed reforms are rejected	Economic crisis leads to recall of Necker	**MAY** Necker persuades Louis to summon the Estates-General. **JUNE** Third Estate declares itself to be the National Assembly. **JULY** Mob storms Bastille. **AUGUST** National Assembly issues Declaration of the Rights of Man.

Economic mismanagement and growing discontent

Louis XIV had further sought to neutralize aristocratic dissent by exempting the nobility from paying taxes, the burden of which thus fell upon the peasantry and the bourgeoisie. This burden steadily increased through the 18th century as France flexed its muscles on the world stage, fighting a number of wars to maintain its position in Europe and to build and defend its overseas empire. In this last ambition it was largely unsuccessful, losing Canada and India to Britain in the Seven Years' War, which ended in 1763. The economy was also weakened by the extensive system, flowing down from the Crown, of patronage and monopolies, which stifled trade and industry.

Louis XIV's successor, Louis XV, proved a weak and indecisive ruler, dominated by his mistresses; and the faction, intrigue and corruption that swirled around the court as a consequence brought the monarchy into increasing disrepute. Things only got worse under the inept and lacklustre Louis XVI, who came to the throne in 1774. Louis's decision to give military support to the Americans in their struggle for independence from Britain, although successful in that aim, brought France to the brink of bankruptcy. The attempts of Louis's finance ministers to introduce economic reforms were thwarted by opposition from the aristocracy and Louis's own wife, Marie-Antoinette.

The events of 1789 Things came
to a head in May 1789, when, in order to resolve the economic crisis, Louis was persuaded to summon – for the first time since 1614 – the Estates-General, the

Marie-Antoinette

Louis XVI's wife, the Austrian princess Marie-Antoinette, was widely criticized by anti-monarchists for her perceived extravagance and lack of sympathy for her impoverished subjects (although it is unlikely that she ever actually said 'Let them eat cake' when told that the people had no bread to eat). Scurrilous rumours abounded, especially about her supposedly insatiable sexual appetites – as in America, those of a republican bent adopted the language of 'virtue', pointing out the decadence and depravity of their oppressors.

1791

JUNE Louis and his family attempt to flee France. **AUGUST** Prussia and Austria threaten to intervene in support of Louis. **SEPTEMBER** Louis accepts new constitution. **OCTOBER** National Assembly replaced by Legislative Assembly, which urges war against Austria.

1792

SEPTEMBER Austro-Prussian invasion defeated at Valmy. New National Convention declares France a republic. **NOVEMBER** Radical Jacobins led by Danton oust moderate Girondist government. **DECEMBER** Louis put on trial.

> **❝The fundamental source of all sovereignty lies in the nation . . . The law is the expression of the general will.❞**
>
> **Declaration of the Rights of Man and of the Citizen,** August 1789

assembly representing the three estates: the clergy, the nobility and the bourgeoisie. The second estate, the nobility, proved unwilling to consider any kind of change, giving the initiative to the third estate, the bourgeoisie, the middle classes, whose commercial ambitions had been thwarted by unfair taxes, restrictions on trade and economic mismanagement. The third estate declared itself to be the National Assembly, and when the king sent troops to Paris, seemingly in a move against this rebellious new body, the mob stormed the Bastille (a fortress holding a number of political prisoners) in order to seize arms in its defence. The French Revolution was underway.

The revolutionaries in Paris and elsewhere established a National Guard to defend the National Assembly. Meanwhile, the army was divided, and did nothing. The National Assembly set about abolishing the privileges of the aristocracy, and in August issued the Declaration of the Rights of Man and of the Citizen, which asserted the liberty and equality of all men. In October, Louis and his family were obliged to leave Versailles and take up residence in Paris, where they would be close to the people to whom they were now accountable.

The bloodbath After a failed attempt to flee the country in 1791, Louis was brought back to Paris and forced to give his agreement to the new constitution, which severely limited his powers. These developments did not go unnoticed among the other countries of Europe, most of which remained absolute monarchies. In August 1791 Leopold II of Austria and the king of Prussia jointly declared that they would not rule out armed intervention in support of the French king, and in December Louis himself was writing to a number of crowned heads suggesting concerted military action 'as the best means of putting a stop to the factions here'.

timeline

1793

JANUARY Louis executed. **FEBRUARY** France annexes Austrian Netherlands. Britain, Austria, Prussia, Netherlands, Spain and Sardinia form coalition against France. **MARCH** Outbreak of anti-revolutionary revolt in the Vendée region. **JULY** Beginning of Reign of Terror. **OCTOBER** Execution of Marie-Antoinette. **DECEMBER** Vendée revolt crushed.

1794

APRIL Danton executed. **JULY** Robespierre overthrown and executed, ending Reign of Terror.

In August 1792 the Austrians and Prussians invaded, with the stated intent of restoring Louis to his full power. The invaders were driven back at Valmy, and the revolutionaries then turned on their fellow Frenchmen, massacring hundreds of suspected counter-revolutionaries. In November, France was declared a republic, and the following year Louis and his queen were convicted of treason and sent to the guillotine.

This was just the beginning. In the face of further foreign threats and internal revolts, the Jacobins – the radical faction – eclipsed the moderate Girondin party and established a virtual dictatorship under the Committee of Public Safety, dominated by Maximilien Robespierre. In the subsequent 'Reign of Terror', tens of thousands of suspected counter-revolutionaries were guillotined. This bloodbath only came to an end when Robespierre himself was overthrown in a coup in July 1794 and executed.

The excesses of the Terror so alarmed governments in other European countries such as Britain that any calls for political or social reform at home were regarded as both dangerous and treasonable, and ruthlessly crushed. The progressive spirit of the Enlightenment, which had helped to fuel the revolutions in both France and America, was snuffed out by a renewed mood of fear and reaction. In France itself, political turmoil continued through the 1790s, until stable government was restored by a fiercely ambitious young army officer called Napoleon Bonaparte.

> **❝When the last king is hanged with the bowels of the last priest, the human race can hope for happiness.❞**
>
> *La Bouche de fer* **[The Iron Mouth], a revolutionary journal, 11 July 1791**

in a nutshell
Established the principles of liberté, égalité and fraternité, but at the cost of much bloodshed

1795	1796–7	1798	1799
Batavian Republic established by local radicals in the Netherlands with the aid of Revolutionary France. National Convention replaced by the Directory of Five.	Napoleon Bonaparte defeats Austrians in Italy. French establish 'sister' republics in northern Italy.	Establishment of republics in Rome and Switzerland	Bonaparte takes power in France as 'first consul'

29 The Napoleonic era

'What will history say?' Napoleon once asked. 'What will posterity think?' Both his contemporaries and those who came after him were divided in their judgements of Napoleon Bonaparte, the young Corsican artillery officer who became Napoleon I, Emperor of the French, and ruler of the largest empire in Europe since the days of the Romans.

In France itself Napoleon is still widely revered, and his burial place in Les Invalides in Paris has become a shrine to that most sacred of French sentiments, *la gloire*. Beyond the frontiers of France, many – particularly in the 19th century – hailed him as a colossus, the archetype of the 'great man', who through sheer energy and willpower came to straddle the globe. Others denigrated him as a vainglorious tyrant who in the name of liberty would have reduced the whole world to slavery.

From brigadier to emperor The two and a half decades of European conflict known as the Revolutionary and Napoleonic Wars commenced in August 1792, when Austria and Prussia attacked Revolutionary France. Britain and other European allies joined in the following year, and it was in December 1793 that Napoleon Bonaparte first came to national prominence, when he played a leading role in the recapture of the naval port of Toulon from the British. Bonaparte was promoted to the rank of brigadier general – aged only twenty-four.

timeline

1792	1793	1796	1797	1798
Austro-Prussian invasion of Revolutionary France repelled at Valmy	France annexes Austrian Netherlands (modern Belgium). British defeated at Toulon.	Bonaparte defeats Austrians in Italy. Savoy and Nice ceded to France. French establish Lombard Republic in northern Italy.	Bonaparte scores further victories in northern Italy, where French proclaim Cisalpine Republic and Ligurian Republic	Establishment of 'sister' republics in Rome and Switzerland (Helvetian Republic). French fleet defeated by British under Horatio Nelson at Battle of the Nile.

Subsequently Bonaparte became involved in internal upheavals, quelling a royalist mob in Paris in October 1795 with his famous 'whiff of grapeshot'. He went on to conduct a brilliant campaign against the Austrians in Italy in 1796–7, obliging the Austrians to hand over the Austrian Netherlands (modern Belgium) to France. Although his campaign in Egypt in 1798 ended in defeat at the hands of the British, his star in France remained in the ascendant, and in November 1799 he seized power as 'first consul', with virtually dictatorial powers. After a brief period of peace in 1802–3, the war continued, and in 1804 Bonaparte horrified many of his republican admirers around the world when he declared himself to be the Emperor Napoleon I. He had rightly calculated that his military successes against the enemies of France had earned him sufficient popularity at home, not least in the army, to make such a bold step.

Although his intention of invading Britain was thwarted by Nelson's fleet at Trafalgar in 1805, Napoleon was triumphant on the continent of Europe, inflicting defeat after defeat on the Austrians, Russians and Prussians. By 1809 they had all made peace with France, leaving Britain to fight on alone. Much of western, southern and central Europe was now under Napoleon's control – as a part of the French empire, or as a kingdom ruled by one of his family (as in Spain and Naples), or as a dependent state – such as the Confederation of the Rhine, established by Napoleon in Germany to replace the Holy Roman empire.

> **❝So he too is nothing but a man. Now he also will trample all human rights underfoot, and only pander to his own ambition; he will place himself above everyone else and become a tyrant.❞**
>
> **Ludwig van Beethoven,** on hearing that the hero and defender of the French Republic had made himself emperor, May 1804. Beethoven tore up the title page of his third symphony, with its dedication to Napoleon, and renamed it the Eroica.

1799	1800	1802	1803	1804	1805
Bonaparte takes power in France as first consul	Bonaparte defeats Austrians at Marengo, establishing French dominance in Italy	France makes peace with Britain and its allies	Resumption of hostilities in Europe	Bonaparte becomes Emperor Napoleon I	Napoleon defeats Austrians at Ulm and occupies Vienna. Nelson defeats French and Spanish fleet at Trafalgar. Napoleon defeats Austrians and Russians at Austerlitz.

Napoleon as a commander

Napoleon's effectiveness as a general lay in a combination of factors. These included an ability to keep the enemy guessing as to his intentions, followed by a sudden concentrated strike at the enemy's weakest point. Such tactics required a mastery of manoeuvre and rapid deployment, combined with flexible logistics. France had responded to the outbreak of the Revolutionary Wars by conscripting a massive citizen army, and with a huge reserve of conscripts at his disposal, Napoleon could afford to expend men: 'You can't stop me,' he once boasted to the foreign minister of Austria, Count Metternich, 'I spend 30,000 men a month.' Despite this callousness, his troops held *l'Empereur* in reverence, not least because he recognized talent over privilege, and promoted many men from the ranks, most famously Marshal Ney.

Folie de grandeur Napoleon's imposition of his brother Joseph as king of Spain in 1808 proved to be a costly mistake, bogging down large numbers of French troops in a brutal war against Spanish guerrilla forces. Napoleon made an even bigger misjudgement in 1812, when he decided to invade Russia. The French *Grande Armée*, although defeating the Russians at Borodino, found itself ill-equipped to deal with the freezing Russian winter, and found it could not follow its usual practice of living off the land, as the Russians had conducted a ruthless scorched-earth policy as they retreated towards Moscow. Nearly half a million French soldiers had begun the campaign; less than one-tenth returned.

The Russian disaster persuaded Prussia and Austria to again ally themselves with Britain against Napoleon. They scored a major victory at Leipzig in 1813, and the following year the Duke of Wellington, who had been fighting the French for years in the Iberian Peninsula, led his British forces over the border into France itself. With Paris in the hands of the allies, Napoleon abdicated and went into exile on the island of Elba, off the coast of Italy. The restored French monarchy was not popular, however, and Napoleon returned from exile to try one more throw of the dice. The French army rallied around him, and in June 1815 faced the British and the Prussians at Waterloo. It was, in Wellington's words, 'a close-run thing', but Napoleon was defeated, captured and sent into exile on the remote island of St Helena in the South Atlantic. He never returned.

timeline

1806	1807	1808	1809
Creation of French-dominated Confederation of the Rhine. French defeat Prussians at Jena and Auerstädt. Napoleon makes his brother Joseph king of Naples and his other brother Louis king of the United Provinces (the Netherlands).	Russians and Prussians make peace with Napoleon. French invade Portugal.	French invade Spain; Napoleon's brother Joseph installed as king. British under Wellington intervene, beginning Peninsular War.	Napoleon defeats Austrians at Wagram. French annex Papal States. Wellington defeats French at Tallavera.

The impact of Napoleon Maximilien Robespierre, before engineering the Great Terror, had warned his fellow citizens against one of their victorious generals establishing a 'legal dictatorship'. This is precisely what Napoleon did in 1799, although he declared at the time he seized power that 'the Revolution is established upon its original principles: it is consummated'. Although Napoleon's rule was far from liberal – he believed, for example, that freedom of the press made the job of governing impossible, and dealt ruthlessly with his domestic political opponents – he did preserve some of the values of the French Revolution, which he feared was degenerating into anarchy. His most enduring legacy was the Napoleonic Code, a system of civil law rolled out across his empire and its dependent states and allies. This embodied many of the values of the Revolution and the Enlightenment, including equality (although not, in Napoleon's version, for women), individual liberty, separation of church and state, and religious toleration. To this day, the Napoleonic Code provides the model for many civil law codes in Europe and around the world.

> **❝Conquest has made me what I am; only conquest can maintain me.❞**
>
> **Napoleon Bonaparte,**
> **30 December 1802**

Following Napoleon's defeat, the victorious allies sought to undo the new dispensation, restoring the old, absolutist monarchies and empires that cut across ethnic boundaries. After 1815, the forces of reaction in power across Europe did all they could to extinguish the radical and nationalist aspirations that had been kindled by the French Revolution. But after decades of repression, these were to burst into flames once more in 1848.

in a nutshell
Whether as tyrant or liberator, Napoleon transformed Europe

1812	**1813**	**1814**	**1815**
Napoleon's disastrous Russian campaign. Outbreak of War of 1812 between Britain and USA over British interdiction of US trade with France.	British defeat French at Vitoria. Napoleon defeated at 'Battle of the Nations' at Leipzig. British enter France. US forces defeat British at Battle of the Thames in Ontario.	Allies occupy France; Napoleon exiled to Elba. Congress of Vienna assembles to work out terms of the peace. British burn Washington DC.	US forces defeat British at New Orleans, not having heard that peace had been agreed. Napoleon returns to France, but is defeated at Waterloo.

30 The Industrial Revolution

In the century and a half after 1750, the economies and societies of much of Europe and North America were completely transformed. Whereas wealth had previously been predominantly grounded in land, it increasingly flowed out of industry, whether mining or manufacturing, both of which were revolutionized by new technologies.

There was a massive growth in towns and cities, as people flocked from the countryside to work in the new factories. In so doing, many exchanged rural poverty for urban degradation and squalor – a phenomenon that can still be witnessed in many newly industrialized countries around the world. But the transformation also created a new managerial and entrepreneurial middle class, who gained more and more political power at the expense of the old landed aristocracy.

The Industrial Revolution began in Britain and then spread to other parts of Europe and the USA. Various factors contributed to Britain becoming the first country to undergo widespread industrialization. First of all, there was a large accumulation of capital for investment in new enterprises. This derived both from wealthy landowners who had improved their estates and thereby increased their profits, and from Britain's increasing dominance of world trade – particularly the Atlantic trade, where fortunes were made out of slaves, sugar, tobacco and other commodities. Britain had by the middle of the 18th century acquired an extensive overseas trading empire,

timeline

1709	1712	1730	1760	1768	1769
Abraham Darby builds coke-fired blast furnace to produce cast iron	Thomas Newcomen invents first practical steam engine	Jethro Tull invents seed drill, a device for sowing seeds efficiently. Around this time 'Turnip' Townshend introduces four-crop rotation.	Beginning of canal-building boom in Britain	Richard Arkwright patents 'water frame', water-powered spinning machine	James Watt improve Newcomen's steam engine, giving major boost to Industrial Revolution

which not only provided such raw materials, but also a growing market for manufactured goods. Also of importance in Britain's industrial growth was its physical geography, with its extensive shoreline with plenty of natural harbours giving access to overseas markets, its many navigable rivers and its reserves of coal and iron ore in close proximity.

Mechanization and the factory system Mechanization was the key that unlocked the Industrial Revolution. In the pre-industrial period, manufacturing had been carried out by self-employed individuals in their homes, or in small workshops in which a master-craftsman oversaw the work of journeymen and apprentices. Commonly, one person would undertake all the tasks involved in producing an item, from start to finish. However, in *The Wealth of Nations* (1776) the pioneering economist Adam Smith had pointed out the inefficiencies of this craft-based approach. Taking the example of a pin factory, Smith said that one man working alone would struggle to complete one pin a day, whereas if ten different workers each undertook one stage in the process, the factory might produce 48,000 pins a day. Such a division of labour, Smith argued, also encouraged the development of new machinery.

In Britain the textile industry (based on home-grown wool and imported American cotton) witnessed a string of innovations to mechanize spinning and weaving. The self-employed hand-loom weavers could not compete with the new factories with their new machines, and were obliged to

> **❛The race that lives in these ruinous cottages . . . or in dark, wet cellars, in measureless filth and stench . . . this race must really have reached the lowest stage of humanity.❜**
>
> **Friedrich Engels, in *The Condition of the Working Class in England,* 1845, describes life for the many in Manchester, one of the great industrial cities of Britain**

1776	**1779**	**1781**	**1785**	**1793**	**1804**
Adam Smith outlines free-market capitalism in *The Wealth of Nations*	Samuel Crompton invents the spinning mule, the standard spinning machine for over a century. Cast-iron bridge built over River Severn.	Watt adds rotary motion to steam engine	Edmund Cartwright patents power loom. Steam power first used in cotton mills.	Eli Whitney improves cotton gin, for separating seeds from fibres	Richard Trevithick builds first working steam locomotive

The Agricultural Revolution

Another kind of revolution was in progress alongside the Industrial Revolution. In the 18th century the whole way that food was produced began to be placed on a more rational footing – partly under the influence of Enlightenment thinking. However, agricultural improvement had a human cost. In Britain large areas of common land were 'enclosed' by wealthy landowners, who obtained the legal right to do so via their friends in Parliament. The people who had worked this common land were evicted, leading to terrible suffering in places such as the Scottish Highlands, where humans were cleared from the land to make way for a more profitable animal – the sheep. Similar developments occurred elsewhere in Europe.

But with large areas of land now under their control, wealthy landowners could introduce scientific improvements, such as four-field crop rotation, selective breeding (especially of animals) and the use of new crops such as turnips to keep animals alive during the winter, rather than slaughtering most of them at the end of autumn. Technology, particularly in the realm of mechanization, also played a key role: notable innovations ranged from Jethro Tull's seed drill of 1730 to John Deere's steel plough of 1837, which made it possible to farm the hard soils of the US Midwest for the first time. The increased food production that resulted from these improvements made it possible to feed the growing numbers of people, both in Europe and North America, who worked in factories rather than on the land.

surrender their independence and go to work for the mill-owners in return for pitiful wages. In some places, disgruntled weavers – known as Luddites – smashed the new machines. When caught, the leaders of this agitation were either executed or transported to Australia.

The Steam Age Initially, the new machinery was powered by water mills, but with improvements in the steam engine, coal became the principal source of power. Coal (in the form of coke) also provided the heat necessary for smelting iron ore, and the burgeoning demand for coal led to the exploitation of deeper and deeper seams.

timeline

1811–12	1812	1821	1823	1825	1829
Outbreak of machine-wrecking in England	Henry Bell builds the *Comet*, the first working paddle steamer	Michael Faraday demonstrates electric motor	British government adopts the improved road-building technique pioneered by John McAdam	First public steam line opened between Stockton and Darlington. Thomas Telford completes suspension bridge over Menai Strait.	Robert Stephenson's *Rocket* locomotive achieves 58 kph (36 mph), encouraging railway development elsewhere

One of the biggest impacts of coal and steam was on transport. For centuries, bulk goods had been moved by boat on rivers and coastal waters rather than by road, as roads were poorly maintained and often, especially in winter, impassable. The 18th century witnessed a massive expansion of waterborne transport, in the form of new networks of canals linked into the existing natural waterways. Although there was also at the same time a major programme of road improvement, the most significant revolution in transport was the coming of the railways, heralded by the opening of the Stockton and Darlington line in 1825. Soon networks of railways were proliferating all over Europe, North America and elsewhere. The railways made possible the cheap bulk carriage not only of goods, but also of passengers, giving rise both to commuting, as cities grew ever larger, and to a widening of horizons, as people could travel further and further afield. A similar impact was experienced once steam power was applied to ships, making transatlantic travel, for example, almost routine.

In its turn, steam power began to be superseded by electricity and the internal combustion engine. In the later 19th century, Britain's economic rivals, Germany and the USA, were more effective in adopting these new technologies, allowing them to pull ahead. By the beginning of the 20th century, the USA had become the world's leading industrial power.

❝We remove mountains, and make seas our smooth highway; nothing can resist us.❞

Thomas Carlyle puts a positive spin on technological advance in *Signs of the Times*, 1829

in a nutshell
The Industrial Revolution created a new prosperity, but at a human cost

1839	1840s	1843	1844	1857	1869	1908
Charles Goodyear invents process for vulcanizing rubber	Railway boom in Europe	Isambard Kingdom Brunel builds the *Great Britain*, first large ship driven by screw propellers	Samuel Morse transmits first message by telegraph	Bessemer process enables cheap production of mild steel	Completion of Union Pacific Railroad, first transcontinental rail link across USA	Henry Ford begins mass automobile production with his Model T

31 Nationalism in Europe

The 19th century saw great changes in the political map of Europe, of comparable significance to the economic and social transformation wrought by the Industrial Revolution. In the south-east of the continent, a number of new countries emerged as the old empire of the Ottoman Turks began to disintegrate (see p. 79), while in central and southern Europe two powerful new states were created: Italy and Germany.

These new states were based on ethnicity, and in the 19th century more and more people defined themselves by their ethnic or national identity, principally based on the language they spoke. In order to shore up this identity, many creative artists of the period celebrated an often mythologized past and drew extensively on folk music and folk tales, thus helping to create what were often new national 'traditions'.

Although in western Europe, nation-states such as Britain and France had been long established, elsewhere on the continent the picture, at the end of the Napoleonic Wars in 1815, was very different. Germany was a patchwork of mostly minor principalities, largely dominated by Austria. Austria's own empire included Poles, Czechs, Slovaks, Hungarians, Slovenes, Croats and Italians, as well as German-speakers. Italy, like Germany, had no political unity, being merely – in the words of Prince Metternich, the Austrian foreign minister – 'a geographical expression'.

timeline

1798	1804–13	1814–15	1820	1821–9	1825
United Irishmen revolt against British rule in Ireland	Successful Serb revolt against Turkish rule	Congress of Vienna restores *anciens régimes* across Europe	Liberal and nationalist revolts in Spain, Portugal and Naples	Greek War of Independence against Turkey	Decembrist revolt in Russia

The Revolutions of 1848 The defeat of Napoleon in 1815, and the restoration of the old absolutist monarchies and empires, put a lid on the hopes that had been raised by the French Revolution. The burgeoning middle classes, their wealth deriving from commerce and industry, had hoped for greater political power at the expense of the old landed aristocracy, and thus many espoused the cause of liberalism – whereby the power of the absolute monarchs would be replaced by a constitution and a legislative assembly in which they would be represented. In those parts of Europe where people found themselves under a foreign ruler, calls for constitutional reform often coincided with demands for the right of national self-determination.

After a number of abortive uprisings in the preceding decades, in 1848 revolutions broke out in many parts of Europe. The unrest started in France, where, as elsewhere, there was also a socialist element involved, as the peasantry and the urban working class found themselves not only disenfranchised but suffering from hunger and unemployment. The French king was deposed, and the Second Republic declared.

Uprisings followed in Germany, Czech-speaking Bohemia, Poland, Italy, Hungary, Sicily and even in Vienna itself. In the Austrian-dominated German Confederation, nationalists formed the Frankfurt Parliament, which called for liberal reforms and German unification. In Prussia, King Frederick William IV was obliged to agree to the creation of a constitution and a national assembly, and to support the goal of German unification, while in the Austrian empire, the Bohemians and Hungarians achieved a measure of independence. Constitutions were also granted in a number of the Italian states. It was, many thought, 'the springtime of the peoples'.

But many of these gains were short-lived. In France, the Second Republic was overthrown in 1851 in a coup by the nephew of Napoleon I, Louis-Napoléon Bonaparte, who declared himself to be the Emperor Napoleon III.

1830	**1831, 1834**	**1832–4**	**1848–9**	**1859**	**1860**
Revolution in France creates conservative constitutional monarchy under Louis Philippe. Belgian revolt leads to independence from Netherlands. Polish revolt against Russian rule.	Unsuccessful revolts by radical democratic 'Young Italy' movement led by Giuseppe Mazzini	Left-wing revolts suppressed in France	Revolutions across Europe	Austrians defeated at Magenta and Solferino and expelled from Lombardy	Garibaldi liberates Sicily and Naples

Bismarck's wars

Bismarck's first territorial acquisition for Prussia was Schleswig-Holstein, control of which had long been disputed with Denmark. In 1864 he made a temporary alliance with Austria and then attacked and defeated Denmark. Two years later he provoked the Seven Weeks' War with Austria, and the defeat of the latter left Prussia as the pre-eminent power in northern Germany. Bismarck's final move was to play on the insecurities of the independent southern German states, who were fearful of falling victim to Napoleon III's military adventurism. To bring them on side, Bismarck goaded France into launching the Franco-Prussian War of 1870–1, which ended in French defeat and set the seal on German unification.

Frederick William refused the offer of the crown of a united Germany, and Austria's domination of the German Confederation was restored. Austria also crushed the revolts in Bohemia, Hungary and northern Italy, and absolutist imperial rule was restored.

Italian and German unification

After 1848, the two most significant developments in 19th-century European nationalism, the unification of Italy and Germany, were largely engineered by the chief ministers of two kingdoms, Piedmont and Prussia.

Piedmont, a constitutional monarchy in north-west Italy, was more advanced economically and industrially than the other Italian states, and its prime minister from 1852, Camillo di Cavour, set about uniting Italy under its leadership through a mixture of diplomacy and war. In 1859, having promised the cession of Nice and Savoy to France, Cavour secured French military support in expelling the Austrians from Lombardy. In 1860 the radical Italian guerrilla leader Giuseppe Garibaldi launched a campaign in which he and his 1,000 Redshirt volunteers swept aside the Spanish dynasty that ruled Sicily and Naples. Determined to maintain Piedmontese control over the process of national liberation, Cavour sent troops to the Papal States to forestall Garibaldi's ambitions there. In 1861 the kingdom of Italy was established, and Garibaldi recognized Victor Emmanuel II of Piedmont as king of the united country. The last remaining pieces of the jigsaw soon

timeline

1861	1863	1864	1866	1867	1870
Kingdom of Italy declared	Poles and Lithuanians revolt against Russian rule	Prussia defeats Denmark and takes Schleswig, while Austria takes Holstein	Prussia defeats Austria and annexes Hanover, Nassau and Hesse-Cassel. Italy acquires Venetia from Austria.	Formation of Prussian-dominated North German Confederation. Creation of dual monarchy of Austria-Hungary, giving latter more autonomy. Fenian Rising against British rule in Ireland.	Outbreak of Franco-Prussian War. Italy takes Rome from pope. Formation of Home Rule movement in Ireland.

fell into place. After Italy gave support to Prussia in its successful 1866 war against Austria, the latter was obliged to hand over Venetia in the north-east, while Italy's historic capital, Rome, was finally acquired in 1870.

Diplomacy, war and realpolitik also marked the route to German unification, which was masterminded by Otto von Bismarck, chief minister of Prussia. Bismarck was – in contrast to the revolutionaries of 1848 – a militaristic conservative, espousing a strategy of 'blood and iron' and engineering three wars in order to bring all the German states under the domination of Prussia. In 1871 King William of Prussia was duly declared Kaiser of a new German empire – which now included the resource-rich former French provinces of Alsace and Lorraine.

> **We have made Italy. Now we must make Italians.**
> **Massimo d'Azeglio,** at the first meeting of the parliament of unified Italy in 1861

Thus the birth of a powerful new German state – the most populous and one of the most industrially advanced in Europe – gave rise to three-quarters of a century of bitter Franco–German enmity, which was to contribute to the outbreak of two devastating world wars. However, the spark that set off the first of these conflagrations flashed a long way from the Franco-German frontier. It came in June 1914 on the other side of Europe, in Sarajevo.

in a nutshell
The growth of nationalism contributed to the outbreak of the First World War

1871	1878	1905	1908	1919
Proclamation of German empire	Congress of Berlin: Romania, Serbia and Montenegro granted independence from Turkey; Bulgaria gains autonomy	Norway gains independence from Sweden	Austria annexes Bosnia-Herzegovina	At Paris Peace Conference, various nation-states are created or revived, including Poland and Czechoslovakia. Alsace and Lorraine are returned to France.

32 Slavery

'Am I not a man and a brother?' This, the motto of the Committee for the Abolition of the Slave Trade established in Britain in 1787, sums up the fundamental and unanswerable moral objection to slavery. The British and American abolitionist movements largely arose from the evangelical revival that occurred in the later 18th century, while in places such as Revolutionary France, abolitionism emerged from the humanitarianism of the Enlightenment, and its concept of fundamental human rights.

Opponents of abolition found it convenient to deny the fraternity of the black man, and argued that being owned by a white man exposed the slave to civilized values to which they would be blind back in Africa. More fundamentally, these upholders of slavery argued – in an era when property rights were regarded by many as trumping virtually all other rights – that abolition would amount to nothing less than theft.

The Atlantic trade Slavery had existed as an institution for thousands of years. The economies of Greece, Rome and other ancient civilizations all depended on slave labour, and slavery appears to be sanctioned in the Bible. In medieval Europe slavery as such was rare; true, there were serfs, peasants who were tied to their lord's land, but serfs had certain rights that distinguished them from slaves. By the early modern period even serfdom had disappeared in much of western Europe.

timeline

1440s	16th C.	1772	1780	1781
Portuguese begin slaving expeditions to Africa	English adventurers such as Francis Drake become involved in Atlantic slave trade	Slavery ruled illegal in England	Pennsylvania passes 'Act for the Gradual Abolition of Slavery'; other Northern states of the USA follow suit	On the orders of the captain, the crew of the slave ship *Zong* throw 183 sick African slaves into the sea; their insurance does not cover death by sickness, but it does cover death by drowning. The case gives impetus to the abolitionist cause.

The Arabs and later the Ottomans owned and traded slaves, many of them African; alongside ivory and gold, slaves were one of the continent's most important exports. The Arabs had trading posts down the east coast of Africa, while slaves from West Africa were sent north via the trans-Saharan caravan routes. Barbary corsairs from North Africa also raided the shipping lanes and coasts of Europe for slaves (see p. 97).

> **To abolish [slavery] would not only be robbery to an innumerable class of our fellow-subjects, but it would be extreme cruelty to the African savages ...**
>
> **James Boswell,** 23 September 1777, as recorded by him in *The Life of Samuel Johnson* (1791)

The European trade in slaves from Africa was initiated by the Portuguese in the 15th century, and the demand for slave labour increased dramatically following the establishment of sugar and tobacco plantations in the New World. This gave rise to the notorious and highly profitable 'triangular trade' (see p. 101), in which, by the 18th century, Britain was the major player, forcing a total of perhaps 3.5 million Africans into slavery in the Caribbean and the southern American colonies, such as Georgia, Virginia and the Carolinas. This number equalled the combined total transported by Britain's European rivals, the Portuguese, French and Dutch. The Africans themselves were also involved in the trade – kingdoms such as Benin and Ashanti flourished on the back of supplying slaves to the insatiable Europeans. The conditions in which the slaves were transported across the Atlantic were appalling: crammed tightly in the fetid air below decks, large numbers – sometimes as many as one in five – succumbed to disease. Their bodies were thrown overboard to the sharks.

The campaign for abolition From the start, some Europeans could see the cruelty of what Africans now call the *Maafa*, a Swahili word meaning 'great tragedy'. 'What heart could be so hard,' asked one Portuguese man who witnessed the arrival of a contingent of African captives in 1445, 'as not to be pierced with piteous feeling to see that

1787	1791	1794	1802	1807	1808	1831
Formation in Britain of the Committee for the Abolition of the Slave Trade	Outbreak of slave revolt in French colony of Haiti	National Convention abolishes slavery in France and its colonies	Napoleon reimposes slavery in France and its colonies	Britain bans slave trade in its empire	USA bans further import of slaves, though domestic trade continues	Suppression of Nat Turner's Revolt, the largest slave revolt in US history

company? For some kept their heads low and their faces bathed in tears, looking upon one another; others stood groaning . . .' Their anguish only increased when 'it was needful to part fathers from sons, husbands from wives, brothers from brothers . . .'

Such expressions of abhorrence were rare until the mid-18th century, when the Enlightenment discourse of rights and liberties began to coincide with a sharpening of the Christian conscience. In England, this manifested itself in the emergence of Methodism and other evangelical groupings such as the Clapham Sect, while in America there was the so-called Great Awakening. To these evangelicals, slavery was an abomination before the Lord.

Toussaint L'Ouverture

Some slaves were not content to sit back and let white abolitionists agitate on their behalf. Many ran away, sometimes setting up independent communities in the wilderness, but few actually took up arms against their oppressors. A notable exception was the slave insurrection that broke out in the French colony of Haiti in 1791, led by a freed African slave called Toussaint L'Ouverture. In 1794, after a string of military successes, he made his peace with the French, who that year abolished slavery and appointed Toussaint lieutenant governor. In 1801, contrary to the wishes of Napoleon, Toussaint overran the neighbouring Spanish colony of Santo Domingo, freed its slaves, and made himself governor general of the whole island of Hispaniola. In 1802 Napoleon's forces invaded. Toussaint laid down his arms in exchange for a promise that slavery would not be reintroduced. However, Napoleon went back on his word, and Toussaint was taken prisoner, dying in captivity the following year. Although an ambivalent figure, Toussaint was to many a martyr to liberty. 'Thy friends,' wrote Wordsworth in a poem addressed to Toussaint, 'are exultations, agonies, / And love, and man's unconquerable mind.'

timeline

1833	1848	1861	1861–5	1863	1865
Slavery banned throughout British empire	Slavery abolished in French colonies	Emancipation of the serfs in Russia	US Civil War between free Northern states and slave-holding Southern states, who had formed the secessionist Confederacy	President Lincoln issues Emancipation Proclamation, freeing slaves in the Confederate states	Thirteenth Amendment to the US Constitution ends slavery in the USA

A key moment came in 1772, in the case of James Somersett, a slave brought to England from Massachusetts by his master. Lord Mansfield presiding over the Court of the King's Bench ruled that slavery was against the laws of England, and as a result Somersett and thousands of other slaves in England were emancipated. The ruling was based on legal rather than humanitarian arguments, and did not extend to the British empire, but it gave great encouragement to the abolitionists.

In Britain, the most prominent campaigner was William Wilberforce, the MP for Hull and a member of the Clapham Sect. Wilberforce decided that the first object should be the abolition of the slave trade, rather than slavery itself, and to this end worked tirelessly in Parliament, while committees were formed around the country to agitate for abolition. Wilberforce initially met with much opposition on economic grounds, but as the West Indies trade declined, resistance dwindled, and in 1807 a bill was passed that banned the importation of slaves into any British colony. The Royal Navy was given the task of enforcing the ban, but it was not until 1833 that a bill was passed that ended slavery itself throughout the British empire. France followed suit in 1848, but the continued existence of slavery in the Southern states of the USA was a suppurating sore that was only lanced by a bloody civil war (see p. 136).

> **Knock off the chains Of heart-debasing slavery; give to man, Of every colour and of every clime, Freedom, which stamps him image of his God.**
>
> **James Grainger,** *The Sugar Cane,* **1764, book 4**

in a nutshell
The abolition of slavery was a crucial milepost in the advance of humanitarianism

1869	1876	1886	1888	1962	2003
Portugal bans slavery in its African colonies	Slavery officially ended in Ottoman empire	Spain ends slavery in Cuba	Brazil abolishes slavery	Saudi Arabia bans slavery	Slavery criminalized in Niger

33 The expansion of the USA

When the American colonies declared their independence in 1776, the embryonic United States of America comprised just thirteen states strung along the eastern seaboard – a small fraction of the continent of North America. By 1900 the country extended from the Atlantic in the east to the Caribbean in the the south and the Pacific in the west.

By this date the USA had also established itself as the dominant power in the western hemisphere, and had acquired an overseas empire. It had also turned into the industrial giant that was to emerge as the leading superpower of the 20th century.

The territorial expansion of the USA was partly driven by massive immigration: between 1820 and 1900 the population increased eight-fold, to 76 million, with wave after wave coming from Ireland, Germany, Scandinavia, Italy and eastern Europe. There were also economic factors: the West contained rich resources, from land suitable for cattle or wheat or fruit, to gold and furs and timber. But there was also a powerful ideological element. This was the idea of US 'exceptionalism', the belief that God had inspired the early settlers – such as the Pilgrim Fathers – to come to America, that the USA was formed (in the words of the pledge of allegiance) as 'one nation under God', and that it was part of God's plan that the USA should extend its sway 'from sea to shining sea'. In 1845 the journalist and diplomat John L. O'Sullivan famously summarized the

timeline

1607	1620	1754–63	1763	1776	1783
Virginia Company founds colony at Jamestown, first permanent English settlement in North America	Pilgrim Fathers establish first English settlement in New England, at New Plymouth, Massachusetts	French and Indian War	British ban further settlement west of the Appalachians	Declaration of Independence	Treaty of Paris recognizes independence of USA, with extended boundaries

idea when he spoke of 'our manifest destiny to overspread the continent allotted by Providence for the free development of our yearly multiplying millions'. As the torch-bearer of liberty, the USA had not so much a right as a divinely ordained duty to spread its light across the land.

Colonial encroachment When the Europeans first arrived in North America, the continent was inhabited by a great diversity of Native American peoples, with an array of different languages and different cultures. In the forests of the north-east were hunter-gatherers, in the Mississippi basin maize farmers, on the Great Plains nomadic buffalo hunters, in the semi-deserts of the south-west pueblo farmers, while in the Pacific north-west the people thrived on the abundance of the seas and rivers.

At first, the native peoples guardedly welcomed their contacts with the Europeans, from whom they could acquire such desirable items as guns and iron tools. But contact with the Europeans also brought diseases to which the Native Americans had no immunity. As the population of European settlers grew, there was an increasing hunger for land, leading to encroachments on traditional tribal territories, conflict, and dispossession. For many decades in the 18th century, the Iroquois Confederacy of the north-east successfully resisted the European advance, through a combination of war and diplomacy, exploiting the rivalries between the British and French, and then the enmity between the colonists and the mother country during the struggle for independence.

> **❝Many, if not most, of our Indian wars have had their origin in broken promises and acts of injustice upon our part.❞**
> **President Rutherford B. Hayes,**
> **Annual Message to Congress,**
> **3 December 1877**

'Westward the course of empire takes its way' This famous line by the Irish philosopher Bishop George Berkeley, penned in 1752, proved to be prophetic. With the achievement of US nationhood, the

1803	1811	1813–14	1819	1823	1830
Louisiana Purchase: US acquires French territory west of Mississippi	Native American alliance under Shawnee chief Tecumseh defeated by US forces at Tippecanoe Creek	Creek War ends in cession of territory to USA	US acquisition of West and East Florida from Spain	Monroe Doctrine: President James Monroe declares US intention to resist any further attempt by European powers to establish colonies in the Americas	Indian Removal Act allows for eviction of 'Five Civilized Nations'

much resented ban on settlement west of the Appalachians imposed by the British in 1763 was nullified. The British had rightly calculated that any such drift westward would lead to more wars with the indigenous peoples, and they did not wish to end up bearing the cost. With this barrier lifted, settlers surged over the Appalachians, laying claim to Native American lands, and by the end of the 18th century two new states had been admitted to the Union: Kentucky and Tennessee.

The Treaty of Paris of 1783, by which Britain recognized the independence of the USA, set the new country's western boundary at the Mississippi, beyond which lay the French territory of Louisiana – a territory vastly larger than the present state of that name, stretching as it did from British Canada to the Caribbean. The treaty also set the USA's southern boundary at the thirty-first parallel, the northern frontier of the Spanish territory of Florida. The USA doubled in size when in 1803 President Thomas Jefferson purchased Louisiana from the French for $15 million; by a further treaty in 1819 the USA acquired Florida from Spain. Texas, which had largely been

The fate of the Native Americans

The relentless land hunger of the 19th century witnessed a rapid deterioration in the situation of the Native Americans. The 'Five Civilized Nations' of the south-east – the Creek, the Cherokee, the Seminole, the Choctaw and the Chicasaw – had developed their own constitution based on that of the USA. Some even owned plantations, with black slaves to work them. But in the 1830s they were evicted from their lands by the US government, and forced to relocate to the west of the Mississippi. The advance of the white man was relentless, and conflict was inevitable – as was the outcome. By 1900 many Native Americans were confined to reservations, far from their ancestral lands, their rich cultural heritage a subject of contempt or touristic curiosity.

timeline

1838	1845	1846	1846–8	1848	1861–5
Trail of Tears: 15,000 Cherokee forcibly marched westward to Oklahoma; 3,000 die en route	Annexation of Texas. Coinage of the phrase 'manifest destiny'.	USA acquires Oregon Territory from Britain	Mexican War; USA acquires vast new areas in the west	Discovery of gold in California sparks gold rush	American Civil War

settled by Anglo-Americans, fought a war of independence from Mexico in 1836, and in 1845 was annexed by the USA as the twenty-eighth state. This sparked a war with Mexico. The American victory in that war in 1848 led to further annexations of Mexican territory – California, and all or part of the present states of New Mexico, Arizona, Nevada, Utah, Colorado and Wyoming. The USA had a number of border disputes with British Canada, especially in the Pacific north-west, but these were finally resolved in 1846, when the USA acquired what are now the states of Washington, Oregon and Idaho. Alaska was purchased from Russia in 1867, and Hawaii – which became the fiftieth state of the Union in 1959 – was annexed in 1898.

The federal government encouraged westward migration by selling off parcels of land at bargain-basement prices – or even, after the Homestead Act of 1862, for nothing. Settlement and commerce were supported by a network of canals linking the great rivers, and later by the railroads; the first transcontinental line was completed in 1869. Here too the government played a role, making substantial loans and land grants to the railroad companies. This westward expansion was not free from trauma, however. The question as to whether slavery should be allowed in these new territories was one of the contributory factors in the outbreak of the American Civil War (see p. 136). And the vicious and perfidious treatment meted out to the native inhabitants of these lands was one of the great tragedies of the 19th century.

in a nutshell
The spectacular growth of the USA was often at the expense of its indigenous inhabitants

1862	1867	1869	1876	1889	1890	1898
Homestead Act offers free western land to new settlers	Purchase of Alaska from Russia	Completion of first transcontinental railroad	Lakota and Cheyenne massacre General Custer's Seventh US Cavalry at Little Big Horn	Oklahoma Land Rush: federal government opens up Cherokee territory to white homesteaders	Last Native American resistance crushed by massacre of Sioux at Wounded Knee	Spanish–American War: USA acquires Philippines, Guam and Puerto Rico. Annexation of Hawaii.

34 The American Civil War

The founding fathers of the USA were aware of the moral ambivalence of their position: at the same time as fighting for the freedom of their fellow whites from tyranny and oppression, they continued to hold black slaves.

Slavery in the USA was largely restricted to the Southern states, where large numbers of African slaves worked on the vast tobacco and cotton plantations on which the Southern economy depended. The economies of the Northern states were much more dependent on industry and small-scale farming, and it was in the North that the first calls for the abolition of slavery – often religiously inspired – originated. Starting with Pennsylvania in 1780, the Northern states introduced legislation for the gradual abolition of slavery. But calls for a federal ban throughout the Union were countered by those who argued that the US Constitution protected the status of slavery: the Fifth Amendment prohibited uncompensated seizure of property, while the Tenth Amendment reserved to the states all powers not specifically delegated to the federal government. Thus it was the right of each state to determine whether slavery should be permitted on its territory. Even many moderate abolitionists felt that Congress had no power in the matter.

The extension of slavery Conflict arose, however, when it came to the status of slavery in the new territories. Cotton had become economically much more significant after 1793, when Eli Whitney had

timeline

1791	1803	1820	1850	1854
Tenth Amendment to Constitution appears to enshrine right of the states, rather than federal government, to determine the issue of slavery	Louisiana Purchase	Missouri Compromise: Missouri admitted to the USA as a slave state, while Maine admitted as a free state	Compromise of 1850: extension of slavery in new territories is restricted, but slavery protected where it exists	Fugitive Slave Act: Northern states obliged to return runaway slaves to their owners. Kansas-Nebraska Act: the new territories are allowed to decide for themselves whether to permit slavery; violence ensues. Formation of Republican Party.

improved the cotton gin, a device for separating the seeds from the fibre, and there was increasing pressure to extend cotton plantations based on slave labour into the new territories of the south-west. The result was the Missouri Compromise of 1820, by which no new slave states north of the thirty-sixth degree of latitude were to be admitted to the Union, with the exception of Missouri. Tensions between abolitionists and pro-slavers grew after the USA acquired further vast areas of western land following the Mexican War of 1846–8. The Compromise of 1850 sought to defuse the situation, restricting slavery in the new territories while protecting the institution where it already existed.

The Compromise of 1850 was overturned, however, by the Kansas-Nebraska Act of 1854, which allowed the inhabitants of these new territories to decide for themselves whether or not to permit slavery. Violence between pro-slavery forces and radical abolitionists such as John Brown ensued, and in 1859 Brown and a number of supporters seized the federal arsenal in Harpers Ferry, in what is now West Virginia, in an abortive attempt to initiate a general slave uprising in the South.

> **Where Slavery is, there Liberty cannot be; and where Liberty is, there Slavery cannot be.**
>
> **Charles Sumner**, senator, 5 November 1864

The broken Union John Brown was hanged, but his action gave the abolitionists a martyr, and at the same time heightened Southern fears of the consequences of emancipation. These fears were heightened even more when in 1860 the Republican candidate in the presidential election, Abraham Lincoln, was voted into office. The new Republican Party was more sympathetic to the cause of abolition than any previous party had been, but it was not a top priority for Lincoln, who, although a supporter of emancipation, insisted that the Constitution protected slavery where it existed, and who had publicly stated that he was not in favour of 'bringing about in any way the social and political equality of the white and black races'.

1860

Election of Republican Abraham Lincoln prompts secession of Alabama, Florida, Georgia, Louisiana, Mississippi and South Carolina

1861

FEBRUARY Formation of Confederacy. **APRIL** Confederate forces attack Fort Sumter. Arkansas, North Carolina, Tennessee and Virginia join Confederacy. **JULY** Confederate victory at Bull Run.

1862

FEBRUARY Union forces take Fort Donnelson and Fort Henry in Tennessee. **APRIL** Grant defeats Confederate counter-offensive at Shiloh. **MAY** Naval battle between ironclads *Monitor* and *Virginia*; US Navy takes naval base at Norfolk, Virginia. **SEPTEMBER** Confederate advance on the North stopped at Antietam. **DECEMBER** Union defeat at Fredericksburg.

Despite such assurances, even before Lincoln's inauguration the Southern states began to secede from the Union, forming the Confederate States of America with Jefferson Davis as their president. In April 1861 Confederate forces opened fire on Fort Sumter, a Union stronghold in South Carolina. Lincoln called for 75,000 volunteers to crush the rebellion. Thus began four years of bitter civil war that were to cost the lives of nearly two-thirds of a million men.

The 'war between the states' Despite the greater economic and manpower advantages of the industrial North, Lincoln was at first hampered by the ineptitude of his generals, as compared to the flair of such rebel commanders as Robert E. Lee and Thomas 'Stonewall' Jackson. Initially, Lincoln kept quiet on the issue of slavery, for fear of alienating

After the Civil War

Lincoln's successor, Andrew Johnson, pursued the former's policy of reconciliation of the South, overseeing the rapid readmission to the Union of the secessionist states. This angered the radical Republicans in Congress, who wished to see a top-to-bottom 'Reconstruction' of Southern society and politics, and nearly succeeded in impeaching Johnson, who was left as a lame duck.

The radicals then took charge of Reconstruction, putting the former Confederate states under the control of the army, and then holding elections in which freed slaves could vote, but from which former leading Confederates were barred. This resulted in the installation of radical Republican state governments and violent opposition by conservative, racist groups such as the Ku Klux Klan. Over time, people in the North turned their backs on the South, and Southern Democrats gradually reassumed power, introducing the so-called Jim Crow laws that denied most blacks their civil rights, including the right to vote. These rights were only restored after great struggles – by Martin Luther King among others – in the 1950s and 1960s.

timeline

1863
JANUARY Emancipation Proclamation.
MAY Union defeat at Chancellorsville.
JULY Decisive Union victory at Gettysburg. Grant captures Vicksburg, Mississippi, cutting Confederacy in two.

1864
SEPTEMBER Union forces begin scorched-earth policy in Shenandoah valley, and capture Atlanta, Georgia. **NOVEMBER–DECEMBER** Georgia laid waste by Union forces in 'March to the Sea'. **NOVEMBER** Lincoln re-elected.

1865
APRIL Confederate surrender. Assassination of Lincoln; succeeded by Vice-President Andrew Johnson.

those slave states – such as Maryland and Missouri – that had remained within the Union. But pressure from radical Republicans led him to issue the Emancipation Proclamation, which took effect on 1 January 1863. This freed all slaves within the seceding states (but not in those slave states remaining within the Union); all such freed slaves, if fit, were to join the Union forces. Thus Lincoln dressed up this partial abolition as 'military necessity', and at the same time Northern blacks were, for the first time, admitted into the armed forces, albeit in segregated regiments commanded by white officers.

> **❝If I could save the Union without freeing any slave, I would do it; and if I could save it by freeing all the slaves, I would do it . . .❞**
>
> **President Abraham Lincoln,** 22 August 1862

That year witnessed a turning of the tide in favour of the North. In July, General George Meade repelled Lee's attempted invasion of Pennsylvania at Gettysburg, and Union forces under Ulysses S. Grant took the rebel stronghold of Vicksburg in Mississippi. The following year Grant was appointed commander-in-chief, and began a campaign of total war against the South, whose resources were eventually exhausted. On 9 April 1865 Lee's army surrendered to Grant at Appomattox Court House.

Lincoln had been re-elected the previous autumn, and in his second inaugural address, on 4 March 1865, had held out a promise of reconciliation to the Southern states, then on the verge of defeat. Within days of victory, on 15 April, Lincoln was assassinated by a Southern sympathizer. The Thirteenth Amendment to the Constitution, abolishing slavery throughout the Union, took effect from 18 December 1865.

in a nutshell
The Civil War ended slavery in the USA

1866	**1867**	**1868**	**1870**	**1872**
Bills giving relief and civil rights to freed slaves are passed over Johnson's veto	Reconstruction Acts place former Confederate states under military government	Fourteenth Amendment enshrines equal protection under the law for whites and blacks, and bars former Confederate officials from state and federal office	Fifteenth Amendment guarantees voting rights to African American men	Amnesty Act restores rights of former Confederate officials to vote and hold office

35 The rise of socialism

The Industrial Revolution created a new ruling class of bourgeois industrial capitalists. It also created a burgeoning urban working class, who laboured in often dangerous conditions for pitiful wages and who were forced to live in squalor and extreme insecurity.

There were a number of responses to the oppressed and impoverished condition of the working class. Some middle- and upper-class philanthropists campaigned for legislation to improve working conditions. Many workers attempted to band together to form trade unions, to agitate for higher wages and healthier workplaces. Attempts to limit the power of the new labour movement, or to crush it entirely, prompted many to call for political action, either through the democratic process, or through violent revolution.

Trade unionism Trade unions have their origins in the medieval craft guilds, societies that regulated entry into – and standards within – different skilled artisanal trades. With the advent of the Industrial Revolution many artisans, unable to compete with larger concerns, were obliged to surrender their independence and go to work in factories. When they attempted to band together to campaign for better wages and conditions, they met with vehement opposition from employers. Governments, alarmed by the bloody upheavals of the French Revolution, interpreted any such activity on the part of the working classes as

timeline

1799–1800	1802	1804	1821	1824–5	1838
Combination Acts prohibit trade unions in UK	First Factory Act in UK	Napoleonic Code bans trade unions in France	Saint Simon outlines his vision of socialism in *Du système industriel*	Repeal of UK Combination Acts, permitting trade unions in certain crafts, but strikes remain illegal	'People's Charter' calls for parliamentary reform in Britain, including universal male suffrage

threatening not only property rights, but also the safety of the realm. As a result, trade unions were widely banned – in Britain, for example, by the Combination Acts of 1799 and 1800, and in France by Napoleon's penal and civil codes, which reined back the universal human rights declared by the French Revolutionaries.

Only gradually through the 19th century was legislation against trade unionism relaxed in a number of countries, and the formation of craft unions was followed by new unions that organized large numbers of unskilled workers. In places such as Russia, however, trade unionists had to operate clandestinely, while in the USA employers used the full weight of the law, backed by armed thugs and even troops, to break strikes.

> **❝A political combination of the lower classes as such and for their own objects, is an evil of the first magnitude.❞**
>
> **Walter Bagehot,** *The English Constitution,* 1867

Democratic vs revolutionary socialism As trade unions struggled to defend the interests of their members, many trade unionists began to think that only a complete transformation of society would bring about justice and equality. They drew on the ideas of socialism, a word first coined by the French theorist Henri de Saint Simon (1760–1825), who envisaged an industrial state freed from poverty, and in which science would replace religion. Also influential was the British philanthropist Robert Owen (1771–1825), who set up a model industrial community at New Lanark in Scotland, with improved housing and Britain's first infant school, and went on to set up a number of self-sustaining cooperative communities, such as that at New Harmony, Indiana, established in 1825.

Fundamental to the socialist vision was that society and the economy should be ordered not so that the individual should be free to follow his or her own course, but for the collective good. Whereas the free-market liberal believed that every human had it within their own power to improve their lot, the socialist believed that the fate of individual

1844	**1848**	**1848–9**	**1864**	**1868**
Foundation of cooperative movement with opening of first cooperative shop in Rochdale, England	Marx and Engels issue *Communist Manifesto*	Socialists join in liberal and nationalist revolutions across Europe, which all eventually fail	Formation of First International, association of labour and socialist organizations of which Marx becomes leader	Formation of Trades Union Congress in UK. French workers given limited right to unionize.

Improving working conditions

As economic liberalism – with its watchwords of free enterprise and free trade – spread amongst the commercial and industrial middle classes, any attempt to regulate business was regarded by many as tyrannical government interference. Nevertheless, in some countries legislation was introduced to end the worst abuses. In Britain, for example, the Factory Act of 1802 made it illegal to oblige children under fourteen to work more than eight hours a day. Further legislation on working hours and health and safety followed in Britain and later in other countries (a maximum twelve-hour day was introduced in France in 1848, for example), increasingly as a result of campaigning by trade unions. In the USA, in contrast, there was strong ideological resistance to such regulation, summed up in 1905 by a Supreme Court judge who stated that 'limiting the hours grown and intelligent men may labour to earn their living' were 'mere meddlesome interferences' with individual rights. There were exceptions: the automobile manufacturer Henry Ford voluntarily reduced the working hours in his factories, arguing that if workers had no leisure time they would not buy his products.

humans is largely determined by their environment, and that the state should intervene to ensure, at the very least, equality of opportunity and reasonable standards of living, via the provision of education, health care, minimum wages, pensions, unemployment benefit and so on.

More radical socialists, following Karl Marx (1818–83) and Friedrich Engels (1820–95), the founders of modern communism, believed that social justice could only be achieved by bringing the whole of the means of production – industry, land, roads, railways – into collective ownership. Marx and Engels, who issued their *Communist Manifesto* in 1848, held that history is determined by blind economic forces and the struggle between the classes. The Industrial Revolution had seen the overthrow of feudalism and the power of the landed aristocracy. In turn, they predicted, the

timeline

1871	1878	1884	1886	1889
Anarchist and socialist revolutionaries establish Paris Commune, which is brutally crushed after two months, driving socialists and trade unionists underground. Trade unions legalized in UK.	German Social Democratic Party banned	Trade-union activity made legal in France	Formation of non-socialist American Federation of Labor, the only US trade-union federation to survive the First World War	Formation of Second International of social democratic parties, which is split between pro- and anti-war factions in 1914

new capitalist bourgeoisie that had achieved power would be violently overthrown by the oppressed urban proletariat, who would introduce socialism as a stage before the state 'withered away', to be replaced by perfect communism. This ideal society, where everybody lived in harmony, would be based on the premise: 'From each according to his ability, to each according to his needs.'

The way socialist movements developed in different countries depended largely on the attitude of governments. In places such as Britain, where trade-union activity was increasingly tolerated and where by the end of the 19th century the vote had been extended to the majority of the male population, it was possible for socialist parties – such as the British Labour Party (which is said to owe more to Methodism than to Marx) – to achieve parliamentary representation for the labour movement. But in more repressive countries such as tsarist Russia and imperial Germany, it seemed to many that the Marxist revolutionary approach was the only option.

Today, although communist ideology has long been abandoned in Russia and elsewhere, the principles of democratic socialism still have some influence around the world. Even in countries with centre-right governments, the state still has an enormous stake in the economy and society – in everything from maintaining the roads to regulating utility prices and running the education system – to an extent that would have been undreamed of even two centuries ago.

in a nutshell
The ideas of socialism have transformed even capitalist societies

1890	1900	1905	1917	1918–19	1919	1924
Ban on German Social Democratic Party lifted	Formation of Labour Representation Committee in UK (renamed Labour Party in 1906)	Abortive revolution in Russia	Successful Bolshevik Revolution in Russia	Abortive communist uprisings in Germany	Formation of Third International (Comintern) of world communist parties	First Labour government in UK

36 Women's rights

At the first women's rights convention in the USA, held at Seneca Falls, New York, in July 1848, Elizabeth Cady Stanton made a long overdue amendment to the American Declaration of Independence. 'We hold these truths to be self-evident,' she thundered, 'that all men *and women* are created equal.'

Three-quarters of a century was to pass before women in America and Britain gained the vote, and the battle to establish the principle of equal rights in law and custom around the world is a long way from being won.

Through history there have been occasional voices calling for greater empowerment of women, but the modern women's movement originated in the later 18th century. In 1789, in the wake of the French Revolution, the National Assembly issued the 'Declaration of the Rights of Man and of the Citizen', but declined to extend civil and political rights to women. In response, in 1791 the playwright 'Olympe de Gouges' published a 'Declaration of the Rights of Woman and the Female Citizen'. In the following year in England, Mary Wollstonecraft published A *Vindication of the Rights of Women*, a book that argued for better education for girls, to enable them to realize their full potential as human beings.

The battle for women's suffrage At the time Mary Wollstonecraft and Olympe de Gouges were writing, middle- and upper-class girls were trained to do little more than read, write, sew, draw and sing, and women were regarded as mere adornments, suppliers of heirs, chattels of their fathers and husbands, to whom they had to submit in everything. Unmarried women could own property and run their own

timeline

1791	1792	1848	1865	1869
Olympe de Gouges publishes a 'Declaration of the Rights of Woman and the Female Citizen'	Mary Wollstonecraft publishes A *Vindication of the Rights of Women*	US campaign for women's suffrage begins at Seneca Falls Convention	Elizabeth Garrett Anderson becomes first woman in UK to qualify as a doctor	Formation of National Woman Suffrage Association in USA. John Stuart Mill publishes *The Subjection of Women*. Launch of French journal *Le Droit des femmes*.

businesses, but in Britain, for example, as soon as they married, their property became their husband's. Similar restrictions operated in other countries. In France, for example, the Napoleonic Code of 1804, which influenced the civil codes of many other European countries, stressed the rights of husbands and fathers at the expense of those of women.

As a consequence of entrenched male dominance in almost every sphere of society, women were barred from the professions, from higher education, and from voting or holding political office. For feminists, there was one important first step to take. Susan B. Anthony, Stanton's long-term colleague in the US movement for women's rights, summed this up when she wrote, 'There never will be complete equality until women themselves help to make laws and elect lawmakers.' Women had to have the vote, before anything else would change, and in 1869 Anthony and Stanton founded the National Woman Suffrage Association. They were particularly incensed that the Fifteenth Amendment to the Constitution had just asserted that 'The right of citizens of the United States to vote shall not be denied . . . on account of race, colour or previous condition of servitude.' There was no mention of gender. In those less enlightened times, one of Anthony and Stanton's supporters complained that the Amendment gave the vote to 'Patrick, Sambo, Hans and Ung Tung', but denied it to educated middle-class women.

> **❝If women be educated to dependence . . . and submit, right or wrong, to power, where are we to stop?❞**
>
> **Mary Wollstonecraft,
> *A Vindication of the Rights of Women,* 1792**

At much the same time, the campaign for women's suffrage was getting underway in Britain. In 1866 the philosopher and Liberal MP John Stuart Mill presented a petition to Parliament demanding that women be given the vote, and the following year saw the formation of the National Society for Women's Suffrage, later superseded by the National Union of Women's Suffrage Societies, led by Millicent Fawcett. These 'suffragists' campaigned peacefully, in contrast to the 'suffragettes' of Emmeline Pankhurst's

1878	**1882**	**1890**	**1893**	**1897**	**1900**
London University begins to award degrees to women, first in UK to do so	UK act of Parliament gives married women full rights over their own property	Formation in USA of National American Woman Suffrage Association, which allies itself with other progressive causes	New Zealand becomes the first country in the world to give women the vote in national elections	Formation of suffragist National Union of Women's Suffrage Societies in UK	Women in France win right to enter legal profession

Women's Social and Political Union, formed in 1903. For Pankhurst, 'The argument of the broken window pane is the most valuable argument in modern politics.' The suffragettes – by throwing stones through windows, chaining themselves to railings and going on hunger strike once arrested – alienated many, but they brought enormous publicity to the cause.

The first country to give the vote to women was actually New Zealand, in 1893. Country after country followed – Australia in 1902, Germany and Britain in 1918, the USA in 1920. France and Italy waited until 1945, Switzerland until 1971, Oman until 2003. In the first ever local elections held in Saudi Arabia in 2005, women were not allowed to vote.

Women and war work

Women from the labouring classes had always worked in the fields and in domestic service, and from the later 18th century large numbers were also employed in factories. Single middle-class women could work as teachers, but it was not until the later 19th century that a few women began to gain access to higher education and professions such as medicine. During the First World War, and again during the Second, millions of women in Britain and America were recruited to work in sectors traditionally reserved for men, such as heavy engineering and, indeed, the armed forces. In the Second World War, the Nazis refused to adopt such a policy, maintaining that a woman's role should be confined to *Kinder, Küche und Kirche* ('children, kitchen and church'); this policy impeded industrial productivity, significantly undermining the German war effort. Even in Britain and America, after the war women were encouraged to surrender their jobs to the returning menfolk. There was an immense 'baby boom', and millions of women found themselves tied down once more by their domestic and parenting roles. It seemed that the status quo had returned – but for many women, the war had given them a glimpse of freedom and power.

timeline

1903	1913	1918	1920	1928	1949	1960
Formation of Women's Social and Political Union – the British suffragettes	In USA, Alice Paul forms militant suffragette National Women's Party	Women gain vote in Britain (only if over thirty) and Germany	Women gain vote in USA and Canada	All women over twenty-one gain vote in UK	Simone de Beauvoir publishes *The Second Sex*	In Sri Lanka, Sirimavo Bandaranaike becomes the world's first woman prime minister

Towards full equality In 1949 the French philosopher Simone de Beauvoir published *The Second Sex*, in which she asserted that 'One is not born a woman; one becomes one' – in other words, much of what people think of as 'femininity' is in fact a cultural construct rather than a biological fact. De Beauvoir's book had little impact until the second great wave of feminism began to emerge in the 1960s, kicking off with Betty Friedan's book *The Feminine Mystique* (1963). In tune with the radical youth politics of the time, the new feminists campaigned under the banner of the 'women's liberation movement'. The new feminists agitated not just for equality of pay and opportunity in the workplace, but also for access to family planning and childcare, and against male violence and exploitation and all forms of discrimination on grounds of gender. Some went further, arguing for a thoroughgoing realignment of the relations between men and women. A few advocated a complete separation from the male world, adopting a lesbian lifestyle as a political gesture.

> ❛The false division of human nature into "feminine" and "masculine" is the beginning of hierarchy.❜
>
> **Gloria Steinem,** in the *Observer*, **15 May 1994**

Although women have won victories such as the UK Equal Pay Act of 1970, women's average earnings in the Western world still lag far behind those of men. And although the representation of women in politics, government, board rooms, the professions and the armed forces is greater than it used to be, they still form a tiny minority in positions of power and influence. And outside the West, billions of women still remain second-class citizens, and struggle for even the most basic of human rights.

in a nutshell
Many victories won, many still to win

1963	1968	1970	1972	1973	1975
Betty Friedan publishes *The Feminine Mystique*	Abortion becomes legal in UK	Germaine Greer publishes *The Female Eunuch.* Equal Pay Act in UK.	US Congress passes Equal Rights Amendment, but this is never fully ratified	Supreme Court ruling in case of Roe vs Wade makes abortion legal in USA	Sex Discrimination Act sets up Equal Opportunities Commission in UK. Margaret Thatcher becomes the first female leader of a major British political party.

37 The First World War

The First World War – 'the Great War' as it was known at the time – was a cataclysm that tore the heart out of Europe, destroying a generation of young men and sowing the seeds of further conflict. For four years, the combatants fought a war of attrition, unable to break the stalemate, unwilling to negotiate a peace, but prepared to expend men on an industrial scale.

Quite why the war started has been a subject of debate among historians. Some point to imperial and industrial rivalries, some to the contradictions within the capitalist system, some to the system of polarized military alliances, some to a chapter of accidents and unintended consequences. It may well have been a combination of all these.

The road to war By 1914, the great powers of Europe had formed themselves into two armed camps. On the one hand there was Germany, Austria-Hungary and Italy; on the other France and Russia, both of whom had also entered into informal 'ententes' with Britain. Britain, the dominant world power through the 19th century, had increasingly come to regard Germany as its greatest industrial, imperial and military rival, and from 1903 the two were locked in a naval arms race.

In 1871 the newly unified Germany had, after defeating the French, annexed the provinces of Alsace and Lorraine. What Germany feared

timeline

1879	1882	1894	1899	1902	1904	1907
Formation of Dual Alliance between Germany and Austria-Hungary	Italy joins Dual Alliance to form Triple Alliance	France forms alliance with Russia	German engineers help Turks build railways, and German officers train Turkish army	Britain forms alliance with Japan	Britain and France enter Entente Cordiale	Britain agrees informal entente with Russia

above all else was encirclement by hostile powers. It now faced France in the west, anxious to recover the lost provinces, and France's ally Russia in the east. Since the mid-19th century Russia had claimed leadership of all the Slavic peoples of eastern Europe, especially in the volatile Balkans. Here Russia came head to head with Germany's ally Austria, which controlled Slovenia and Croatia, and which in 1908 annexed Bosnia-Herzegovina. Russia was also alarmed by the material and military support Germany was giving to Turkey, its traditional enemy in the Balkans.

It was in the Balkans that the fuse was lit. On 28 June 1914 Archduke Franz Ferdinand, heir to the Austrian throne, was assassinated by a Serb nationalist in Sarajevo, the capital of Bosnia. Austria blamed Serbia, Russia's staunchest ally in the Balkans, and issued a threatening ultimatum. Serbia appealed to Russia, which, following Austria's declaration of war against Serbia on 28 July, began to mobilize its vast army. Russian mobilization was the trigger for Germany to activate its Schlieffen Plan, a strategy to avoid fighting a war on two fronts. The Plan involved delivering a quick knock-out blow to France by means of a surprise attack through neutral Belgium, before Russia could complete its mobilization. In accordance with the Schlieffen Plan, therefore, on 1 August Germany declared war on Russia, and on 3 August it declared war on France. The following day German troops entered Belgium, prompting Britain – which had guaranteed Belgian neutrality – to declare war on Germany.

> **❝If there is ever another war in Europe, it will come out of some damned silly thing in the Balkans.❞**
>
> **Otto von Bismarck,** Chancellor of Germany until 1890

Global conflict All the participants had expected the war to be over by Christmas. It was not to be. Fighting on the Western Front was initially relatively mobile – and on the Eastern Front was to remain so. But after the French and the British stopped the German advance on Paris at the Marne in September, the two sides began to dig in, and by October they faced each other from opposing lines of trenches extending from the

North Sea to the Swiss frontier, with neither side able to make a decisive breakthrough. With the Russian army now fully mobilized, the Germans now faced their worst nightmare: a war on two fronts.

There were, of course, more than two fronts in the conflict, justifying its status as a 'world war'. On the Western Front, the Germans were faced by the armies of Belgium, France, Britain and its empire, and, by the end, the USA. On the Eastern Front, the Russians fought the Germans in the north, and the Austrians in Galicia and the Carpathians. In the Balkans, Serbia (with limited support from France and Britain) fought Austria and, from 1915, Bulgaria. Italy, which had held back in 1914, joined the Allies (Britain, France, Russia, etc.) in 1915 on the secret promise of receiving

Stalemate and slaughter

For four years the opposing sides faced each other on the Western Front. The generals dreamed of the great breakthrough, when their artillery would knock a hole in the enemy's defences through which the infantry – and even the cavalry – could charge en masse, carrying all before them. Attempts to make such a breakthrough, in offensives lasting weeks or months, nearly always ended in failure or at best an advance of a mile or two, at the cost of hundreds of thousands of casualties. On the first day of the Battle of the Somme alone, the British army lost 20,000 men killed outright.

Military technology at that time overwhelmingly favoured the defenders, who could shelter from artillery bombardments in deep trenches and concrete blockhouses, and then with rapid-firing machine-guns mow down the attackers as they became mired in the mud and the barbed wire entanglements of no-man's land. Towards the end of the war, new tactics and weapons – such as tanks and aircraft – began to end the stalemate. But the slaughter had been on an unimaginable scale: some 9.8 million men – perhaps as many as 12 million – were killed in the fighting, more battle deaths than in any conflict before or since.

timeline

1916

JANUARY Allies withdraw from Gallipoli. **FEBRUARY–DECEMBER** Battle of Verdun costs half a million French and German lives.
MAY Battle of Jutland in North Sea, after which German fleet is confined to port. **JULY–NOVEMBER** Anglo-French offensive on the Somme costs over a million casualties. **AUGUST** Romania joins Allies.

1917

MARCH Revolution in Russia forces abdication of tsar. **APRIL** USA declares war on Germany. Mutinies break out in French army. **JULY** Arabs capture Aqaba from Turks. Launch of major British offensive at Ypres. **OCTOBER** Italian army overwhelmed by Austro-German offensive at Caporetto. **NOVEMBER** Bolshevik Revolution in Russia. **DECEMBER** British take Jerusalem from Turks.

territory in the north from Austria, thus opening another front. Turkey joined the Central Powers (Germany and Austria) in October 1914, and an Allied attempt to knock it out of the war by invading the Gallipoli peninsula in 1915 was a bloody failure. There was also fighting in the Middle East, the Caucasus and Africa. One of the most important theatres was the Atlantic Ocean and the North Sea, where Britain used its naval superiority to blockade Germany; for its part, Germany waged a successful submarine campaign against Allied shipping.

The extension of the German submarine campaign to neutral shipping was instrumental in bringing the USA into the war in 1917. Americans had a traditional aversion to becoming involved in foreign entanglements, but once they joined the Allies their vast industrial capacity and reserves of manpower made Allied victory almost inevitable. This duly came on 11 November 1918, when an armistice was signed. Russia, following the Bolshevik Revolution of 1917, had made a separate peace with Germany. But by 1918 the latter – with its resources exhausted, its population nearing starvation, and with mutinies breaking out in the armed forces – was near collapse.

> **❝It is easier to make war than to make peace.❞**
>
> **Georges Clemenceau,**
> French prime minister, in a speech, July 1919

The victors were not magnanimous. The terms of the Treaty of Versailles forced on Germany in 1919 were punitive, and created resentments that were to foster the rise of Nazism. Far from being 'the war to end all wars', as many hoped, the First World War proved to be merely the first act in a global conflict that was to resume twenty years later, at the cost of even more lives.

in a nutshell
An unnecessary war, fought on an unprecedented scale

1918

JANUARY US President Wilson announces Fourteen Points peace programme. **MARCH** Treaty of Brest-Litovsk: Bolsheviks take Russia out of the war. Germans begin Spring Offensives on Western Front. **AUGUST** Allies begin counter-offensives on Western Front. **OCTOBER** British and Arab forces occupy Damascus. German naval mutiny. **NOVEMBER** Revolution in Berlin. Armistice on all fronts.

1919

JANUARY Opening of Paris Peace Conference.
JUNE Germany signs Treaty of Versailles.

38 Lenin and Stalin

Karl Marx had predicted that the revolution heralding the victory of communism would begin in his native Germany. With its large industrial proletariat, Germany fulfilled the conditions he regarded as necessary for the next great stage in the class struggle – the overthrow of the bourgeoisie.

Marx would never have believed that the first successful communist revolution would take place in Russia, a backward land that was only just emerging from centuries of feudalism.

What Marx had not foreseen was the ease with which the working classes could be seduced by nationalism. When war broke out in 1914, millions of men abandoned working-class solidarity and volunteered for the slaughter. In Russia the tsarist regime handled the war with particular ineptitude, causing suffering on an unimaginable scale. It was this situation that the communist revolutionary Vladimir Ilych Lenin set out to exploit when he returned to Russia from exile in 1917.

The road to revolution While many European states moved towards democracy in the 19th century, imperial Russia remained an autocracy: 'Every country has its constitution,' quipped one Russian; 'ours is absolutism moderated by assassination.' Repression provoked radical opposition, such as the Decembrist revolt of 1825, and the assassination of Tsar Alexander II in 1881. Alexander had tried to introduce a modicum of modernization, for example by emancipating the serfs in 1861, but his successors, Alexander III and Nicholas II, turned their backs on reform, regarding themselves as divinely sanctioned fathers of their people.

timeline

1902	1903	1904–5	1905	1914	1915
Lenin publishes *What Is to Be Done?*, emphasizing role of party elite in bringing about revolution	Russian Social Democrats split between Bolsheviks under Lenin and Mensheviks; Stalin joins Bolsheviks	Russo–Japanese War	After failure of Revolution of 1905, Lenin goes into exile abroad	Outbreak of First World War	Nicholas II takes command of Russian armed forces

Nicholas II attempted to assert Russian power in the Far East, leading to a humiliating defeat in the Russo–Japanese War of 1904–5. Defeat and general discontent prompted the Revolution of 1905, marked by massacres of peaceful demonstrators, uprisings, mutinies and a general strike. The tsar agreed to the formation of a *duma*, or parliament, and then, having brought moderate opinion over to his side, proceeded to crush the revolt. Some reforms followed, but Nicholas was indifferent to the appalling conditions in which the emerging urban proletariat lived and worked.

Life for the workers and peasants was made immeasurably worse by the First World War. As Nicholas took command of the armed forces, Russia suffered reverse after reverse, and government at home was left in the equally incapable hands of the Empress Alexandra and her right-wing circle. By 1917, military casualties exceeded 8 million, and a million more men had deserted. The peasants stopped sending produce to the cities, leading to food shortages. On 8 March 1917 (February in the old Russian calendar) revolution broke in Petrograd (St Petersburg). Soldiers and workers formed a soviet (council), and other soviets sprang up elsewhere. The tsar ordered the Petrograd garrison to suppress the revolt, but the garrison mutinied, and on 15 March Nicholas abdicated. A moderate provisional government was set up, but the soviets represented a significant alternative centre of power.

> **In such a country it was quite easy to start a revolution, as easy as lifting a feather.**
>
> **V. I. Lenin,** addressing Seventh Congress of the Bolshevik Party, 7 March 1918

The Bolshevik coup On 16 April, Lenin arrived in Petrograd from exile in Switzerland. Lenin was the leader of the Bolshevik ('majority') faction of the Russian Social Democratic Workers' Party, which had split in 1903. The Bolsheviks believed a single, small group of professional revolutionaries could and should lead the revolution to a successful conclusion. The Menshevik ('minority') faction, in contrast, believed that a mass party needed to be built before the revolution could take place.

1917	1918	1919	1920	1921
MARCH Revolution in Petrograd. Formation of soviets. Tsar abdicates in favour of provisional government. **APRIL** Lenin returns to Russia. **NOVEMBER** Bolsheviks seize power.	Beginning of Russian Civil War. **MARCH** Treaty of Brest-Litovsk: Bolsheviks make peace with Germans. **JUNE** Introduction of 'War Communism'. **JULY** Tsar and his family shot by the Bolsheviks.	Red Army retakes Ukraine	Red Army retakes most of Siberia. End of Civil War.	Kronstadt naval mutiny. Introduction of New Economic Policy.

As soon as he arrived in Petrograd, Lenin called for a transfer of power from the provisional government to the soviets. The failure of the provisional government to end Russia's involvement in the war or to implement land reforms or end food shortages fuelled unrest. The Bolsheviks gained a majority in the Petrograd soviet, and in November (October in the old Russian calendar) staged a revolution and seized power.

The establishment of the Soviet Union The new government made peace with Germany, signing a peace treaty in March 1918. The Bolsheviks were then faced with an internal civil war, in which the Red Army, led by Leon Trotsky, fought the anti-Bolshevik Whites. Despite pro-White military interventions by various Western powers, the Red Army was victorious by 1920, and in 1922 the Bolsheviks, having reconquered many non-Russian parts of the old Russian empire that had declared their independence, proclaimed the Union of Soviet Socialist Republics.

From Red Terror to Great Purge

In 1918 Lenin let loose the Cheka (secret police) against his political opponents in a process called the Red Terror. His use of arrest, execution and confinement of suspected enemies in a 'Gulag' of labour camps, where many more died in appalling conditions, was expanded under Stalin. During the collectivization of agriculture, the entire class of kulaks (rich peasants) was eliminated, with millions of deaths; millions more died in famines in Ukraine and Kazakhstan in 1932–4. Stalin then turned his attention to real or suspected enemies within the minority nationalities, the army and the Communist Party itself – including many veterans of the 1917 Bolshevik Revolution, who were tortured into publicly admitting their 'guilt' in a series of show trials in the Great Purge of 1936–8. In all, tens of millions were shot, exiled or sent to labour camps – while Stalin made himself the object of a cult of personality, and kept a steel grip on power.

timeline

1922	1924	1927	1928	1932–3
Formation of Union of Soviet Socialist Republics, encompassing much of old Russian empire. Lenin incapacitated by series of strokes. Stalin becomes general secretary of the Communist Party.	Death of Lenin	Trotsky exiled, clearing the way for Stalin to become supreme leader	Stalin orders confiscation of land from peasants. Start of first five-year plan to improve heavy industry.	Famine in Ukraine

In the wake of the Bolshevik Revolution, Lenin had ordered the break-up of the old estates and the redistribution of land to the peasants. But the exigencies of the civil war obliged him in June 1918 to introduce 'War Communism', under which the state nationalized industry, appropriated private businesses and requisitioned food from the peasants. Productivity collapsed, and there were serious food shortages. This resulted in disaffection and protests, such as the 1921 mutiny at the Kronstadt naval base. In response, Lenin introduced the 'New Economic Policy' (NEP), which restored a measure of free enterprise and made concessions to peasants and consumers. As the economy recovered, so did the grasp on power of the Communist Party (as the Bolsheviks were now known).

> **❝One death is a tragedy, a million deaths a statistic.❞**
>
> **Joseph Stalin,** attributed remark

Lenin's death in 1924 led to a power struggle, chiefly between Trotsky and Joseph Stalin. Stalin proved to be the more ruthless operator, and in 1927 Trotsky – who had wanted to spread the revolution across Europe – was expelled from the party and went into exile. Stalin embarked on a policy of 'socialism in one country', abandoning the NEP and introducing a series of five-year plans, which involved a massive acceleration in industrialization and the repossession of land from the peasants, who were forced to work on collective farms. In the process millions upon millions died, as Stalin stamped himself on the USSR as absolute dictator, a position he was to hold until his death in 1953.

in a nutshell
Russia exchanged one tyranny for another

1936–8	1939	1940	1941	1944–5	1945	1953
Millions killed in Great Purge	Stalin signs Non-Aggression Pact with Hitler. Red Army occupies eastern Poland.	Trotsky assassinated in Mexico, probably on Stalin's orders. USSR annexes Baltic States.	Nazi invasion of USSR	Red Army sweeps through countries of eastern Europe, which become Soviet satellites	Beginning of Cold War	Death of Stalin

39 The shadow of Fascism

The First World War left the countries of Europe exhausted, impoverished and embittered – a perfect breeding ground for political extremism. Many returning soldiers felt the politicians had not only abandoned them, but also dishonoured their millions of dead comrades. The war had all been for nothing, and with the return of peace the politicians offered no security and no hope. Democracy had failed. What was needed to restore national pride was a strong, charismatic leader who could bend the whole of society to his will.

It was this mood that gave birth to Fascism, an extreme form of militaristic nationalism that took root in a number of European countries in the 1920s and 1930s, most notably in Italy and Germany. Fascism is not a coherent international ideology like Marxism, but tends to take on local characteristics – for example, German Nazis were much more anti-Semitic than the supporters of Mussolini in Italy. But in general Fascists espouse violent authoritarianism, share a hatred of foreigners, ethnic minorities, socialists, communists, liberals and democrats, and yearn for military conquest.

The rise of Mussolini and Hitler Following the Bolshevik seizure of power in Russia in 1917, fear of communist revolution propelled many middle-class people in Europe into the arms of the far right. In Italy, the most prominent of the far-right parties was the *Fasci di Combattimento* – the

timeline

1918	1919	1920	1922	1923	1925
NOVEMBER End of First World War	**JANUARY** Spartacist (communist) revolt in Berlin suppressed by right-wing *Freikorps* militia. **JUNE** Treaty of Versailles.	Failure of right-wing coup attempt, the 'Kapp Putsch', in Germany	Fascist 'March on Rome'; Mussolini becomes prime minister of Italy	Failure of Nazi Beer Hall Putsch in Munich	Hitler publishes *Mein Kampf*

Fascists – who took their name from the *fasces*, the bundles of rods enclosing an axe carried by magistrates in ancient Rome as a symbol of their authority. In 1922, under their leader Benito Mussolini, a journalist and brilliant orator, 25,000 black-shirted Fascists made their famous 'March on Rome', where King Victor Emmanuel II was persuaded to ask Mussolini to form a government. Mussolini went on to establish a single-party dictatorship, with himself as *Il Duce* ('the leader').

In Germany, during the chaos following the end of the First World War, groups from both the communist left and the far right unsuccessfully tried to seize power. In 1923, one of the far-right parties, the National Socialist German Workers' Party – the Nazis – attempted to overthrow the government of Bavaria in the so-called 'Beer Hall Putsch'. The Nazi leader, a former corporal called Adolf Hitler, spent a short time in jail as a consequence, where he wrote *Mein Kampf* ('My Struggle'), in which he asserted the superiority of the blond, blue-eyed 'Aryan' race of the Germanic and Nordic countries over Africans, Slavs, Gypsies, Jews and other *Untermenschen* ('sub-humans'). Hitler declared that it was the destiny of the German race to create a *Lebensraum* ('living space') in the rich agricultural lands of western Russia. In addition, Hitler played on the resentment felt by many Germans at the severity of the Treaty of Versailles, and peddled the popular myth that the German army, far from being defeated in 1918, had been 'stabbed in the back' by the democratic politicians.

With the onset of the Great Depression – which Hitler blamed on Jewish bankers – the Nazis experienced an upswing in their popularity. In the election of 1932 they became the largest party in the Reichstag (the German parliament), and in January 1933 Hitler became chancellor (prime minister). When the Reichstag was burned down in February, the Nazis blamed the communists and proceeded to arrest opposition politicians. By

> **❝The broad mass of a nation . . . will more easily fall victim to a big lie than to a small one.❞**
>
> **Adolf Hitler,** *Mein Kampf,* 1925

1926	1929	1930	1931	1932	1933
Mussolini makes himself dictator	Wall Street Crash ushers in Great Depression	Economic and political crisis leads President Hindenburg to rule by decree in Germany	Japanese army occupies Manchuria	Nazis become largest party in Reichstag	Formation of Falange, Spanish Fascist party. **JANUARY** Hitler appointed chancellor. **FEBRUARY** Reichstag fire. **MARCH** Enabling Act allows Hitler to rule by decree. Jews expelled from civil service, and Jewish shops and firms boycotted. **OCTOBER** Germany leaves League of Nations.

The Treaty of Versailles

Following its defeat in the First World War, Germany was obliged to sign the punitive Treaty of Versailles, in which it was forced to admit to starting the war. Germany lost all of its overseas possessions and much territory in Europe, including Alsace and Lorraine to France, and a corridor giving Poland access to the Baltic Sea, so splitting Germany in two. The Rhineland was occupied by Allied troops. Conscription was banned, and Germany's armed forces were limited to 100,000 men, with no tanks, military aircraft or large warships. Finally, Germany was forced to pay vast sums in reparations to Britain and France

August 1934 Germany had become a single-party dictatorship, with Hitler known simply as the *Führer* ('leader'). The Nazi Party controlled every aspect of German life, and enforced its will by means of the Gestapo (secret police) and SS paramilitaries. In addition to eliminating their political enemies, the Nazis stepped up their persecution of the country's Jewish population.

Dreams of empire While Hitler declared the advent of a new German Reich that would last a thousand years, Mussolini sought to build an empire to rival that of ancient Rome, and in 1935 ordered his army to invade the independent African kingdom of Abyssinia (Ethiopia). One of the provisions of the Treaty of Versailles had been the creation of the League of Nations, an international body that was supposed to prevent any future aggression by one state against another, and thus put an end to all wars. However, the League had done little more than express disapproval after Japan occupied Manchuria in 1931, and, following the Italian invasion of Abyssinia, it did nothing apart from imposing ineffective economic sanctions.

Germany had followed Japan out of the League in 1933. The following year Hitler defied the Versailles treaty by reintroducing conscription and began a massive programme of rearmament. It was this more than anything that returned the country to full employment during the Great Depression. In 1936 Hitler ordered the German army to reoccupy the Rhineland, and formed an alliance with Mussolini known as the Rome–Berlin Axis.

timeline

1934

MAY Fascist coup in Bulgaria. **JUNE** Paramilitary leader Ernst Röhm, Hitler's rival in the Nazi Party, is murdered alongside 150 of his supporters in the 'Night of the Long Knives'. **AUGUST** After Hindenburg's death, Hitler becomes *Führer*, with powers of both chancellor and president.

1935

JANUARY People of Saarland vote for reunification with Germany.
MARCH Hitler reintroduces conscription.
SEPTEMBER Nuremberg Laws strip German Jews of their civil rights.
OCTOBER Italian invasion of Abyssinia.

1936

MARCH German troops reoccupy Rhineland.
JULY Beginning of Spanish Civil War between right-wing Nationalists (supported militarily by Germany and Italy) and left-wing and democratic Republicans. **OCTOBER** Formation of Berlin–Rome Axis. **NOVEMBER** Germany and Japan form Anti-Comintern Pact aimed at USSR; Italy joins 1937.

Hitler then turned his attention to extending the boundaries of the German Reich. Versailles had left many ethnic Germans as minorities within other states, and Hitler exploited this. *Anschluss* (union) with Austria had been forbidden by the Versailles treaty, but there were many Nazi sympathizers in Austria, and when in March 1938 German troops entered the country, they were widely welcomed. Britain and France protested, but, desperate to avoid another war, did nothing – a policy subsequently dubbed 'appeasement'.

Hitler now pressed the case of the ethnic Germans in the Sudetenland area of Czechoslovakia, who demanded to join the Reich. As the crisis deepened, the British and French prime ministers, Neville Chamberlain and Edouard Daladier, joined Hitler and Mussolini in Munich to find a peaceful solution. On 30 September 1938 they signed the Munich Agreement, which – without consulting the Czechoslovak government – transferred the Sudetenland to Germany.

When Hitler proceeded to occupy the remainder of Czechoslovakia in March 1939, Chamberlain realized that appeasement was not the answer, and when Hitler began to demand the return of the Polish Corridor and the free city of Danzig (Gdansk), Britain and France declared that they would provide military assistance should Poland's frontiers be threatened. On 1 September 1939, having agreed a Non-Aggression Pact with the Soviet Union, Hitler called their bluff and launched an invasion of Poland. Two days later, Britain and France declared war.

> **❛I believe it is peace for our time.❜**
>
> **Neville Chamberlain,**
> on the Munich Agreement,
> 30 September 1938

in a nutshell
Discontent with the outcome of the First World War paved the way for the Second

1937	1938	1939
JULY Japan launches full-scale invasion of China	**MARCH** German troops occupy Austria, which becomes part of the German Reich. **SEPTEMBER** In Munich, Britain and France agree to German annexation of Czech Sudetenland. **NOVEMBER** *Kristallnacht*: Jewish shops, homes and synagogues burned throughout Germany.	**MARCH** German forces occupy the remainder of Czechoslovakia. Britain and France declare they will defend Poland. **APRIL** Nationalist victory in Spanish Civil War. Italy invades Albania. **AUGUST** Nazi-Soviet Non-Aggression Pact. **SEPTEMBER** Hitler invades Poland, beginning Second World War.

40 The Great Depression

'In no nation are the fruits of accomplishment more secure,' President Herbert Hoover told his fellow Americans on taking office on 4 March 1929. 'I have no fears for the future of our country. It is bright with hope.'

His mood of optimism was shared across the USA: never had the stock market been so highly valued, as people enthusiastically speculated in the ongoing success of the capitalist system. Seven months after Hoover's inaugural address, disaster struck. On 24 October 1929, 'Black Thursday', the US Stock Exchange on Wall Street crashed. On that day alone, 13 million shares changed hands, as speculators realized that the real value of their investments bore no relation to the inflated sums they had paid for them. In a few days, $30 billion had been wiped off the value of stocks.

It was not the first speculative bubble to have burst, but the repercussions of the Wall Street Crash were both longer-lasting and wider-ranging than anything the world had seen before. As US banks panicked and recalled huge sums in loans they had made to European countries, particularly Germany, the Crash ushered in the Great Depression, a decade-long period of global economic collapse, and high unemployment.

The path to economic collapse The Great Depression – also called the Slump – was not brought about by the Wall Street Crash alone. The expense of the First World War had caused the combatant countries

timeline

1919	1920	1921	1922	1923	1924
Treaty of Versailles forces Germany to pay reparations after defeat in First World War	Short-lived postwar boom	Unemployment in UK soars to 2.5 million. USA imposes tariffs on agricultural imports.	Beginning of German hyperinflation. Mussolini's Fascists come to power in Italy.	**JANUARY** French and Belgian troops occupy Ruhr valley after Germany fails to pay reparation instalment. **NOVEMBER** German mark falls to 4.2 trillion to the dollar.	**JANUARY–OCTOBER** Britain's first Labour government. **SEPTEMBER** Dawes Plan reschedules German reparations.

to accumulate massive debts – largely owed to US banks – and it had also skewed industrial production towards armaments, and boosted the demand for agricultural products. With the coming of peace, industry experienced a brief boom, but soon found that the market for manufactured goods was limited. Similarly, as demand for agricultural products – from wheat to cotton to rubber – decreased, farmers were faced with falling prices. In America, many were forced to mortgage their farms to the banks, while countries that relied on exporting agricultural produce were obliged to borrow large sums.

As well as making loans to US farmers and foreign states, the US banks had happily lent money to stock-market speculators. But when Wall Street crashed, many speculators were left penniless, and the banks – if they did not themselves go bust – implemented a severe squeeze on credit. Thousands of farmers lost their properties as the banks foreclosed on their mortgages, forcing numerous families, especially in the Midwest, off the land and onto the road in search of work. The banks also called in overseas loans, which further reduced the demand for US exports, as few could afford to buy them. In 1930 the USA introduced import tariffs to protect US industry and agriculture, a move described by one historian as 'a virtual declaration of economic war on the rest of the world'. Other countries responded by introducing their own protectionist measures. There was a general failure to recognize the global nature of the crisis, and, instead of working cooperatively, the world's leading powers scuttled into their own blinkered corners.

> **❛Brother, can you spare a dime?❜**
>
> **Yip Harburg song,** 1932, which has come to symbolize the Great Depression in America

From laissez-faire to New Deal In the USA, President Hoover initially believed the crisis was just a temporary blip. But as the US unemployment rate rose to one in four in the USA, and one in three in some other countries, even Hoover had to admit there was a problem – but he did not believe that it was the responsibility of the federal government. In the 1932 presidential election, Hoover was swept out of office by Franklin

1925	**1926**	**1929**	**1930**
US President Calvin Coolidge opposes reduction of British and French war debt	Failure of General Strike in Britain	**MARCH** Herbert Hoover becomes president of the USA. **MAY** Labour Party forms minority government in Britain. **JUNE** Young Plan reschedules German reparations; bitterly opposed by Nazis. **OCTOBER** Wall Street Crash.	**JUNE** President Hoover signs Smoot-Hawley tariff bill, leading to international trade wars. **SEPTEMBER** As German unemployment reaches 3 million, Nazis win 107 seats in Reichstag.

Delano Roosevelt, who promised a 'New Deal' for the American people. Roosevelt went along with the ideas of the British economist John Maynard Keynes, who held that the traditional laissez-faire capitalist approach of keeping government spending and government involvement in the economy to a minimum only perpetuated economic downturns. Roosevelt set about subjecting banking, prices and production to strict government control, offered federal loans to forestall bankruptcies and foreclosures on mortgages, and embarked on a massive programme of public-works projects, by which the government brought millions back into employment, and thus pumped large sums back into the economy. By 1934 unemployment began to fall, and the economic situation slowly began to improve.

The effect of reparations

In 1919 the British economist J. M. Keynes had warned of the disastrous consequences of the Treaty of Versailles (see p. 158). Germany had been one of the biggest economies in the world, but the requirement imposed on it by the treaty to pay vast sums in reparations severely hampered its return to economic health, and so a major market was denied to exporters in other countries. By 1923 Germany was suffering hyperinflation – to such an extent that it required a wheelbarrow to carry enough banknotes to buy a loaf of bread.

Although the German economy recovered to some extent, helped by a rescheduling of reparations and a massive US bank loan in 1924, the Wall Street Crash brought more financial difficulties, and in 1930 a further rescheduling was arranged, together with another large loan. But it made no difference: as German banks collapsed and unemployment soared, in 1932 the international community eventually agreed to cancel all reparations. But the damage was done: in that year's election, the Nazis became the biggest party in the German Reichstag. In 1919 Keynes had foreseen something of the kind. 'But who can say how much is endurable,' he had written, 'or in what direction men will seek at last to escape from their misfortunes?'

timeline

1931

AUGUST Labour government in Britain collapses over public-spending cuts; replaced by Conservative-dominated National Government. **SEPTEMBER** Britain abandons Gold Standard. **DECEMBER** Unemployment in USA reaches 8 million.

1932

Unemployment in Germany exceeds 6 million. Britain introduces 'imperial preference', abandoning free trade in favour of imports from the British empire. **JUNE** Britain and France cease to pay war debts to USA. **JULY** Nazis become biggest party in Reichstag. **NOVEMBER** F. D. Roosevelt elected US president, on basis of 'New Deal'.

1933

MARCH Hitler assumes dictatorial powers in Germany. **APRIL** USA abandons Gold Standard. **JUNE–JULY** Failure of World Economic Conference in London.

"While it isn't written in the Constitution, nevertheless it is the inherent duty of the federal government to keep its citizens from starvation."

President F. D. Roosevelt, quoted in *America in Midpassage*, 1939

Other governments, such as the Conservative-dominated National Government in Britain, preferred to concentrate on cutting government expenditure and raising protective tariffs. Traditional heavy industries such as ship-building were left to their fates, leading to unemployment rates as high as 70 per cent in the north-east, prompting a number of 'hunger marches' on London, such as the 1936 'Jarrow Crusade'.

In Germany, the effects of the Depression were particularly acute, and helped Hitler to power in 1933. The Nazis blamed international Jewish bankers for the suffering of the German people, and promised to restore national pride. In their latter aim they succeeded, reducing unemployment by a variety of means – principally by the reintroduction of conscription and a massive programme of rearmament, as Hitler prepared the country for another war. As the 1930s rolled on, and international tensions began to rise, other countries, such as Britain, embarked on programmes of rearmament, and these injections of government money served to stimulate the economy and reduce unemployment. But it was really only the outbreak of the Second World War that brought the Great Depression finally to an end.

in a nutshell
The worst economic slump of the 20th century

1934	**1935**	**1936**	**1939**
US industrialists begin to organize opposition to New Deal policies. **FEBRUARY** Workers' uprising in Austria suppressed by right-wing government. **MAY** Soil erosion turns much of Midwest into a 'Dust Bowl'.	US Supreme Court rules some New Deal legislation unconstitutional	Left-wing Popular Front governments elected in Spain and France. Jarrow Crusade in Britain. J. M. Keynes publishes his vastly influential *General Theory of Employment, Interest and Money.* **SEPTEMBER** France abandons Gold Standard. **NOVEMBER** Roosevelt re-elected.	Outbreak of Second World War

41 The Second World War: Europe

By the late 1930s, the world was preparing for another war. In the Far East, an increasingly militaristic Japan had been pursuing an aggressive policy of territorial expansion since its occupation of Chinese Manchuria in 1931. The world sat back and did nothing. In 1935, Mussolini, the Italian dictator, ordered his troops into Abyssinia. Again, the world did nothing.

In 1937 Japan launched an all-out war of conquest in China itself. The international community did not lift a finger. In 1938 Hitler annexed Austria, and at the Munich Conference Britain and France agreed to his annexation of the Sudeten area of Czechoslovakia. Hitler went on to occupy the whole of the country, and then started threatening Poland, demanding the return of former German territory lost after the First World War.

At last, Britain and France woke up to the danger, and declared that they would come to Poland's aid should it be invaded. Of more concern to Hitler, however, was the Soviet Union, and to avoid the prospect of a war on two fronts, on 23 August 1939 he shocked the world by agreeing a Non-Aggression Pact with Stalin, his greatest ideological enemy. On 1 September, German tanks rolled into Poland. Two days later, Britain and France declared war.

timeline

1931	1935	1936	1937	1938
Japanese army occupies Manchuria	Italian invasion of Abyssinia	**OCTOBER** Formation of Berlin–Rome Axis. **NOVEMBER** Germany and Japan form. Anti-Comintern Pact aimed at USSR; Italy joins 1937.	Japan launches full-scale invasion of China	**MARCH** Germany annexes Austria. **SEPTEMBER** At Munich, Britain and France agree to German annexation of Czech Sudetenland.

Dark days Being on the other side of Europe, there was little that either Britain or France could do to help the Poles. For six months there was a period of tense stand-off known as the Phoney War, which came abruptly to an end in April 1940, when Hitler overran Denmark and invaded Norway. Then in May he launched his Blitzkrieg ('lightning war') on the Low Countries and France, using fast-moving tanks and motorized infantry to punch holes in the enemy's defences, and aircraft to support the attack and terrorize the civilian population with aerial bombing. Both the British and French armies were taken by surprise, and were forced into headlong retreat.

The British prime minister Neville Chamberlain, who had sought to appease Hitler in 1938 by acceding to his territorial demands, resigned. He was replaced by the robust and defiant figure of Winston Churchill, who told the British people he had 'nothing to offer but blood, toil, tears, and sweat'. After the British Expeditionary Force, surrounded in Dunkirk, was evacuated at the end of May, and France signed an armistice with Germany, Britain was left to fight Hitler alone. 'We shall never surrender,' Churchill famously told the British people.

> **❝What is our policy? . . . to wage war against a monstrous tyranny, never surpassed in the dark, lamentable catalogue of human crime.❞**
>
> **Winston Churchill,** first address as prime minister to the House of Commons, 13 May 1940

Across the Atlantic, President F. D. Roosevelt, though sympathetic to Britain's plight, was constrained by strong isolationist sentiment in the USA from entering the war on the British side. However, he supplied huge amounts of material aid via Atlantic convoys, which found themselves under constant attack by German U-boats, Hitler's aim being to starve the British into submission. During the summer of 1940, he prepared to launch an invasion across the English Channel, and as a first step set out to destroy Britain's military airfields. In this aim he was thwarted by the Royal Air Force, which, during the Battle of Britain, shot down so many German bombers that Hitler turned instead to night-time raids on British cities – the Blitz – in which tens of thousands of civilians were killed.

1939

MARCH German forces occupy the remainder of Czechoslovakia. **APRIL** Italy invades Albania. **AUGUST** Nazi-Soviet Non-Aggression Pact. **SEPTEMBER** Hitler invades Poland; Britain and France declare war; Soviet Union occupies eastern Poland. **NOVEMBER** Soviet Union attacks Finland.

1940

APRIL German forces overrun Denmark and invade Norway. **MAY** Germany invades Low Countries and France. **JUNE** French government signs armistice with Germany and proceeds to collaborate with occupiers. Italy enters war. **JULY–AUGUST** Battle of Britain. **SEPTEMBER** Beginning of London Blitz. Italians invade Egypt from Libya. **OCTOBER** Hungary and Romania join Axis.

The tide turns The war moved to different fronts. In September 1940 Italy attacked the British in Egypt, and were later reinforced by the German Afrika Korps. The two sides fought to and fro across the deserts of North Africa until British and Commonwealth troops scored a decisive victory in 1942 at El Alamein. By this time the USA had entered the war and landed in north-west Africa, and in July 1943 the Allies invaded Sicily. Italy agreed to an armistice, but German troops occupied the country and fiercely resisted the Allied advance.

All these were sideshows compared to the massive scale of operations on the Eastern Front. In June 1941 Hitler abandoned his Non-Aggression Pact with Stalin and launched a massive invasion of the Soviet Union. The Red Army, weakened by Stalin's purges of the later 1930s, reeled. The Germans treated the Russians as not only ideological enemies because of their communist system, but also as *Untermenschen* (sub-humans) because of the supposed inferiority of the Slavic 'race' to which they belonged. In

Cracking the Enigma code

Long before the war the Germans had developed a sophisticated encryption device, the Enigma machine, which scrambled top-secret military communications into codes that could only be unscrambled using another Enigma machine. In 1939 the British set up an equally top-secret project at Bletchley Park, where hundreds of mathematicians and linguists eventually found a way of deciphering Enigma radio signals – and in the process created one of the world's first computers. The intelligence thus gained played a key role in a number of decisive campaigns – perhaps most notably the Battle of the Atlantic, where by 1943 the Allies knew exactly where the German U-boat packs were going to strike. This proved invaluable in protecting the huge flow of men and materials across the Atlantic during the build-up to D-Day.

timeline

1941	1942	1943
MARCH US Senate passes Lend-Lease bill to give aid to Britain. Italians invade Greece. Bulgaria joins Axis. **APRIL** Germans invade Yugoslavia and Greece. **JUNE** Germany invades Soviet Union. **DECEMBER** USA enters the war after Japanese attack on Pearl Harbor.	**MAY** Thousand-bomber raid on Cologne. **NOVEMBER** Allies defeat Axis armies at El Alamein, Egypt. Allied landings in north-west Africa. Red Army encircles Germans at Stalingrad.	**FEBRUARY** Germans surrender at Stalingrad. **MAY** Axis forces surrender in North Africa. **JULY** Allied invasion of Sicily; fall of Mussolini. Red Army defeats Germans at Kursk in largest tank battle in history. **SEPTEMBER** Allied invasion of mainland Italy, which agrees armistice.

consequence, the suffering of the Soviet people as well as the Soviet armed forces was on a horrendous scale: perhaps 20 million died in the course of the war. But Hitler, like Napoleon before him, had underestimated the size, the climate and the resources of Russia. As Stalin pulled Russian industry behind the Urals, churning out tanks and aircraft in unprecedented numbers, the Germans suffered in the bitter Russian winter and were weakened by over-extended supply lines. Stalin had no qualms in sacrificing wave after wave of infantry, who were sent into battle with NKVD (secret police) machine-guns at their backs. The turning point on the Eastern Front came at Stalingrad on the Volga, where through the winter of 1942–3 a whole German army was encircled and forced to surrender. The Soviets then went on the offensive, advancing westward into eastern Europe.

> **❝I ask you: Do you want total war? Do you want it, if necessary, more total and more radical than we can even imagine it today?❞**
>
> **Joseph Goebbels,** Nazi propaganda minister, speech following the German surrender at Stalingrad, February 1943

Stalin had long demanded that his Western Allies open a second front. This eventually occurred when US, British and Commonwealth forces landed on the beaches of Normandy on D-Day, 6 June 1944. As the Western Allies advanced through France and the Low Countries and eventually crossed the Rhine into Germany itself, on the other side of the continent the Red Army was approaching Berlin. Hitler committed suicide on 30 April 1945, and on 7 May all German forces unconditionally surrendered to the Allies. No one quite knows the full extent of the human cost of the conflict around the world: estimates suggest that in excess of 50 million people died as a direct or indirect consequence of the fighting.

in a nutshell
The bloodiest war in history

1944

MARCH Germans occupy Hungary. **MAY** Allies capture Monte Cassino, strategic defensive position in Italy. **JUNE** Allies enter Rome. D-Day landings. **AUGUST** Allies land in south of France. Paris liberated. **SEPTEMBER** Allied airborne operation fails to secure strategic bridge at Arnhem, Netherlands. **DECEMBER** The Battle of the Bulge: Germans launch counter-offensive in the Ardennes.

1945

FEBRUARY Red Army takes Budapest. **MARCH** Allies cross Rhine. **APRIL** Execution of Mussolini by Italian partisans. Red Army attacks Berlin; suicide of Hitler. **MAY** Unconditional surrender of all German forces.

42 The Second World War: Asia and the Pacific

In a few decades at the end of the 19th century, Japan transformed itself from an isolated medieval state to a modern industrial power. Mimicking the great Western powers, the country also developed imperial ambitions, taking Taiwan and Korea from China in the war of 1894–5, and putting a stop to Russian expansion in the Far East in the war of 1904–5.

During the 1920s Japan – short of land and resources for its burgeoning population – experienced severe economic difficulties, and many people, particularly in the army, believed that only strong military government and territorial expansion could solve the country's problems. Their ardently militaristic and xenophobic nationalism centred round the emperor, a figurehead who was nevertheless worshipped as a living god.

Some elements in the army began to take matters into their own hands. Japan had gained the right to station troops to protect its South Manchurian Railway, and when in September 1931 a section of the railway was blown up near the city of Mukden (modern Shenyang), the army blamed the Chinese and used it as an excuse to occupy the whole of Manchuria. The League of Nations condemned the occupation, but Japan simply left the League.

timeline

1931	1932	1933	1934	1936	1937
Japanese army occupies Manchuria	Japanese set up puppet regime in Manchuria, renamed Manchukuo, under Puyi, the last Chinese emperor, who had been deposed in 1912	Japan leaves League of Nations	Japan renounces international treaties limiting its navy	Germany and Japan form Anti-Comintern Pact	**JULY** Japanese invasion of China. **DECEMBER** Sack of Nanjing, Chinese capital.

Japanese ambitions The militarists increasingly gained control of the government in Japan, which repudiated international limits on its naval strength, and saw itself, alongside Germany and Italy, as one of the most unjustly treated countries in the world. Japan allied itself with Germany and Italy, and in 1937 launched an all-out attack on China. The Japanese occupied much of the coast, and the capture of the then Chinese capital was followed by the 'Rape of Nanking', in which as many as 300,000 Chinese civilians were massacred. Nevertheless, resistance by Chinese nationalists continued.

> **❝Our national situation has reached an impasse . . . the only path left open to us is the development of Manchuria and Mongolia.❞**
>
> **Lieutenant Colonel Ishiwara Kanji,** one of the army officers involved in the annexation of Manchuria in 1931

The USA – which had its own interests and territories in the Pacific (including Hawaii, Guam and the Philippines) – grew alarmed at Japanese expansionism, and sought to restrict Japanese access to strategic raw materials, such as coal, iron ore and oil. For its part, especially after the outbreak of war in Europe in 1939, Japan had its eye on the colonies of Britain, France and the Netherlands in southern and south-eastern Asia, which it intended to absorb into a 'Greater East Asia Co-Prosperity Sphere'. This was dressed up as a liberation of Asian peoples from colonial rule, but in fact the intention was to swap European for Japanese domination, acquire strategic raw materials (such as Malayan rubber and Burmese oil), and at the same time to create a market for Japanese manufactured goods.

Japan demanded that all passage of supplies to the Chinese nationalists through French Indochina and the British colonies of Burma and Hong Kong should stop. To enforce this, in July 1941 Japanese troops occupied French Indochina, resulting in the US government freezing all Japanese assets in the USA. Prince Konoe, the Japanese premier, tried to broker a deal, but when the US government insisted that Japan withdraw from China and also from its alliance with Germany and Italy, Konoe resigned,

1938

OCTOBER Japanese capture Guandong (Canton).
NOVEMBER Japanese announce their plan for Greater East Asia Co-Prosperity Sphere.

1940

MARCH Japanese establish puppet Chinese government in Nanjing.
SEPTEMBER Japan signs Tripartite Pact with Germany and Italy, creating Rome–Berlin–Tokyo Axis.

1941

JULY Japanese occupation of French Indochina; US freezes Japanese assets. **AUGUST** Britain and Netherlands impose embargoes on Japanese trade.
DECEMBER Japanese attack on Pearl Harbor; USA declares war. Japan proceeds to attack Malaya, Guam, Philippines, Wake Island, Burma, Borneo and Hong Kong.

and was replaced in October 1941 by General Hideki Tojo. Tojo, while continuing to negotiate with the USA, was in fact planning all-out war. On 7 December 1941, while talks continued in Washington, Japanese carrier-borne aircraft attacked the US naval base at Pearl Harbor, on Oahu in the Hawaiian Islands. It was, President F. D. Roosevelt told Congress the following day as he requested a declaration of war, 'a date which will live in infamy'. But, by bringing an end to American isolationism and given America's huge resources, the attack ensured that, given time, the war was as good as lost as far as Japan and Germany were concerned.

The road to perdition The same day as Pearl Harbor, Japanese forces attacked US and British bases elsewhere in east Asia and the Pacific. There followed one of the most spectacular offensive campaigns in history, and by the middle of 1942 Japan had occupied most of the island groups of the western Pacific, plus the Philippines, northern New Guinea, the Dutch East Indies (modern Indonesia), Hong Kong, Thailand, Malaya, Singapore

The atomic bomb

In 1939 the great physicist Albert Einstein, who as a Jew had been obliged to flee to the USA from Nazi Germany, wrote to President F. D. Roosevelt to warn him that the Germans might already be working on nuclear weapons. As a consequence, Roosevelt authorized the Manhattan Project, which in utmost secrecy assembled a team of the world's top physicists and engineers to develop an atomic bomb. The first device was tested in the New Mexico desert on 16 July 1945, prompting the Project's director, Robert J. Oppenheimer, to quote a line from the ancient Hindu poem, the *Bhagavadgita*: 'I am become death, the destroyer of worlds.' It was the birth of the nuclear age: as Oppenheimer remarked two years after the atomic bombing of Hiroshima and Nagasaki: 'The physicists have known sin; and this is a knowledge that they cannot lose.'

timeline

1942

JANUARY Japanese invasion of Dutch East Indies, New Guinea and Solomon Islands. **FEBRUARY** Surrender of Singapore, Britain's most important naval base in the Far East. **MAY** Battle of the Coral Sea prevents planned Japanese landings at Port Moresby, New Guinea. **JUNE** US navy wins decisive Battle of Midway. Japanese complete conquest of Philippines. **AUGUST–DECEMBER** Beginning of Allied counter-offensives on Guadalcanal (Solomon Islands), New Guinea and Burma.

1943

FEBRUARY End of Japanese resistance on Guadalcanal. **AUGUST** US forces land on Ellice Islands (Tuvalu). **NOVEMBER** US landings on Bougainville. US forces capture Gilbert Islands.

and Burma, and was threatening India itself, the jewel in Britain's imperial crown. The campaign was accompanied by appalling acts of brutality, the Japanese then regarding all other races as inferior species, and treating any soldiers who surrendered to them rather than fighting to the death as contemptible cowards, to be used as slave labour and subjected to starvation, beatings and summary execution.

> **❝I fear we have only awakened a sleeping giant, and his reaction will be terrible.❞**
>
> **Admiral Yamamoto,** (attributed), **commander of the Japanese fleet that attacked Pearl Harbor**

The Japanese advance was turned back in June 1942 at the Battle of Midway, in which the Japanese lost four aircraft carriers and 248 aircraft. It proved to be the turning point in the Pacific War. The Japanese did not have the resources to replace such losses at anything like the rate that the Americans could. Although there were still years of hard fighting left, from this point on the Japanese were forced into a desperate retreat. By mid-1944 the Americans had retaken islands close enough to Japan to provide bases from which their bombers could begin the devastation of Japanese cities. But the closer the Americans came to Japan itself, the stiffer the Japanese resistance. Faced with Japan's refusal to surrender, and the prospect of enormous casualties should they attempt an invasion of the Japanese home islands, the Americans decided to deploy a horrendous new weapon. On 6 August they dropped an atomic bomb on the city of Hiroshima, instantly killing 78,000 people. A second bomb was dropped on Nagasaki three days later. On 15 August Emperor Hirohito made his first ever radio broadcast to his people, announcing the unconditional surrender of all imperial Japanese forces to the Allies.

in a nutshell
Japan overextended itself in taking on the USA

1944	**1945**
FEBRUARY US forces complete capture of Marshall Islands. **JUNE** Allies repel attempted Japanese invasion of India at Kohima and Imphal. Japanese fleet defeated at Battle of the Philippine Sea. **SEPTEMBER** Beginning of Allied counter-attacks in Burma. **OCTOBER** US naval victory at Battle of Leyte Gulf.	**FEBRUARY** US forces meet with fierce resistance on Iwo Jima. Beginning of firebombing of Tokyo. **APRIL** Japanese use kamikaze tactics against US forces invading Okinawa. Japanese resistance ends on Okinawa and much of Philippines. **AUGUST** Atomic bombs dropped on Hiroshima and Nagasaki. USSR declares war on Japan. Japan accepts surrender terms.

43 The Holocaust

In a few short years, between 1939 and 1945, some 6 million Jews – two-thirds of Europe's Jewish population – were systematically murdered by the Nazis. The magnitude of the horror contained within this bald statement is almost impossible to grasp.

Nor is it easy to comprehend the motives of the perpetrators, who took that most hateful and twisted of human delusions – belief in the superiority of one race over others – to its logical conclusion. It was not the first nor the last example of genocide, but it was on a scale that humanity has not so far surpassed.

The word 'holocaust', first used in this context by historians in the 1950s, comes from a Greek word meaning 'burned whole', and was applied in the Old Testament to animal sacrifices in which the victim was entirely consumed by fire – the allusion being to the burning of the bodies of murdered Jews in the crematoria of the extermination camps. To Jews, the attempted annihilation of European Jewry is simply the *Shoah*, the Hebrew word for 'catastrophe'.

The roots of anti-Semitism Jewish communities had settled around the Mediterranean during Roman times, and from there spread throughout Europe. In those lands ruled by Muslims, such as medieval Spain, they were generally tolerated, but the Christian church tended to regard Jews as 'Christ killers', leading to intermittent bouts of persecution – such as the massacres of Jews during the religious fervour of the First Crusade and later at the time of the Black Death, which many claimed

timeline

1933	1935	1937	1938
Nazis come to power in Germany. Jews expelled from civil service, and Jewish shops and firms boycotted.	Nuremberg Laws strip German Jews of their civil rights. Heinrich Himmler, head of the SS, starts a breeding programme to produce an 'Aryan master race'.	**JULY** Opening of Buchenwald concentration camp. German Jews forced to wear yellow Star-of-David badges. **DECEMBER** Jews in Romania excluded from professions and barred from owning land.	**NOVEMBER** *Kristallnacht*: Jewish shops, homes and synagogues burnt throughout Germany, in revenge for murder of German diplomat in Paris by a German-Polish Jew

had been caused by Jews poisoning the wells. With their separate religion and culture, Jews, like other outsider groups through history, were groundlessly suspected of all sorts of abominations – such as the sacrifice of Christian children – and became a convenient scapegoat when things went wrong. Some countries, such as England in the late 13th century and Spain in 1492, expelled their Jewish communities altogether. It was almost 400 years before Jews were allowed back into England.

In western Europe, Jewish communities tended to be prosperous, middle-class and relatively assimilated – significant numbers even converted to Christianity. Many worked in commerce and banking – often because the professions, the civil service and the army had been barred to them – and their financial success often inspired envy, or worse.

Other victims of the Nazis

Jews were not the only victims of the Nazi doctrine of 'racial hygiene': nearly 400,000 Gypsies were also killed, together with untold numbers of Slavs, homosexuals and people with mental or physical disabilities. Also targeted for extermination were Jehovah's Witnesses, communists, socialists, and any others regarded by the Nazis as enemies of the state. In addition, over 3 million Soviet prisoners of war – more than half of those taken by the German army – died during their captivity, so appalling were the conditions in which they were kept. In all, the Nazis killed an estimated 14 million people whom they regarded as *Untermenschen* ('sub-human').

Towards the 'final solution' During the later 19th century there emerged a perversion of Darwin's theory of evolution by natural selection that held that, to ensure the future of the human race, only the fittest specimens, in both physical and mental terms, should be allowed to breed. A pseudo-science of 'eugenics' arose, which identified all those who should be prevented from having children – the mentally ill, criminals, alcoholics, those of limited intellectual capacity, those born with physical defects, and so on. Alongside eugenics, a new form of racism emerged, which identified

1939
SEPTEMBER Hitler invades Poland, beginning Second World War

1940
Nazis begin massacres of Jews in Poland, and confine Jews to ghettoes.
JULY Collaborationist Vichy government in France introduces anti-Jewish measures.

1941
JUNE Nazi invasion of Soviet Union followed by mass murder of Jewish populations. Hungary formally allies itself to Nazi Germany, but refuses to hand over its 800,000-strong Jewish population. **SEPTEMBER** In two days, SS troops shoot 33,771 Ukrainian Jews at Babi Yar, a ravine outside Kiev.

some 'races' as 'superior' to others using pseudo-scientific techniques such as measuring skull dimensions, and which advocated maintaining the 'purity' of the 'superior races' by preventing mixed marriages. Into this heady brew, the Nazis threw in a strong dose of traditional anti-Semitism to come up with a determination to find a 'final solution to the Jewish question'.

> **We Germans must finally learn not to regard the Jew ... as people of our own kind ...**
>
> **Heinrich Himmler,** leader of the SS, 5 March 1936

After Hitler came to power in Germany in 1933, Jews were expelled from the civil service, and Jewish shops and businesses were boycotted. Two years later, the Nuremberg Laws deprived Jews of their German citizenship and forbade them from marrying 'Aryans' (as the Nazis described the blond and blue-eyed Germanic and Nordic 'race'). On 9 November 1938, on *Kristallnacht* ('the night of broken glass'), attacks were made on Jewish homes, shops and synagogues across Germany, and nearly 100 Jews were murdered. Many wealthier Jews had already fled Germany, but many remained, and it became increasingly difficult for would-be refugees to find a country that would accept them.

The Second World War gave the Nazis the opportunity to fulfil their genocidal policies, not only in Germany, but in all the countries they conquered. As the German army swept through Poland in 1939, and then on into Russia in 1941, they were accompanied by *Einsatzgruppen* ('task forces') of SS troops whose job it was to eliminate Soviet political commissars and round up and 'resettle' the Jewish population. 'Resettlement' was a euphemism for extermination, and by early 1942 the *Einsatzgruppen* had killed more than half a million Jews, mostly by shooting. But things were going too slowly for the Nazi leadership, and in January 1942 a group of senior officials met in the Berlin suburb of Wannsee to discuss the achievement of the 'final solution'.

The outcome was a ruthlessly efficient system for the industrialization of murder. Vast camps were built in Poland, at places such as Auschwitz and

timeline

1942	**1943**	**1944**
JANUARY At the Wannsee Conference, senior Nazi officials determine 'the final solution of the Jewish question'. **JULY** French authorities round up 30,000 Parisian Jews for deportation to the death camps.	**APRIL–MAY** Uprising in Jewish ghetto of Warsaw; 60,000 are killed when it is crushed. **OCTOBER** SS attempt to round up Jews in Denmark largely thwarted by the Danish authorities and civilians.	**MARCH** German troops occupy Hungary, and deportations of the Jewish population begin

Treblinka. Trainload by trainload, the Jews of Nazi-occupied Europe were transported in cattle trucks to the camps. As they disembarked, doctors identified the fitter ones and these were put to work as slave labour. Others became the subject of brutal medical experiments. The majority – men, women, children, babies – were herded away, ordered to strip and ushered into what they thought were shower blocks. But then the doors were locked, and from the ceiling there flowed not water, but Zyklon-B, a lethal gas containing hydrogen cyanide. It took the victims up to twenty minutes to die. One SS doctor, after he had witnessed his first gassing, recorded in his diary that 'Dante's hell seemed like a comedy in comparison.' Once all were dead, the bodies were carted off to the crematoria, which were soon belching smoke both by day and by night.

Even as the Red Army advanced remorselessly towards the German Fatherland, the Nazis diverted precious resources into maintaining the rate of extermination, even evacuating camp inmates westward in appalling 'death marches'. It was madness on an unimaginable scale, but the men and women involved in carrying out the 'final solution' were not inhuman monsters but ordinary men and women who had been so indoctrinated that they believed they were just doing their job, efficiently and in accordance with the Führer's will. The realization of the darkness that had settled in the heart of Europe – Germany, the land of Schiller, Goethe and Beethoven – brought about a profound shift in the continent's view of itself. Indeed, humanity as a whole could never look at itself in the same way ever again.

> ❝I was the accuser, God the accused. My eyes were open and I was alone – terribly alone in a world without God and without man.❞
>
> Elie Wiesel, *Night*, 1958, an account of his experiences as an inmate at Auschwitz and Buchenwald

in a nutshell
Genocide on an unsurpassed scale

1945	1945–6	1961
JANUARY Soviet troops liberate Auschwitz, where only 3,000 prisoners remain alive; around 1 million have been killed. **APRIL** US forces liberate Dachau concentration camp, near Munich.	Nuremberg Trials: Nazi leaders put on trial for war crimes and crimes against humanity; twelve out of twenty-two are sentenced to death	Israeli agents kidnap Adolf Eichmann, who had been put in charge of implementing the 'final solution' and who escaped to Argentina after the war. Eichmann is tried in Jerusalem and executed in 1962. The prosecution of lesser Nazi war criminals continues into the 21st century.

44 The Cold War

World affairs in the second half of the 20th century were dominated by a long period of armed hostility between the capitalist USA and the communist Union of Soviet Socialist Republics (the USSR or Soviet Union) together with their respective allies. This period of heightened tension was dubbed the 'Cold War' – a term first used in 1947 – as it never quite broke out into a 'hot' global conflict.

The USA and the Soviet Union had emerged from the Second World War as the world's two superpowers, and, although they never directly fought each other, these fervent ideological enemies conducted a number of proxy wars against the other's allies, and built up enormous stockpiles of nuclear weapons that threatened the very future of humanity.

The Iron Curtain The antipathy between the capitalist West and the communist Soviet Union dated back to the 1917 Bolshevik Revolution in Russia. However, when Hitler invaded the Soviet Union in 1941, the principle of 'my enemy's enemy is my friend' came into play, and the UK, USA and USSR made common cause in the war against Nazi Germany. As Allied victory became more and more certain, the 'Big Three' – President F. D. Roosevelt of the USA, British prime minister Winston Churchill and Soviet leader Joseph Stalin – met at Yalta in February 1945, and agreed that those areas of eastern Europe that had been liberated from the Nazis by the Red Army should remain under Soviet influence. Within three years there were pro-Soviet communist governments installed in the eastern occupation zone of Germany, and also in Poland, Hungary,

timeline

1945	1946	1947	1948	1949
FEBRUARY Yalta Conference. **MAY** Germany divided into four Allied occupation zones, with the Soviets in the east.	**SEPTEMBER** Civil war breaks out in Greece between communists and royalists	**MARCH** Truman Doctrine. **JUNE** USA announces Marshall Plan, massive aid package aimed at preventing communist revolution in western Europe. **OCTOBER** Beginning of anti-communist 'witch hunt' in USA.	**JUNE** Soviets blockade US, British and French sectors of Berlin. **JUNE** Yugoslavia breaks away from Soviet bloc.	**APRIL** USA, Canada and European allies form anti-Soviet North Atlantic Treaty Organization (NATO). **OCTOBER** Communists take power in China.

Czechoslovakia, Bulgaria, Romania, Yugoslavia and Albania. An 'Iron Curtain' had descended across Europe.

By this time, the wartime Allies had long fallen out. Even before the end of the Second World War, fighting had erupted in Greece between communists and non-communists, the latter supported by the British. Soon afterwards, the Turkish government found itself faced with a communist insurgency, and in 1947 President Truman enunciated the 'Truman Doctrine', committing the USA to containing the spread of communism around the world.

Nuclear stand-off

At the end of the Second World War the USA was the only country to possess the atomic bomb. But in 1949 the USSR exploded its first atomic weapon, and a nuclear arms race was underway. The USA tested its first hydrogen bomb – a much more powerful weapon – in 1952, and before long the Soviet Union had also produced its own hydrogen bomb. With the subsequent development of intercontinental ballistic missiles, launched from land or from submarines, both sides had the capacity to destroy each other, whoever attacked first. This principle of 'mutually assured destruction' (MAD) lay behind the theory of deterrence, which held that the very possession of nuclear weapons by both sides ensured that they would never be used. It was a high-risk strategy.

While the West feared the spread of communism, the Soviets feared that they were under imminent threat of attack. From their point of view they had brought the benefits of their system to previously benighted peoples, while creating a buffer between the USSR and a potentially resurgent Germany, whose war against them had cost the lives of at least 20 million Soviet citizens. For many of those in eastern Europe subjected to Soviet domination, however, they had merely exchanged one tyranny – that of Nazi occupation – for another. When reforming governments in Hungary in 1956 and Czechoslovakia in 1968 attempted to pursue a more independent line, their ambitions were ruthlessly crushed by Soviet tanks. Until the end of the Cold War, only Yugoslavia, Albania and Romania had managed to break away from Moscow's steel grip.

1950	1955	1956	1961	1962	1963
JUNE Outbreak of Korean War (until 1953)	**MAY** Eastern European states join USSR in Warsaw Pact, a military alliance	**NOVEMBER** Soviet forces crush Hungarian Uprising	**APRIL** US-backed invasion of pro-Soviet Cuba is defeated at Bay of Pigs. **AUGUST** Construction of Berlin Wall.	**OCTOBER** Cuban Missile Crisis	**AUGUST** USA, USSR and UK sign Nuclear Test Ban Treaty

❝**At the present moment in world history nearly every nation must choose between alternative ways of life. The choice is too often not a free one . . .**❞

President Harry S. Truman, from the 'Truman Doctrine', 12 March 1947

Conflict beyond Europe While in Europe two armed camps glowered at each other across the Iron Curtain, elsewhere in the world ideological polarization resulted in armed conflict. In 1949, after years of civil war, the communists took power in China, and the following year war broke out in Korea. After its liberation from Japan in 1945 Korea had been divided into a communist northern sector and a capitalist southern sector, and in 1950 North Korea launched an attack on the South, in a bid to reunite the country. Under the aegis of the United Nations, the USA, Britain and their allies intervened to throw back the invaders. The UN force succeeded in this aim, then advanced northward towards the Chinese border. China had warned that it would not tolerate such a move; 'If the lips are gone,' the Chinese said at the time, referring to their North Korean ally, 'the teeth will feel the cold.' Millions of Chinese troops poured over the border, pushing the UN forces back south again. After two years of stalemate, both sides signed an armistice, although technically North and South Korea are still at war.

The Korean War was a relatively short-lived affair compared to the fighting in Vietnam, a country that had also been divided between a communist North and a capitalist South. The Vietnam War (see p. 184) was to tie up large numbers of US troops and huge amounts of resources, in the belief that, if South Vietnam fell to communism, all the neighbouring countries of south-east Asia would soon follow, in a so-called 'Domino Effect'. From the communist point of view, the war was to liberate south-east Asia from Western imperialism.

timeline

1965	1968	1969	1972	1973
Escalation of US involvement in Vietnam War	**AUGUST** Warsaw Pact forces topple liberalizing communist government in Czechoslovakia	**NOVEMBER** Beginning of Strategic Arms Limitation Talks (SALT) between USA and USSR	**FEBRUARY** US President Nixon visits China. **MAY** Nixon visits Moscow and signs Anti-Ballistic Missile Treaty with USSR.	**MARCH** Last US troops leave Vietnam. **SEPTEMBER** CIA backs military coup in Chile.

Closer to home, the Americans were particularly sensitive to any suggestion of Soviet penetration in Latin America, which it traditionally regarded as its own sphere of influence. This led the USA to support a number of oppressive right-wing military juntas in the region, and even to back the overthrow of democratically elected socialist governments, as occurred in Chile in 1973. However, the USA proved unable to oust Fidel Castro's left-wing regime in Cuba, despite backing an unsuccessful invasion by anti-Castro exiles in 1961 and imposing trade embargoes. In 1962 the USSR stationed missiles on the island, and President Kennedy threatened to use nuclear weapons unless they were removed. As the world held its breath, the Soviets backed down.

Such brinkmanship was rare, and both sides, realizing that all-out nuclear war would in all probability lead to the extinction of the human race, sought a means of achieving 'peaceful coexistence'. During the 1970s, the USA moved to isolate the USSR by opening a process of détente with communist China, which had broken away from the Soviet bloc in the later 1950s. This prompted the Soviets to seek to improve relations with the USA, and the two sides agreed to limitations on the sizes of their nuclear arsenals – although at the same time continuing to fight proxy wars in places as diverse as Angola, Nicaragua and Afghanistan. But in the end, the Soviet Union found it could not compete with the vastly superior resources and hugely successful economy of the USA. As a consequence, not only did the Soviets let go of their empire in eastern Europe, but the USSR itself ceased to exist (see p. 192).

> **From Stettin in the Baltic to Trieste in the Adriatic an iron curtain has descended across Europe.**
>
> **Winston Churchill,** speech at Fulton, Missouri, 5 March 1946

in a nutshell
The period when humanity came closest to destroying itself

1975	1979	1985	1989	1989–91
Communists take power in Cambodia, South Vietnam and Laos	**JUNE** USA and USSR sign Strategic Arms Limitation Treaty. **DECEMBER** Soviet forces invade Afghanistan.	**MARCH** Mikhail Gorbachev becomes Soviet leader and begins process of liberalization and economic reform	**FEBRUARY** Soviet forces withdraw from Afghanistan	Collapse of communist regimes across eastern Europe and USSR

45 The end of empire

At the end of the Second World War, nearly all of Africa and much of southern and south-eastern Asia were governed by European powers, who also possessed many territories around the Caribbean and in the Indian and Pacific Oceans. Within three decades, the vast majority of colonial peoples had gained their independence, sometimes peacefully, sometimes through wars of liberation. By the end of the 20th century, there was barely a vestige of empire left. It was a rapid dismantling of an imperial dream that had taken centuries to realize.

There were a number of factors that brought about this transformation. One of the most significant was the creation within many colonies of Western-educated elites, who were trained up to help the colonial power in local administration and development. These elites absorbed Western values of freedom, equality and democracy, which in turn led to demands for national self-determination – demands that were increasingly backed by liberal and socialist opinion back in the mother countries. A more immediate factor was the Second World War, which left most European countries close to bankruptcy, and unable to afford the huge cost of maintaining an empire. That war had also given greater confidence to colonial peoples, who had seen how an Asian country, Japan, had swept the all-powerful Europeans out of south-east Asia and much of the Pacific.

timeline INDEPENDENCE DATES

1945–9	1950–4	1955–9
1946 Philippines (USA); Jordan (UK); Syria (France) **1947** India, Pakistan (UK) **1948** Burma, Ceylon (UK; Ceylon renamed Sri Lanka 1972) **1949** Indonesia (formerly Dutch East Indies)	**1951** Libya (UK and France; previously an Italian colony 1911–42) **1954** Laos, Cambodia, Vietnam (formerly French Indochina; Vietnam partitioned until 1975)	**1956** Morocco, Tunisia (France); Sudan (UK and Egypt) **1957** Malaya, Ghana (UK) **1958** Guinea (France)

Paving the way By the early 20th century, Britain had granted independence to its colonies of 'white settlement' – Canada, Australia, New Zealand and South Africa. These precedents encouraged the growth of nationalism in India, by far the most populous – and also the most developed – of Britain's non-white colonies. The Indian National Congress had been formed in 1885, and from the 1920s, under the leadership of Mahatma Gandhi and Jawaharlal Nehru, it became increasingly militant and well-organized, and largely unsatisfied by the granting by the British of small degrees of self-rule. At the same time, as Congress pressed for independence, the Muslim League demanded the creation of a separate Muslim state – Pakistan – in the sub-continent. Gandhi and his followers pursued a policy of non-violent civil disobedience, culminating in the Quit India campaign launched in 1942, which prompted the British to imprison most of the Congress leadership for the rest of the Second World War.

> ❛The moment the slave resolves that he will no longer be a slave, his fetters fall . . . Freedom and slavery are mental states.❜
>
> Mahatma Gandhi, *Non-Violence in Peace and War*, 1949

The Labour government elected in Britain at the end of the war in 1945 was more sympathetic than its predecessors to the spirit of Indian nationalism. It also faced a postwar financial crisis that made it imperative to shed its imperial burden as soon as possible. The result was that independence was granted in 1947, when the sub-continent was hastily partitioned into Hindu India and Muslim Pakistan. Although independence had been won by non-violence, terrible atrocities followed its achievement: partition led to massive movements of refugees in both directions, during which hundreds of thousands died in sectarian massacres.

Processes of transition By and large, Britain's withdrawal from empire was a peaceful affair. There were exceptions, however. Through the 1950s, for example, British forces combated the pro-independence Mau Mau movement in Kenya. In the eyes of the British, the Mau Mau were

1960	**1961–4**	**1965–9**
Mauritania, Senegal, Mali, Côte d'Ivoire, Upper Volta (now Burkina Faso), Togo, Dahomey (now Benin), Niger, Chad, Central African Republic, Cameroon, Gabon, Congo-Brazzaville, Madagascar (all France); Cyprus, Nigeria (UK); Somalia (UK and Italy); Congo (Belgium)	**1961** Sierra Leone, Tanganyika (UK; Tanganyika unites with Zanzibar to form Tanzania 1964) **1962** Algeria (France); Uganda, Jamaica, Trinidad and Tobago (UK); Rwanda, Burundi (Belgium); Western Samoa (New Zealand) **1963** Sarawak, Sabah, Singapore, Kenya, Zanzibar (UK) **1964** Malawi, Zambia, Malta (UK)	**1965** Gambia, Maldives (UK) **1966** Botswana, Lesotho, Barbados, Guyana (UK) **1967** South Yemen (UK; unites with North Yemen 1990) **1968** Swaziland, Mauritius (UK); Equatorial Guinea (Spain); Nauru (Australia)

The struggle for Algerian independence

The most intractable of colonial situations tended to arise where large numbers of Europeans had settled in the territory concerned. This was the case in Zimbabwe (formerly Rhodesia) and South Africa, where white minorities insisted on clinging on to power long after other African countries had achieved black majority rule.

One of the bitterest of such conflicts was the struggle for independence in Algeria. The coastal region had been extensively settled by the French, and was, in law, a part of metropolitan France. A campaign for independence was launched by indigenous Muslims in 1954, and before long a bitter war was underway, with atrocities committed by both sides. Divisions of opinion in France over the war led, in 1958, to the fall of the Fourth Republic. The army and the settlers expected the new president, Charles de Gaulle, to take a hard line against the insurgents, but de Gaulle realized the majority of French voters opposed the war, and announced his backing for Algerian 'self-determination'. Elements in the army and extremist settlers formed the Organisation de l'armée secrète (OAS), which mounted a terrorist campaign to try to hinder the process. However, despite attempted military coups and assassinations, de Gaulle successfully negotiated an end to hostilities, and independence was granted in 1962.

terrorists, but to many of their fellow Kenyans they were freedom fighters – a dichotomy widely observed throughout the process of decolonization.

The other leading European colonial power, France, had a similarly chequered record. Although most of its extensive African empire had achieved independence peaceably by 1960, after the Second World War the French violently resisted independence movements in Indochina, which had been occupied by the Japanese during the war. In Vietnam, the communist-dominated Viet Minh had declared independence after the

timeline

1970–4

1970 Fiji, Tonga (UK) **1971** Bahrain, Qatar, United Arab Emirates (UK) **1973** Bahamas (UK) **1974** Guinea-Bissau (Portugal); Grenada (UK)

1975–9

1975 Papua New Guinea (Australia); East Timor (Portugal); Mozambique, Angola, Cape Verde, São Tomé e Príncipe (Portugal); Comoros (France); Surinam (Netherlands) **1976** Seychelles (UK); Western Sahara (Spain) **1977** Djibouti (France); **1978** Dominica, Solomon Islands, Tuvalu (UK) **1979** Kiribati, St Lucia, St Vincent and the Grenadines (UK) defeat of Japan, but were forced to withdraw to safe bases when the French returned to reclaim their right to rule. After years of fighting, the Viet Minh secured victory – and independence – in 1954, but the subsequent partition of Vietnam sowed the seeds of the Vietnam War (see p. 184). The French war in Indochina split opinion at home in France; the struggle for independence in Algeria was to prove even more divisive.

❛The wind of change is blowing through this continent . . .❜

Harold Macmillan, British prime minister, speech in Cape Town, South Africa, 3 February 1960

Among the other European powers, the Dutch initially fought to regain control of the East Indies after the defeat of Japan, but in 1949 the colony achieved independence as Indonesia. Belgium hastily granted independence to Congo in 1960, but had previously restricted political activity by the Congolese, who were thus poorly prepared for ruling themselves. As a result, the country quickly descended into a bloody civil war. Portugal desperately held on to its African colonies, fighting local independence movements until 1974, when the right-wing dictatorship in Portugal itself was overthrown.

In 1945, there had been some seventy independent sovereign states. Thirty years later, in 1975, there were more than 170. In the decades that followed, most of Europe's remaining colonies in the Caribbean and Indian and Pacific Oceans also became independent. Although all these countries are now technically sovereign states, many of them still find themselves dominated, both politically and economically, by the West, or by emerging economic superpowers such as China. Some hold that the age of empire has not completely passed.

in a nutshell
A transformation of the map of the world

1980s

1980 Zimbabwe (UK); Vanuatu (UK and France)
1981 Antigua and Barbuda, Belize (UK)
1983 St Kitts-Nevis (UK); **1984** Brunei (UK)
1986 Marshall Islands, Micronesia (USA)

1990s

1990 Namibia (South Africa) **1994** Palau (USA) **1997** Hong Kong (UK; to China)
1999 Macao (Portugal; to China)

46 The Vietnam War

Vietnam was the war that America lost. The US engagement in south-east Asia lasted more than a decade, and in the process divided the nation and left an enduring legacy of bitterness. In all, some 2 million Americans – most of them poor white or African American conscripts – saw combat in the theatre, and US planes dropped more than twice the tonnage of bombs dropped in the Second World War.

The conflict in Vietnam was the 'hottest' episode in the USA's Cold War strategy to contain – or even push back – international communism, which it regarded as a threat to its way of life, a way of life based on 'rugged individualism', democracy and unfettered capitalism. But as the death toll of young Americans grew higher and higher, it became clear that the American people felt they were paying too high a price.

The anti-colonial struggle The nationalist ideals that germinated in Europe's overseas colonies in the first half of the 20th century were often aligned with the anti-imperialist ideals of socialism and communism. One young colonial subject who picked up such ideas while living in France was Ho Chi Minh, who had petitioned President Woodrow Wilson at the 1919 Paris Peace Conference to recognize the rights of the Vietnamese people – then under French colonial rule – to self-determination. He was ignored. Ho Chi Minh went on to found, in 1930, the Communist Party of Vietnam.

timeline

1941	1945	1946	1954
JULY Japanese forces occupy French Indochina. Subsequently USA backs nationalist-communist Viet Minh resistance fighters.	**SEPTEMBER** Ho Chi Minh, leader of Viet Minh, declares independence of Vietnam	**NOVEMBER** Fighting begins between Viet Minh and French colonial forces; USA backs latter	**MAY** Viet Minh decisively defeat French at Dien Bien Phu. **JULY** Geneva Accords: independent Vietnam divided into communist North and non-communist South, pending elections. **AUGUST** President Eisenhower commits USA to defend South Vietnam.

The Japanese occupation of Vietnam during the Second World War gave Ho Chi Minh the opportunity to strengthen the position of his guerrilla movement, the Viet Minh, and after the Japanese defeat in 1945 he declared the country independent. The French had different ideas, and returned in force. The war that followed resulted in victory for the Viet Minh in 1954, and the same year the independence of French Indochina (Vietnam, Cambodia and Laos) was recognized by the Geneva Accords. Vietnam itself was temporarily divided along the seventeenth parallel of latitude, Ho Chi Minh heading a communist regime in the North, while a non-communist government was established in the South. Nationwide elections were to be held in 1956.

When it became clear that the Viet Minh would in all likelihood win the elections, the South – under the despotic US-backed rule of Ngo Dinh Diem – refused to cooperate. By the end of the 1950s a communist guerrilla group, the Viet Cong, was active in South Vietnam, supported by the North via secret supply routes through Laos and Cambodia known as the Ho Chi Minh Trail. The USA sent military advisers to assist the South Vietnamese army, and in 1963 orchestrated the overthrow of the deeply unpopular Diem. However, the administration of President Lyndon B. Johnson came to the conclusion that only the deployment of regular US forces could stem the tide. If South Vietnam fell to the communists, the US strategists believed, then the whole of south-east Asia would follow.

> ❛We could pave the whole country and put parking stripes on it and still be home for Christmas.❜
>
> **Ronald Reagan,** interview in the *Fresno Bee*, 10 October 1965, referring to Vietnam

The morass A suitable pretext came in August 1964 when the North Vietnamese attacked a US naval vessel in the Gulf of Tonkin. As a result, President Johnson gained the approval of Congress for an escalation of America's military involvement. 'We're going to bomb them back into the Stone Age,' boasted Curtis E. LeMay, chief of staff of the US Air Force, as American aircraft were ordered to hit targets in North Vietnam. The

1955	1959	1960	1961	1963
FEBRUARY Eisenhower sends US military advisers to train South Vietnamese army. **OCTOBER** Ngo Dinh Diem declares independent republic of South Vietnam; USA backs his refusal to hold plebiscite on reunification.	North Vietnam and Viet Cong (South Vietnamese guerrillas) begin military campaign to reunite the country	**OCTOBER** Viet Cong form National Liberation Front to attract non-communists to their cause	**MAY** President Kennedy sends 400 special forces troops to Vietnam	**NOVEMBER** USA backs coup overthrowing Diem

first US ground forces were deployed in the South in 1965, and by the end of 1969 the number of American troops deployed in Vietnam had risen to over half a million.

While US forces conducted search-and-destroy missions in the countryside – alienating the Vietnamese peasantry in the process – the Viet Cong simply retreated to their hidden underground tunnels. Nevertheless, US generals continually voiced confidence that victory was in sight. Thus when the North Vietnamese army and the Viet Cong launched a major offensive during the Tet new year holiday in early 1968 it was a tremendous shock to the American public. The American media had more or less unrestricted access to the fighting, and with the war being shown on American TV every evening, attitudes began to change. Even the veteran CBS anchorman Walter Cronkite concluded in February 1968 that 'we are mired in a stalemate', and that the only way out was to begin negotiations with the North. 'If I've lost Walter,' President Johnson commented, 'I've lost Mr Average Citizen.' Although the

The 'Sideshow' in Cambodia

Prince Sihanouk, the ruler of neighbouring Cambodia, had kept his country neutral during the early years of the Vietnam War. In 1970 he was overthrown by a pro-US army general, but this, together with US raids into the country, only served to increase support for Cambodia's communist guerrillas, the Khmer Rouge. The Khmer Rouge captured the Cambodian capital, Phnom Penh, in 1975, and under their leader

Pol Pot attempted a complete transformation of society, forcing city dwellers to work in the countryside, and killing anybody considered to be a counter-revolutionary. In all, as many as 2.5 million Cambodians may have died either of famine or at the hands of Pol Pot's death squads. This reign of terror only came to an end when the Vietnamese army mounted an invasion at the end of 1978 and forced the Khmer Rouge back into the jungle.

timeline

1964	1965	1968	1969
AUGUST Attack on US vessel in Tonkin Gulf prompts Congress to pass Tonkin Gulf Resolution, authorizing escalation of US involvement in Vietnam	**FEBRUARY** US bombs North Vietnamese targets and commits regular ground troops to conflict	**JANUARY** Opening of Tet offensive, followed by increasing protests in US against Vietnam War. **MARCH** At least 350 unarmed villagers massacred by US troops at My Lai. **MAY** Peace talks begin in Paris. **OCTOBER** Complete cessation of US bombing of North Vietnam.	**MARCH** President Nixon orders covert bombing of targets in Cambodia

Tet offensive ended in failure for the communists, it also showed that the US generals' talk of imminent victory was an illusion. As anti-war demonstrators flooded the streets of American cities, Johnson announced that he would not stand for re-election.

The victorious candidate in the 1968 presidential election, Richard Nixon, had won largely on a promise to end the Vietnam War. Although peace talks had begun in Paris, progress was painfully slow, and while the fighting – and domestic protests – continued, Nixon announced a strategy of 'Vietnamization', by which the South Vietnamese army would take over operations as US forces were withdrawn. At the same time, Nixon intensified the bombing of the North, and also illegally ordered air raids and ground incursions into Laos and Cambodia to hit communist supply lines.

> **❝I knew from the start that if I left the woman I really loved – the Great Society – in order to fight that bitch of a war . . . then I would lose everything at home. All my hopes, my dreams . . .❞**
>
> **Lyndon B. Johnson, in the *New York Times Magazine*, 2 November 1980.** The 'Great Society' was Johnson's ambitious programme of domestic civil rights and anti-poverty reforms.

The Paris peace talks resulted in a ceasefire in 1973, allowing the completion of the US withdrawal. When North Vietnamese forces resumed their offensive in 1975, the South Vietnamese army lost all will to resist. By the end of April the North Vietnamese had taken the southern capital, Saigon, and shortly afterwards Vietnam was reunited. Laos and Cambodia also fell to communist insurgents. The war had cost the lives of 58,000 US servicemen – and millions of Vietnamese.

in a nutshell
The USA's biggest foreign policy failure in the Cold War

1970	**1972**	**1973**	**1975**	**1976**
APRIL US ground forces move into Cambodia, prompting increase in anti-war demonstrations. **DECEMBER** Congress repeals Tonkin Gulf Resolution.	**MARCH** North Vietnamese launch major offensive, thwarted by US airpower. **DECEMBER** Nixon orders intensive 'Christmas bombing' of Hanoi.	**JANUARY** Peace deal signed. **MARCH** Last US troops leave Vietnam.	**APRIL** North Vietnamese take Saigon, completing takeover of South Vietnam. Khmer Rouge take power in Cambodia. **NOVEMBER** Communist Pathet Lao take power in Laos.	**JULY** North and South Vietnam reunited

47 The Arab–Israeli conflict

The dispute between the Jewish state of Israel, the Palestinians and other Arab peoples has proved to be one of the most intractable and longest-lasting conflicts in modern history. It is also a conflict that has had powerful impacts beyond the Middle East, whether on the price of oil or on the growth of global terrorism.

Jewish settlement in Palestine – then part of the Turkish Ottoman empire – began in the early years of the 20th century. The settlers were inspired by the ideals of Zionism, a movement founded in the late 19th century by Theodor Herzl who held that the Jewish people – scattered around the world for millennia – should create a Jewish state in their biblical homeland.

The creation of Israel A major impetus to the Zionist cause came in 1917, when the British foreign secretary, A. J. Balfour, declared that his government would 'view with favour the establishment in Palestine of a national home for the Jewish people'. Balfour's aim was to drum up support from Britain's Jewish population for the British cause in the First World War, then underway. After the defeat of Turkey in 1918, the old Ottoman empire was broken up, and Palestine became a League of Nations mandate, administered by Britain.

Jewish settlement in Palestine increased in the 1920s, leading to violent confrontations with the Arab people who already lived there. Not only

timeline

1897	1917	1920	1945	1947	1948
First Zionist Congress	Balfour Declaration	Britain takes control of Palestine	Zionist Irgun guerrillas begin attacks on British in Palestine	UN votes for partition of Palestine; supported by Jews but opposed by Arab League	**APRIL** Jewish extremists from Irgun and the Stern Gang massacre 254 Palestinian Arabs at the village of Deir Yassin. **MAY** Proclamation of state of Israel, followed by First Arab–Israeli War.

were the latter concerned about losing their land, they were also influenced by the new spirit of Arab nationalism. In the First World War the Arabs had aided the Allies by mounting a revolt against the Turks, and had expected to achieve independence as a reward. Instead, much of the former Ottoman empire had been divided between the British and the French.

Violence continued in the 1930s, and plans to partition Palestine between Jews and Arabs were shelved following the outbreak of the Second World War. The experience of the Holocaust prompted many surviving European Jews to seek refuge in Palestine, but the British maintained their prewar policy of restricting immigration. Within Palestine, Zionist guerrilla groups such as Irgun and the Stern Gang conducted a violent campaign against British forces, leading Britain to announce in 1947 that it would hand over its mandate to the United Nations, the successor to the League of Nations. The UN voted for the partition of Palestine between Jews and Arabs, but this only served to intensify the fighting between the two sides. On 14 May 1948, the day before the British mandate was due to end, the Jews in Palestine proclaimed the state of Israel.

The Arab–Israeli Wars Israel's Arab neighbours – Egypt, Jordan, Syria and Lebanon – immediately attacked the infant state. Fighting was fierce, but after a ceasefire was agreed in 1949, Israel found itself in possession of more territory than had been allocated it by the UN – around 80 per cent of the land area of Palestine. The creation of Israel had a terrible human cost: violence against Arab civilians by Jewish extremists forced some 500,000 Palestinian Arabs to flee the country in what has come to be known as the *nakba* (Arabic for 'catastrophe'), leaving only 200,000 behind. These refugees were housed in camps in Gaza and the West Bank, hoping that they would soon be able to return. Their cause

> ❝We shall live at last as free men on our own soil, and die peacefully in our own homes.❞
>
> **Theodor Herzl,** the founder of Zionism, in his book *The Jewish State*, 1896

1949	1956	1967	1970	1973
Armistices agreed between Israel and its Arab neighbours	**JULY** Egypt nationalizes Suez Canal. **OCTOBER–DECEMBER** Second Arab–Israeli War (Suez Crisis).	**JUNE** Third Arab–Israeli War (Six Day War). **NOVEMBER** UN Security Council calls for Israeli withdrawal from Occupied Territories.	**SEPTEMBER** Jordanian army forcefully expels PLO, which moves to Lebanon	**OCTOBER** Fourth Arab–Israeli War (Yom Kippur War). Arab oil producers increase price of oil fourfold.

became the cause of Pan-Arab nationalism, a movement that grew stronger and stronger across the region, especially after the Second Arab–Israeli War – the Suez Crisis of 1956.

The Suez Crisis

In July 1956 President Nasser of Egypt, an ardent Arab nationalist, seized the Suez Canal, jointly owned by British and French interests. Britain and France came to a secret agreement with Israel, by which the latter would invade Egyptian Sinai on the pretext of stopping cross-border raids, and Britain and France would intervene, ostensibly to protect the canal. The campaign started in October, and sparked widespread international condemnation. The USA was particularly incensed, applying considerable financial pressure on Britain and arranging for the UN to demand immediate withdrawal of the Anglo-French force. This duly came about in December. It was the end of Britain's pretension to imperial power – and a triumph for Nasser, who became the hero of the Arab world.

The Third Arab–Israeli War took place in June 1967. Alarmed by Egypt's movement of troops into Sinai, and its demand for the withdrawal of the UN force installed there during the Suez Crisis, Israel mounted a pre-emptive attack on its neighbours. In six days, Israeli forces seized Sinai from Egypt, the Golan Heights from Syria and the West Bank from Jordan. Israel determined to hold on to these captured territories, on the grounds that they gave it more defendable borders, but this only served to create more Arab refugees and more bitterness.

The Fourth Arab–Israeli War came in 1973, during the Jewish holiday of Yom Kippur, when Egypt and Syria launched an attack against Israel on two fronts. Fierce fighting ensued, and the USA went onto heightened nuclear alert when it believed that the USSR was about to commit forces in support of Egypt and Syria. However, a ceasefire was agreed, leaving Israel still in possession of the 'Occupied Territories'. To punish the West's perceived support of Israel, the Arab oil-producing nations imposed a steep hike in the price of oil, leading to a severe global economic recession. The USA, realizing how close to the brink the world had come, put pressure

timeline

1975	1976	1978	1982	1987
Lebanon descends into civil war between Israeli-backed Christian militias on the one side and the PLO and Lebanese Muslim militias on the other	Syria intervenes in Lebanon	**MARCH–JUNE** Israel intervenes in Lebanon. **SEPTEMBER** Camp David Agreement.	**APRIL** Israeli army begins campaign against PLO in Lebanon. **SEPTEMBER** Lebanese Christian militias allied to Israel massacre hundreds of Palestinian civilians in Sabra and Chatila refugee camps.	**DECEMBER** Beginning of Palestinian *intifada* in Occupied Territories

on Israel and Egypt to make peace, resulting in the 1978 Camp David Agreement, by which Israel returned Sinai and Egypt recognized Israel's right to exist.

That was by no means the end of the conflict. In 1982 Israel invaded Lebanon in order to crush the Palestine Liberation Organization (PLO), which continued to mount attacks against Israel. Israel's complicity in the massacre of Palestinian civilians in Lebanon did nothing to dull Arab hostility, nor did its policy of building Jewish settlements in the Occupied Territories, in defiance of the UN. While Palestinians erupted in an *intifada* (uprising) in the Occupied Territories, PLO leader Yasser Arafat began to look for a diplomatic solution – although this was opposed by extreme Islamist Palestinian groups such as Hamas and Hezbollah, supported by Syria and Iran. More moderate political opinion in Israel also favoured negotiation, and in 1993 Israeli prime minister Yitzhak Rabin came to an agreement with Arafat for Palestinian self-rule in the Occupied Territories, and a gradual Israeli withdrawal. Elements in Israel were deeply opposed, and Rabin was assassinated by a Jewish extremist.

> **❛Israel has swallowed a serpent.❜**
> **Palestinian saying,** referring to the Israeli occupation of Gaza and the West Bank

Since then, progress towards a lasting peace in the region has been thwarted by a number of factors. Israel has failed to withdraw from the West Bank, and continues to build settlements there, while Hamas and Hezbollah continue to mount attacks on civilians in Israel itself – often leading to fierce military responses by Israel. All this serves to whip up hatred of Israel – and of the USA, seen as Israel's chief sponsor – across the Middle East, fuelling the murderous ambitions of groups such as al-Qaeda.

in a nutshell
A major threat to international peace and security

1993	1995	2000	2005	2007	2008	2009
SEPTEMBER Israeli–Palestinian peace agreement; violence continues	**NOVEMBER** Assassination of Yitzhak Rabin	**OCTOBER** Renewal of *intifada*	**SEPTEMBER** Israeli forces withdraw from Gaza	Hamas takes control in Gaza; Israel institutes blockade of the territory	**DECEMBER** Israel launches airstrikes against Gaza in retaliation for rocket attacks on southern Israel	**JANUARY** Israeli ground forces enter Gaza, leaving after three weeks of intense fighting

48 The fall of communism

At the end of the 1980s – suddenly and unexpectedly – hard-line communist regimes in eastern Europe, for long thought of as immutable and immovable, toppled like a house of cards, with barely a shot being fired. Even the Soviet Union, the one-time ruler of this empire of puppet states, found itself no longer able or willing to maintain itself as a single sovereign state, and crumbled into a patchwork of new countries.

These monumental transformations came about through a combination of external pressures and an internal appetite for change. The Soviet invasion of Afghanistan in 1979 had been followed by an intensification of the Cold War, especially after Ronald Reagan entered the White House in 1981. Under the amiable surface, Reagan was a diehard Cold War warrior, characterizing the USSR as an 'evil empire'. He was determined to put pressure on the Soviets, especially through an escalation of the arms race, which he knew the USA, with its economic and technological superiority, could win. Cruise missiles were deployed in western Europe, and an ambitious and hugely costly space-based missile defence system announced – the Strategic Defence Initiative, jokingly referred to as 'Star Wars'.

Meanwhile, the inflexible Soviet command economy was creaking under the strain, unable to compete in terms of defence expenditure, or in any other sphere. The gerontocracy that had kept the USSR in a state of

timeline

1985	1988	1989
MARCH Mikhail Gorbachev becomes Soviet leader and begins process of liberalization and economic reform	**MAY** Hard-line communist leadership in Hungary replaced by reformers. **JUNE** Soviet forces intervene to quell ethnic violence in Armenia, Azerbaijan and the Armenian enclave of Nagorno-Karabakh. **NOVEMBER** Political parties legalized in Hungary.	**JUNE** Free multi-party elections in Poland. **AUGUST** In Poland, Solidarity forms coalition with communists. Thousands of East German refugees begin to arrive in West via Hungary and Czechoslovakia. **SEPTEMBER** Communists defeated in free elections in Hungary. Beginning of mass demonstrations in East Germany.

stagnation for decades was dying off, and in 1985 a dynamic younger man, Mikhail Gorbachev, became secretary general of the Soviet Communist Party. The reform-minded Gorbachev instituted two new policies: *glasnost* ('openness'), which allowed much greater freedom of expression, and *perestroika* ('restructuring'), which involved a radical overhaul of the political and economic system. Factories and collective farms were given far greater autonomy, and some degree of private enterprise was allowed. Free multi-party elections were held in 1989 for a new parliament, the Congress of People's Deputies, and in February 1990 the Communist Party renounced its monopoly on power.

> **We must heed the impulses of the times. Those who delay are punished by life itself.**
>
> Mikhail Gorbachev,
> speaking in East Berlin,
> 8 October 1989

Upheavals in the east In June 1989 Gorbachev had announced that the USSR was no longer willing to intervene to 'defend socialism' in its east European allies – the doctrine that had been used to justify military actions in Hungary in 1956 and Czechoslovakia in 1968 (see p. 177). This gave the green light to reformers across eastern Europe. That same month, Poland held multi-party elections, and subsequently Solidarity (a party led by former shipyard worker Lech Walesa) joined a coalition government with the communists. In Hungary, as summer turned to autumn, the communists were overwhelmingly defeated in free elections, and mass demonstrations in East Germany brought about a change in the communist leadership, the opening of the Berlin Wall, and an irresistible drive for unification with capitalist West Germany, achieved the following year. Similar demonstrations – the so-called 'Velvet Revolution' – took place in Czechoslovakia towards the close of the year, resulting in the formation of a coalition government including a former leading dissident, the playwright Václav Havel. The only violent revolution was that in Romania, where, following the bloody suppression of an uprising by the secret police, the army took power in December 1989 and executed the dictator, Nicolae Ceaucescu, and his wife. Change was slower in Bulgaria, but in 1990 free elections were held for the first time.

1989

OCTOBER Hungary declares itself a democratic republic. **NOVEMBER** East German government resigns. Berlin Wall opened. Communist leader of Bulgaria resigns. Mass demonstrations in Czechoslovakia. **DECEMBER** Non-communist government takes power in Czechoslovakia. Violent overthrow of communist regime in Romania.

1990

FEBRUARY Soviet Communist Party agrees to give up its monopoly on power. **MARCH** Lithuania declares its independence from USSR. Free elections in East Germany. **MAY** Latvia and Estonia declare their independence from USSR. Boris Yeltsin elected president of Russian Federation, which declares itself a sovereign state. **JULY** Ukrainian parliament votes for independence. **OCTOBER** Reunification of East and West Germany.

Ethnic and nationalist conflict

The relaxation of the iron grip of communist rule, which had treated nationalist aspirations as reactionary and dealt with them accordingly, led to the opening of a Pandora's box in parts of the former Soviet empire. For example, in the Caucasus, Muslim separatists in Chechnya attempted to break away from the Russian Federation, which led to bloody military intervention and retaliatory acts of terrorism. In Europe itself, the break-up of the former communist state of Yugoslavia in the 1990s into a number of ethnically based republics led to a series of bitter wars and bouts of 'ethnic cleansing', in which brutal tactics – including wholesale massacres – were used to clear certain areas of their populations. Such methods were deployed by a number of different nationalist militias, most notoriously the Bosnian Serbs, who at Srebrenica in 1995 killed more than 7,000 Muslim men in cold blood – the worst such atrocity in Europe since the Second World War.

In the Soviet Union itself, Gorbachev's policies failed to improve the economic situation, and indeed shortages of food and consumer goods actually increased. Although he had become the darling of the West, he was increasingly unpopular at home. Some preferred Boris Yeltsin, the newly elected president of the Russian Federation (the largest constituent of the USSR), who advocated a more rapid rate of reform. At the other end of the spectrum were hardliners in the Communist Party, who in August 1991 attempted a coup against Gorbachev. This collapsed after a couple of days, largely owing to popular outrage stage-managed by Yeltsin. Gorbachev was left as a lame duck, as was the Soviet Union itself. One by one the constituent national republics declared their independence, and on Christmas Day Gorbachev resigned. The Soviet Union formally dissolved itself on 31 December 1991.

The aftermath Economically, the countries of eastern Europe and the former Soviet Union found themselves subjected to a rapid and unmoderated

timeline

1991

JUNE Slovenia and Croatia declare independence from Yugoslavia; fighting breaks out with Serb-dominated Yugoslav army, leading to civil war. **AUGUST** Failed coup against Gorbachev, who suspends Communist Party. Subsequently, remaining Soviet republics declare their independence, and by end of 1991 USSR ceases to exist.

1992

JANUARY UN brokers ceasefire in Croatia. Macedonia and Bosnia-Herzegovina declare independence from Yugoslavia. **APRIL** Serbs begin siege of Bosnian capital Sarajevo. **JUNE** Beginning of secessionist violence in the Caucasus.

transition to unrestrained free-market capitalism, in which small numbers of often unscrupulous entrepreneurs made themselves extremely rich, while others found themselves much worse off. It was a traumatic experience for many, used to full employment, subsidized housing and the safety net of the socialist welfare state – to which, in the course of time, some began to look back with a measure of regret, a rosy-tinted view dubbed Ostalgie in Germany (punning on *ost*, 'east', and *Nostalgie*, 'nostalgia').

> **❛We communists were the last empire.❜**
>
> **Milovan Djilas,** former aide to the Yugoslav communist leader Josef Broz Tito, speaking in 1992

Gradually, most of the countries of eastern Europe achieved sufficient economic equilibrium and democratization for them to be admitted to the European Union. The Russian Federation has taken a different course: while embracing free-market capitalism, it has tended towards an increasingly autocratic style of government, and also attempted to reassert something of the old imperial power exercised during the eras of the tsarist empire and the Soviet Union. This has sometimes led to tensions with the West, but nothing compared to that which prevailed during the Cold War.

To some in the West, the fall of communism was 'the end of history', the final triumph of the values of Western liberal democracy. They had not reckoned with the emergence of an entirely new phenomenon, that of global Islamist terrorism, which sought the utter destruction of the West.

in a nutshell
The rapid disappearance of a dispensation that had prevailed since 1945

1993	1994	1995	1999
JANUARY After a referendum, Czechoslovakia splits into Slovakia and Czech Republic	**AUGUST** Civil war breaks out in Chechnya between pro- and anti-Russian groups. **DECEMBER** Russian forces enter Chechnya.	**JULY** Bosnian Serbs massacre thousands of Bosnian Muslims in Srebrenica. **AUGUST** NATO airstrikes against Bosnian Serbs. **NOVEMBER** Dayton peace agreement ends Bosnian conflict.	**MARCH** NATO begins airstrikes against Serbia in response to atrocities against ethnic Albanians in Kosovo

49 The resurgence of China

At the beginning of the 20th century the glory of imperial China, at one time the most advanced civilization on the planet, had long been eclipsed. Within ten years, nationalist revolutionaries known as the Kuomintang had overthrown the last emperor, the opening move in a century of sometimes cataclysmic upheaval, involving civil war, invasion, revolution, ideological about-turns and – ultimately – astonishing economic growth.

In less than 100 years, China has transformed itself from a backward feudal society into a great industrial and commercial powerhouse – and a force to be reckoned with on the world stage.

Civil war and revolution The leader of the 1911 revolution, Sun Yat-sen, died in 1925, having failed to establish the rule of the new republic over northern China, which was still controlled by fiercely independent warlords. Sun's successor, Chiang Kai-shek, was more of a military man, and campaigned against the warlords while crushing a series of urban revolts by the Chinese Communist Party, which had been formed in 1921. Following Marxist orthodoxy, the communists believed that the revolution could only be brought about by the urban proletariat, but in the 1920s this class in China only comprised a tiny proportion of the total population.

timeline

1911	1921	1922	1925	1927
Nationalist revolution led by Sun Yat-sen	Foundation of Chinese Communist Party	Anarchy in China as regional warlords range unchecked	Unrest in Shanghai and elsewhere against 'unequal treaties' with Western powers. Death of Sun Yat-sen. Chiang Kai-shek begins campaign against warlords, supported by communists.	Nationalists take Nanjing and Shanghai. Chiang Kai-shek turns against the communists, crushing a revolt in Guandong (Canton). Civil war follows.

Towards the end of the 1920s, a new figure emerged among the communist leadership. This was Mao Zedong, who developed a revolutionary strategy based on China's huge peasantry. In 1931 a Chinese Soviet Republic was formed in the mountainous region of Jiangxi, but this came under pressure from the nationalist armies, precipitating the Long March of 1934–5, in which the communists retreated some 6,000 miles (10,000 km) to Yunnan in the remote north-west. Only half of the 100,000-strong army reached its destination, but during the course of the Long March Mao established himself as undisputed leader of the communists.

Civil war continued until the Japanese invasion of 1937 (see p. 169), when communists and nationalists agreed to form an alliance against the common enemy. After the defeat of Japan in 1945 the civil war resumed, and on 1 October 1949 Mao declared the People's Republic of China in Beijing. Chiang Kai-shek and the rump of the nationalist army retreated to the island of Taiwan, where they set up the rival Republic of China.

From communism to capitalism The People's Republic was initially an ally of the USSR (for example in the Korean War; see p. 178), but the two fell out in the late 1950s, turning the Cold War into something of a three-way affair, accentuated in the early 1970s when the USA and China embarked on a policy of détente, improving their mutual relations in a drive to isolate the Soviets.

At home, Mao led China through a succession of massive convulsions, including the Great Leap Forward and the Cultural Revolution (see p. 198).

> ❝No foreign country can expect China to be its vassal, nor can it expect China to accept anything harmful to China's interests.❞
>
> **Deng Xiaoping,** speech to the Twelfth National Congress of the Communist Party of China, 1 September 1982

1931	1934–5	1937	1946	1949	1950
Establishment of Chinese Soviet Republic in Jiangxi. Chinese Manchuria occupied by Japanese army.	Communists retreat in Long March	**JULY** Japanese invasion of China, beginning Second Sino–Japanese War; nationalists and communists form anti-Japanese alliance.	**APRIL** Civil war resumes between communists and nationalists	**OCTOBER** Proclamation of People's Republic of China in Beijing	**FEBRUARY** People's Republic signs treaty of alliance with USSR. **OCTOBER** Chinese occupy Tibet. **NOVEMBER** Chinese intervene in Korean War on side of North Korea.

Mao's death in 1976 was followed by a power struggle in which modernizers such as Deng Xiaoping came to the fore, resulting in a rejection of Mao's belief in permanent revolution. In 1978 Deng emphasized the need for four 'modernizations' – of agriculture, industry, national defence, and science and technology. This involved the reintroduction of capitalist free enterprise, while at the same time maintaining the Communist Party's monopoly on political power. Economic liberalization necessitated an opening-up to the West, required both as a trading partner and a provider of new technologies.

The Great Leap Forward and the Cultural Revolution

Mao's so-called Great Leap Forward of 1958–61 was intended to sweep away traditional customs and ways of thinking, and to mobilize China's vast population to modernize the country through rapid industrialization and the collectivization of agriculture. Resistance from bureaucrats and from within the party, combined with the withdrawal of Soviet technical support and a series of poor harvests, led to failure and famine, in which some 20 million people may have died. By the end of the 1950s a similar number had been 'liquidated' for opposing Mao's policies.

Facing increasing internal party threats to his leadership, in 1966 Mao launched the Cultural Revolution, in which he mobilized millions of radicalized young people, the Red Guards, to purge the party and to restore ideological purity. Party officials, industrial managers, scientists, technicians, academics, teachers and other professionals were subjected to bouts of public criticism and often violent humiliation, and sent off to the countryside to rid themselves of 'bourgeois elitism' by working on the land. Education and industry were neglected, the economy badly damaged, and chaos reigned. Eventually the army stepped in to stop the worst excesses of the Red Guards, but the Cultural Revolution was still underway when Mao died in 1976.

timeline

1953	1958–61	1959	1961	1964	1966	1969
End of Korean War	Great Leap Forward	Anti-Chinese uprising crushed in Tibet	Chinese denounce Soviet leaders as 'revisionist traitors', formalizing split that had been widening since 1956	China tests its first nuclear weapon	**AUGUST** Mao launches Cultural Revolution	Chinese–Soviet border clashes

The consequent influx of Western influence led to widespread demands, particularly among students, for political liberalization. For a while in the spring of 1989 it seemed that pro-democracy demonstrations in Beijing's Tiananmen Square – coinciding as they did with the liberalization then underway in the Soviet Union – might bring about a radical political change. But in early June the aged Chinese leadership moved to crush the demonstrations, and thousands were killed.

Since then, China's human rights record has not improved, but its economy has grown and grown, and vast amounts of goods once manufactured in Europe and North America are now made in China. One consequence of this growth is that China, in order to obtain more and more natural resources for its industries, and to satisfy the increasing consumer demands of its own population, has established an ever-growing presence in areas such as Africa. Many Western businesses are part-owned by Chinese enterprises, and the Chinese government itself owns hundreds of billions of dollars' worth of US Treasury bills, helping to fund America's budget and trade deficits.

A number of questions arise. How long can the Chinese leadership resist the external and internal pressures for democracy? How likely is it that in the next half century China will overtake the USA as the world's greatest superpower? If it does, will we find ourselves dominated by a foreign power with little regard for human rights? China's rise would not be possible without globalization, but globalization is a process that works both ways, so it is a moot point how long the notionally communist leadership in Beijing can cling to their monopoly of power.

> **'China is rising, and it's not going away. They're neither our enemy nor our friend. They're competitors.'**
>
> **Barack Obama,**
> speaking in April 2007

in a nutshell
A rising global power

1971	1976	1977	1989
SEPTEMBER Lin Biao, Mao's designated successor, dies in plane crash while fleeing to USSR, possibly after failed coup attempt. **NOVEMBER** People's Republic of China replaces nationalist Republic of China on UN Security Council, as part of US President Nixon's policy of détente.	**SEPTEMBER** Death of Mao	**JULY** 'Gang of Four', leading supporters of Mao's Cultural Revolution, are expelled from the party as modernizers such as Deng Xiaoping gain the upper hand	**JUNE** Tanks crush pro-democracy demonstrations in Tiananmen Square

50 9/11 and after

Tuesday 11 September 2001 dawned clear and sunny in New York. It was a beautiful late summer morning. Then, as commuters arrived at their offices, reports began to circulate that a plane had accidentally struck one of the Twin Towers of the World Trade Center in Lower Manhattan. As thousands of onlookers stared at the smoke billowing out of the North Tower, they were astonished to see another plane – a large airliner – fly out of a clear blue sky straight at the South Tower and crash into it with a great burst of flames.

It was just fifteen minutes after the first hit at 8.46, and it was immediately clear that this was no accident. At 9.40 a third plane hit the Pentagon, the Department of Defense headquarters in Washington, DC, and within the hour a fourth plane had crashed in the Pennsylvania countryside. The passengers, finding the plane taken over by hijackers and hearing of events in New York and Washington on their mobile phones, had rushed their captors, in the almost certain knowledge that it would cost them their lives.

In all 2,750 were killed in the Twin Towers. A further 184 died at the Pentagon, and forty in Pennsylvania. All nineteen of the hijackers, most of them from Saudi Arabia, were also killed. It was the worst ever attack on mainland America, and it was to change the world for ever.

From East Africa to Afghanistan It soon became clear that the hijackers were associated with al-Qaeda, a hitherto shady Islamist terrorist group headed by a Saudi millionaire called Osama bin Laden. In the 1980s

timeline

1990	1991	1996	1998
AUGUST Saddam Hussein's Iraq invades neighbouring Kuwait	**JANUARY–FEBRUARY** Broad-based UN-sanctioned US-led coalition expels Iraqis from Kuwait, but leaves Saddam in power. **MARCH** Saddam brutally crushes revolts by Kurds in north and Shiites in south.	**SEPTEMBER** Taliban take power in Afghanistan and impose strict *sharia* law	**AUGUST** Al-Qaeda bombings of US embassies in Kenya and Tanzania kill over 300. US request for extradition of bin Laden from Afghanistan is refused by Taliban. **DECEMBER** As Saddam Hussein refuses to cooperate with UN weapons inspectors, US and British planes attack targets in Iraq.

bin Laden had joined the US-backed *mujahedeen* fighting the Soviet occupation of Afghanistan, but by February 1998 he was enjoining Muslims to 'kill the Americans and their allies – civilians and military . . . in any country in which it is possible to do it'. In August of that year, al-Qaeda bombed the US embassies in Kenya and Tanzania, killing over 300 people. Bin Laden, as well as condemning America for its support of Israel, was particularly incensed by the presence of US forces on the soil of Saudi Arabia – the home of Islam's most sacred sites, in Medina and Mecca. US forces had been stationed in Saudi Arabia since the 1991 Gulf War, to deter any further aggression by Saddam Hussein's Iraq, whose occupation of Kuwait had been forcibly ended by a US-led coalition.

> **'The Americans love Pepsi Cola, but we love death.'**
>
> **Placard displayed by an Afghan man in Pakistan,** September 2001

Following the attacks of 11 September 2001, some Americans were prompted to ask why they should be so hated in parts of the Muslim world, but many others enthusiastically backed Bush's call for a 'war on terror', launched in an address to Congress on 20 September. This 'war on terror', designed to defend the Western values of liberty and democracy, ironically involved a disregard for human rights, as those suspected of terrorist involvement around the world were subjected to detention without trial and even torture.

Al-Qaeda's training camps were in Afghanistan, which had been controlled by the Muslim fundamentalist Taliban since 1996. In October 2001 the USA, at the head of a NATO coalition, began airstrikes against Afghanistan with the aim of destroying al-Qaeda bases, and in the following ground campaign ousted the Taliban from power. Bin Laden, together with most of the al-Qaeda leadership, escaped, probably into the lawless region along Pakistan's north-west frontier. Although a pro-Western democratic government was installed in Kabul, it has proved to be endemically corrupt, and unable to extend its power over much of the country. This, together with traditional tribal divisions and dislike of

2001

SEPTEMBER 9/11 attacks on New York and Washington. President Bush announces 'war on terror'. **OCTOBER** US-led coalition begins airstrikes against al-Qaeda and Taliban in Afghanistan. **NOVEMBER** Coalition begins ground campaign in Afghanistan. **DECEMBER** Islamist attack on Indian parliament kills fourteen.

2002

JANUARY Bush asserts that Iraq, Iran and North Korea belong to an 'axis of evil'. **OCTOBER** US Congress authorizes Bush to use force to deprive Iraq of WMD. In Bali, Islamist suicide bombings linked to al-Qaeda kill 202. **NOVEMBER** US Security Council tells Saddam to cooperate with weapons inspections or face 'serious consequences'.

foreign occupiers, and an initial failure by the West to supply much-needed development aid, has led to a strong Taliban insurgency, tying down large numbers of NATO troops.

Debacle in Iraq The 1991 Gulf War had left Saddam Hussein in power in Iraq, a somewhat artificial country created by the British at the end of the First World War out of a part of the former Ottoman empire. There were Kurds in the north, Sunnis in the centre and Shiites in the south, an uneasy cohabitation that Saddam had kept together through ruthless oppression – even using chemical weapons against his own citizens. As well as poison gas, Saddam was suspected of acquiring other weapons of mass destruction (WMD), such as biological and even nuclear weapons, in defiance of UN resolutions. He was also increasingly thwarting the efforts of UN inspectors sent to ensure that he held no WMD.

Assessing the threats

The actions of the USA and its allies in Iraq and Afghanistan do not appear to have diminished the terrorist threat, as bombings in Bali, Spain, London, Kampala and elsewhere attest. Indeed, the invasion of Muslim countries by Western 'crusaders' may actually have increased recruitment to the cause of violent global jihad. This has replaced Cold War nuclear annihilation as the main existential threat in the minds of many in the West, even though much informed opinion holds that climate change presents a far greater risk to global security.

It may never be possible to eliminate entirely the death-loving fervour of Islamist terrorism – suppress one cell, another grows up somewhere else; destroy training camps in one failed state, another failed state opens its doors to the terrorists; knock out the leadership, imitators will arise around the world. A security strategy based on containment and intelligence may prove the best way forward, combined with a determination to address – politically and economically – the causes that lead so many to embrace or sympathize with terrorism.

timeline

2003

FEBRUARY Massive demonstrations around the world against Bush's proposed war against Iraq.
MARCH US-led coalition begins invasion of Iraq.
DECEMBER Capture of Saddam Hussein followed by a massive increase of violence in Iraq.

2004

MARCH Al-Qaeda-inspired bombing of commuter trains in Madrid kills 191.
MAY Islamist terrorists kill over twenty Westerners in Saudi Arabia. **NOVEMBER** US forces retake Iraqi town of Fallujah and in the process almost completely destroy it.

2005

JULY 7/7 suicide bombings in London by British-born Muslims kill fifty-two.
OCTOBER Islamist suicide bombings in Bali kill twenty.

After 9/11 the Bush administration began to suggest that Saddam was in league with al-Qaeda and other Islamist terror groups, and was likely to supply them with WMD, so threatening the West. In fact, Saddam was a secular Arab nationalist of the old school, and had dealt harshly with Islamists within Iraq. But Saddam nevertheless became the target of especial opprobrium by the neoconservatives within Bush's administration, who believed that it was the mission of the USA to export freedom and democracy to the Third World, backed up if necessary by armed force. The fact that Iraq sat on huge oil reserves also made it strategically important. The consequence was that in March 2003 a 'coalition of the willing', primarily comprising the USA and the UK, mounted an invasion of Iraq and overthrew Saddam. There was no clear UN sanction for this action, which was undertaken in defiance of mass popular protests around the world. Not a single WMD – the sole justification for the UK's involvement – was found.

> **Either you are with us, or you are with the terrorists.**
>
> **President George W. Bush,**
> address to Congress,
> 20 September 2001

The invading powers had made insufficient plans for rebuilding Iraq after 'regime change'. The ethnic and religious divisions within the country opened up, leading to civil strife and fierce resistance to the Western occupiers, together with the emergence of an al-Qaeda group in the country. During the invasion and the subsequent insurgency, the infrastructure of Iraq was badly damaged, and tens of thousands – perhaps hundreds of thousands – of Iraqi civilians were killed. Although the last US combat brigades withdrew in August 2010, Iraq remains a dangerously unstable place.

in a nutshell
The beginning of a new age of anxiety?

2006	2007	2008	2009	2010
DECEMBER Saddam Hussein executed	US begins 'troop surge' in Iraq	**MARCH** Red Cross declares that humanitarian situation in Iraq remains amongst the most critical in the world. **NOVEMBER** Pakistani Islamist terrorists kill 173 in Mumbai, India.	**APRIL** UK ends combat operations in Iraq	**JULY** Bombings in Kampala, Uganda, by Somali-based Islamists kill seventy-four

Index

Quercus Publishing Plc
55 Baker Street
7th Floor, South Block
London
W1U 8EW

First published in 2011

A catalogue record of this book is available from the British Library

UK and associated territories: ISBN 978 0 85738 075 3
US and associated territories: ISBN 978 1 84866 131 8

Designed by Patrick Nugent

Printed and bound in China

10 9 8 7 6 5 4 3 2